POLITICS, POLICY, AND CULTURE

POLITICAL CULTURES
Aaron Wildavsky, Series Editor

Political cultures broadly describe people who share values, beliefs, and preferences legitimating different ways of life. This series is distinguished by its openness to a variety of approaches to the study of political cultures; any defensible comparison, definition, and research method is considered. The goal of this series is to advance the study of political cultures conceived generally as rival modes of organizing political and social life.

A single set of common concerns will be addressed by all authors in the series: what values are shared, what sorts of social relations are preferred, what kinds of beliefs are involved, and what the political implications of these values, beliefs, and relations are. Beyond that, the focal points of the studies are open and may compare cultures within a country or among different countries, including or excluding the United States.

Books in the Series

Politics, Policy, and Culture
Dennis J. Coyle and Richard J. Ellis, editors

*The American Mosaic: The Impact of Space, Time,
and Culture on American Politics*
Daniel J. Elazar

The Malevolent Leaders: Popular Discontent in America
Stephen C. Craig

Handling Frozen Fire
Rob Hoppe and Aat Peterse

*Cultures of Unemployment: A Comparative Look at
Long-Term Unemployment and Urban Poverty*
Godfried Engbersen, Kees Schuyt, Jaap
Timmer, and Frans Van Waarden

*Culture and Currency: Cultural Bias
in Monetary Theory and Policy*
John W. Houghton

A Genealogy of Political Culture
Michael E. Brint

Cultural Theory
Michael Thompson, Richard Ellis, and Aaron Wildavsky

District Leaders: A Political Ethnography
Rachel Sady

POLITICS, POLICY, AND CULTURE

EDITED BY
Dennis J. Coyle
and Richard J. Ellis

Westview Press
BOULDER • SAN FRANCISCO • OXFORD

Political Cultures

Copyright © 1994 by Westview Press, Inc.

Published in 1994 in the United States of America by Westview Press, Inc., 5500 Central Avenue, Boulder, Colorado 80301-2877, and in the United Kingdom by Westview Press, 26 Lonsdale Road, Summertown, Oxford OX2 7EW

A CIP catalog record for this book is available from the Library of Congress.
ISBN 0-8133-2098-4—ISBN 0-8133-2099-2 (pbk).

Printed and bound in the United States of America

The paper used in this publication meets the requirements
of the American National Standard for Permanence of Paper
for Printed Library Materials Z39.48-1984.

10   9   8   7   6   5   4   3   2   1

In memory of
Aaron Wildavsky

Contents

PART THREE
THEORY

Preface and Acknowledgments

We would first like to thank the contributors, who have shown the patience expected only of saints and scholars as the book project slowly made its way through the process of compilation, outside review, and publication. Without exception, they have been responsive to our requests and have endured our editing with grace and humor. Many other authors shared their manuscripts with us, and we appreciate their generosity and the opportunity to see how much interesting work is being done in the field of political culture.

We also wish to thank Westview Press, especially for its commitment to a timely publication schedule, and the anonymous reviewers who provided many helpful comments and criticisms. Jennifer Knerr, the acquisitions editor, has brought her enthusiasm and intelligence to this project, and Cindy Hirschfeld, the project editor, has tolerated the twists and turns that an academic manuscript can take, especially one with fourteen contributors. Diane Hess's excellent editing job was restrained yet thorough.

Even with the best of help and the most obliging of contributors, editing a multiauthor volume is a time-intensive and often trying venture. Richard Ellis is thus particularly grateful for the year off from his teaching responsibilities at Willamette University that was made possible by the support he received from the George and Eliza Gardner Howard Foundation, the Earhart Foundation, the Carthage Foundation, and the Lynde and Harry Bradley Foundation. Their support helped make it possible for him to meet the substantial demands of pulling together an edited volume while not altogether neglecting his family. He would also like to thank his coeditor, who for better and for worse had the bright idea of doing this book.

Dennis Coyle thanks his wife, Linda, and children, Erin and Kevin, for their tolerance of the long hours and anxieties of academic life, and particularly the odd behavior of a husband and father who tends to find inspiration at times when all but vampires and nightwatchmen are asleep. He hereby promises that should the tenure gods look kindly on the day of reckoning, he will spend the week after being professionally irresponsible. He would also like to thank his colleagues at the Catholic University of America and the University of Maryland Graduate School at Baltimore for the freedom to pursue work that does not always reside at the safe center of political science and the Earhart Foundation for a summer grant that aided in the completion of this project.

The seed for this book was a panel on political culture at the Western Political Science Association meetings in spring 1992. The fate of that panel is revealing of political culture's promise as well as of its uncertain position within the discipline of political science. The panel proposal was bounced around while the organizers of the conference debated where, if anywhere, it might fit within the existing categories of political science—was this empirical theory? normative theory? public policy? American politics? Eventually the decision was reached to cross-list this anomalous creature within a couple of sections. That political culture does not fit neatly within any of the standard subfields of political science suggests something of its subversive potential to span what are too often sacrosanct boundaries. To view political and social phenomena through the lens of culture, as the pioneering work of Gabriel Almond, Ronald Inglehart, Lucien Pye, and others makes clear, is to cross not only the lines within political science but also to cross over into anthropology, sociology, history, philosophy, and economics.

In many ways, this book complements and extends the approach to cultural analysis taken by *Cultural Theory* (Westview Press, 1990). Our edited volume is intended in part to provide the sort of empirical work and case studies that *Cultural Theory* called for though did not itself contain. A number of chapters also address conceptual criticisms of the "cultural theory" advanced in that book and sometimes directly challenge the theory's validity and coherence. In that same spirit of critical dialogue and empirical testing, we encourage fellow scholars to take up testing, refining, refuting, and reconceptualizing the "grid-group" model that underlies each of the chapters in *Politics, Policy, and Culture.*

Our understanding of culture builds upon two central foundations. First and foremost, of course, is the extraordinarily original work of Mary Douglas, who developed the grid-group framework. Douglas combines an intellectual daring that sends her off in pathbreaking directions with an undue modesty about the importance of her theoretical contributions. Although many scholars have followed in her footprints, two of her students, Michael Thompson and Steve Rayner, deserve special mention for the contributions they have made and continue to make to our understanding of culture. Doubtless they and others will not agree with all that has been done here in the name of grid and group (nor do we), but we hope they find these chapters push forward the dialogue about culture in a constructive and creative fashion.

The second foundation is the scholarship and mentorship of Aaron Wildavsky. We are both fortunate to have had the opportunity to study under and collaborate with Aaron as graduate students at Berkeley. Aaron was unmatched in the energy with which he promoted a cultural approach to the study of politics in the last dozen or so years of his career. Some scholars accustomed to his more mainstream work in political science and public administration may have been a bit puzzled by the strange tongue in which Aaron now spoke. But Aaron made a career of making the unusual acceptable and the peripheral central—transforming the study of budgeting and helping to turn public policy into a recognized academic discipline, to name but two examples. For us, grid-group analysis or, as Aaron preferred to call it, cultural theory, offers an innovative and essential tool for understanding the world, and we hope that it too will someday be part of the standard lexicon of social science.

As editor of the series in which this book appears, Aaron encouraged its publication, and he agreed to contribute a coauthored chapter just before he was diagnosed with terminal cancer. He passed on this devastating news in typical Aaron fashion, sending a letter to confirm that he and Sun-Ki Chai would indeed complete their chapter despite, as he put it, "a few minor impediments like my lung cancer." True to his character, despite the many urgent personal and professional demands on Aaron's time in the final weeks, the chapter that arrived was complete, original, and on time.

Aaron's death left a huge gap in the hearts and minds of many. For Aaron, the professional was personal, and he genuinely cared about the scholars he nurtured, collaborated with, or engaged with in lively conversation and correspondence. His special combination of wit, wisdom, intensity, integrity, creativity, and compassion affected countless people inside and outside of the political science profession. We take partial comfort in the rich body of work he left behind, but we cannot help but wish that Aaron were still here to criticize, to cajole, and to throw more fat on the fire of cultural analysis. To Aaron, and his family, we dedicate this book.

Dennis J. Coyle
Libertytown, Maryland

Richard J. Ellis
Salem, Oregon

Introduction

Richard J. Ellis
and Dennis J. Coyle

This is a book about culture, using that term in a broad sense to encompass social relations as well as values and beliefs. But it is also a book about the stuff of social science: politics, policies, and preferences. Our premise is that to understand the latter we must appreciate the former; that issues, opinions, and institutions are not isolated phenomena but rather intimately connected with basic choices about how we wish to live, choices that are constrained by our cultural context.

The renewed attention to culture is among the most promising developments in social science.[1] This is part of a larger trend in which many social scientists have become dissatisfied with those methods that treat individuals as atomistic, and take preferences as given and interests as self-evident. Recent work in fields such as transaction-cost economics, political psychology, and the "new institutionalism" has placed greater emphasis on social and institutional factors in shaping individual preferences.[2] In political theory, law, and history, the communitarian and republican schools stress the importance of the public realm, particularly democratic deliberation, in molding private aspirations.[3]

It is an invigorating time in social theory, yet also a frustrating one. For although social scientists increasingly recognize that individual preferences must be understood as social products and that explanations framed solely in terms of material self-interest are empirically inadequate,[4] there has not emerged a convincing theoretical account of what types of cultures or institutions shape which preferences or interests and in what kinds of ways. Grounding the individual in a web of social or cultural relationships often seems to come at the expense rather than at the service of theory-building. Context and qualification seem to drive out comparison and generalization. Little wonder, then, that rational choice theories still retain their immense attraction; for they offer, as John Harsanyi says, to "explain a wide variety of empirical facts in terms of a small number of theoretical assumptions."[5]

Cultural theories, if they are to make lasting inroads in the social sciences, must do the same. They must generate a large number of explanations and predictions from a few simple theoretical assumptions. A theory of culture cannot traffic in particularity and uniqueness. Too often in the past culture has been conceptualized in terms of the unique configuration of values, beliefs, and practices that make the Russians different from the Chinese, the Methodists different from the Quakers, or Toyota different from Audi. As long as culture is defined in terms of national, religious, ethnic, racial, or corporate distinctiveness, common measures are impossible and culture must remain little better than another name for the unexplained variance. To get beyond using culture as the anthropologist's veto— "Not in my tribe"—a theory of culture must identify common sociocultural dimensions and types.

Any typology, of course, is doomed to fail in the sense that it will never precisely capture the full variety of social organization. Each historical setting is unique in countless ways. Each person has her own experiences, and any attempt to generalize across individuals or groups inevitably entails distortion. "General ideas," as Tocqueville explained, "do not bear witness to the power of human intelligence but rather to its inadequacy, for there are no beings exactly alike in nature, no identical facts, no laws which can be applied indiscriminately in the same way to several objects at once."[6] Since we lack the ability to perceive the full variety of the human experience, our choice must be either to abandon the quest for understanding or to generalize. And fundamental to generalization is typology.[7] "If we eschew explicit typologies which can be criticized and improved," Mary Douglas warns bluntly, we "expose the whole domain to undeclared, implicit typologies. Either way, behavior is going to be fitted into boxes."[8]

We seek to build a theory of culture, then, in which criteria and categories are fully stated, so that they may not only be well understood but also criticized and improved. We seek categories that are built from common social dimensions and that are mutually exclusive and jointly exhaustive. We seek, moreover, a typology that reflects fundamental choices in politics and society and that can be applied to a wide variety of social settings and political issues. A tall order indeed. Yet we believe that such a theory of culture may be at hand in the "grid-group" analysis pioneered by Mary Douglas.[9]

Douglas's cultural theory[10] does what we believe a theory of culture must do: create measures of culture that allow for comparisons across time and space and relate values and beliefs to social relations and institutions. Fundamental to this method is the assumption that it is through the mundane encounters of everyday life that we develop our values and beliefs and learn how our aspirations—what we wish to do and to own, who we wish to be with—are interrelated with our preferences about social institutions and organization. As John Dryzek puts it, "In remaking our institutions, we also remake ourselves: who we are, what we value, how we interact, and what we can accomplish."[11] Living and valuing are intimately related, and it is in social relations that culture is rooted. "Unless cultural theories can account for the origins of ... attitudes by reference to the institutions that generate and reproduce them," Peter Hall points out, "they do little more than summon up a *deus ex machina* that is itself unexplainable."[12] Culture must not be treated as an uncaused cause purportedly explaining why people behave as they do yet incapable of itself being explained. To do so is to posit a world in which values are disembodied, unattached to human beings and the social institutions they inhabit.

Cultural theory posits that the variability of an individual's involvement in social life can be adequately captured by two dimensions of sociality: "group" and "grid." That is, to what degree do individuals define themselves as members of a group (and act accordingly), and to what degree are individual actions constrained by rules? The group dimension, explains Mary Douglas, taps the extent to which "the individual's life is absorbed in and sustained by group membership."[13] A high group score, then, connotes more than membership in a club; the further right one moves along the group dimension, the more an individual places the welfare of the group before his own and differentiates between those inside the group and those outside. Although the term "grid" may be unfamiliar to social scientists, the concept it denotes is not. In *Suicide,* Emile Durkheim presents much the same idea in his discussion of social "regulation." A highly regulated (or high grid) social context is signified by "an explicit set of institutionalized classifications [that] keeps [individuals] apart and regulates their interactions."[14] The further one moves down the grid, the more individuals negotiate their relationships with others.

At the core of the grid-group model, then, is the claim that these two dimensions—whether one calls them grid and group or structure and boundary or regulation and integration or control and commitment—are fundamental to social life. Together they define four basic ways of life: hierarchy (high group, high grid), egalitarianism (high group, low grid), individualism (low group, low grid), and fatalism (low group, high grid) (see Figure I.1).[15]

Hierarchies are characterized by strong group boundaries and binding prescriptions. Individuals are constrained by an external group boundary and by the demands imposed by stratified roles. In contrast to egalitarianism, hierarchy "has an armoury of different solutions to internal conflicts, [including] upgrading, shifting sideways, downgrading, resegregating, redefining."[16] Hierarchies are characterized by unequal roles for unequal members and deference toward one's betters matched by noblesse oblige on the part of superiors. A bureaucratic civil service and the leadership structure of the Roman Catholic church are examples of hierarchy.

Strong group boundaries coupled with minimal prescriptions produce egalitarian social relations. Equality is the transcendent value for egalitarian groups. Because these groups lack internal role differentiation, relations among group members are ambiguous and resolution of disputes is difficult. Because adherents are bound by group decisions but no one has the right to tell others what to do, consensual decisionmaking is preferred, and schisms may result when the decision

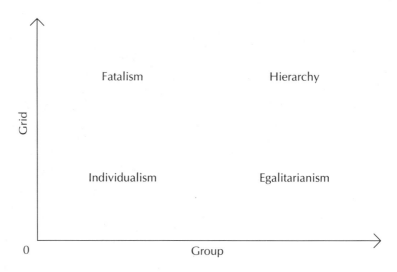

FIGURE I.1 The grid-group diagram.

process breaks down. The Green Party and the Clamshell Alliance are good examples of groups that seek to organize themselves along egalitarian lines.

Persons who are bound neither by group incorporation nor by prescribed roles inhabit an individualistic, or libertarian, social context. In such an environment all boundaries are provisional and subject to negotiation. Self-regulation is the guiding norm, though such a way of life also requires an extraordinary, and perhaps paradoxical, degree of trust and mutual respect of rights. The free market is the most obvious example of an organizing system that aspires to individualist principles (although in practice it may be heavily regulated, in part to counteract the tendency of individuals to seek unfair advantage over others).

The most curious social location on the grid-group map is the low-group, high-grid environment in which a person finds herself subject to binding prescriptions yet excluded from membership in the group for whose welfare decisions are made. She may have little choice about how she spends her time, whom she associates with, what she wears or eats, or where she lives and works. The fatalist, or isolate, endures the social isolation of individualism without the autonomy; the constraint of hierarchy without the support of a loyal group. Slaves and prison inmates are examples of fatalists.

Each of these four types of social relations is justified and sustained by an accompanying pattern of shared beliefs and values (or "cultural biases"). Individualists, for instance, often justify their decentralized social relations by blaming the individual for failure and by portraying human nature as invariably self-seeking. Fatalists reinforce their pattern of social relations through their beliefs that they can do little to help themselves, that life is unpredictable and capricious, and that other persons are dangerous and not to be trusted. Egalitarians may blame "the system" for unconscionable inequalities and socially destructive behavior by arguing that people are naturally good but corrupted by evil institutions. Finally, hierarchists shore up their social relations by blaming deviants when things go wrong and insisting that human beings are redeemable only through institutions.

The grid-group typology, moreover, is not an exotic beast the likes of which has never been seen on the shores of social science. Rather, cultural theorists seek to encapsulate major developments in the social sciences into an explicit typology, with an eye to asking new questions.[17] The fourfold categorization both builds on previous research—particularly regarding hierarchy and markets—and opens up relatively unexplored but important avenues of cultural expression, specifically fatalism and egalitarianism. Sensing that there must be more than markets and hierarchies, organization theorists occasionally mention clans or clubs,[18] for example, but these types do not come from the same matrix and are not built out of the same dimensions as markets and hierarchies. A vital contribution of the grid-group typology is that the egalitarian and fatalist cultures are derived from dimensions that can also produce the more familiar categories of individualism and hierarchy.[19]

Cultural theory bridges old and new in yet another way. Cultural theorists aspire to the analytic rigor and precision of the established social sciences, yet their subject matter is shared meanings and social constructions, terms that have of late become the intellectual property of those who insist that an explanatory social science in search of regularities is impossible. We see no reason that meaning and science should be divorced, that it should not be possible to make statements of regularities that help explain and even predict (or retrodict) the social construction of meaning. Subjectivity need not rule out regularity as long as conferred meanings and social constructions are patterned.[20]

Demonstrating that shared meanings and social constructions are patterned is among the aims of *Politics, Policy, and Culture.* In three sections covering public policy, history, and theory, the authors build the case for cultural theory as an effective, even essential, tool for understanding and explaining much of the world around us.

Hitherto cultural theory has made perhaps its greatest contribution to social scientific understanding in the area of risk analysis. Beginning with Mary Douglas and Aaron Wildavsky's influential study, *Risk and Culture,* cultural theorists have argued that people construct risks so as to bolster their preferred patterns of social relationships.[21] The Greenhouse effect, for instance, is so hotly contested not just because it concerns "the fate of the earth" but because it is a debate about how people should live with one another. For if people become persuaded that nature is fragile and that the slightest wrong step may result in cataclysmic consequences for the human species, then it becomes difficult to resist arguments and policies that would rein in the acquisitive entrepreneur in the name of the collectivity.

Most of this work on risk has been based on interviews, participant observation, and other qualitative methods of research. The opening chapter of Part 1, by Hank Jenkins-Smith and Walter Smith, is significant because it uses quantitative survey research methods to test the validity of cultural theory's hypotheses about risk perception.[22] Using a nationwide telephone survey, Jenkins-Smith and Smith show that citizens' perceptions of nuclear risks are not just a function of the level of information about the safety of particular proposals, or a product of generalized psychological predispositions such as risk acceptance or aversion. Rather, risk perception is embedded in cultural orientations or worldviews. Moreover, they show that culture is far more than just a fancy name for what we already know as ideology. Indeed, cultural bias outperforms ideology in explaining how people perceive nuclear risks.

Dennis Coyle's study of environmental and land-use policies provides further evidence that disputes over policy are inescapably disputes over culture. Coyle unearths three competing conceptions of how the world should be structured that lie beneath the incessant and often arcane debates over zoning, pollution, and the like. The hierarchical voice argues for a well-ordered community made possible by public controls over individuals. The libertarian (or individualist) voice contends that individuals should largely be free to make use of their property as they see fit. Finally, the egalitarian argument focuses on the use of regulatory controls to redistribute resources and power more equitably. The progressive reformers' dream that land-use decisions could be resolved scientifically by appealing to neutral facts proved chimerical because land-use and environmental disputes are normative debates about how we wish to live with each other, a question that cannot be settled by facts alone.

Frank Hendriks's chapter on transportation policy shows that conflict between rival cultures serves a valuable social function by forcing participants to question their own assumptions and explain themselves to others. The absence of a strong egalitarian voice at the time of the building of Birmingham's Inner Ring Road, Hendriks argues, created a systemic blindness on the part of policymakers. The result was a transportation system that has proven inadequate to Birmingham's changing needs. In the contrasting case of Munich's Altstadtring, all three cultures played a vital role in the formation of transportation policy, and the result was a more flexible and livable transportation system that has better met the needs of its citizens.

Brendon Swedlow's study of U.S. policies on mental illness also finds that each cultural perspective taps some part of the truth about the causes and consequences of mental illness. But Swedlow uncovers a quite different policymaking dynamic: Egalitarianism, far from being ignored, often seems dominant. During the 1960s the reigning hierarchical model of paternalistic and coercive state mental hospitals came under increasing attack from egalitarians, who believed that it was the establishment doctors, not the poor patients, who were crazy. Mental health, egalitarians believed, could be addressed only by redressing societal inequalities and by setting up community mental health centers that eschewed hierarchical doctor-patient relationships. Yet deinstitutionalization could never have occurred if it had been an egalitarian remedy alone. Deinstitutionalization succeeded in the United States because egalitarians were joined in their opposition to incarceration in state hospitals by individualists, who saw in these institutions unjustifiable constraints on individual choice and autonomy. Working together for different reasons and in pursuit of different ways of life, individualists and egalitarians transformed the mental health system in America, though in directions that they often did not intend or anticipate. Egalitarianism's failure to provide adequate community mental health centers left mentally ill people on their own; the huge numbers of people let out included many who could not make it on their own in a competitive, individualistic society. One legacy of this policy change is the homeless problem, a problem that, ironically, is now used by egalitarians to indict the establishment. Implicit in Swedlow's chapter is the lesson that hierarchical or paternal relationships have perhaps been underappreciated, at least in this policy domain. Egalitarians and individualists, although good at identifying the abuses of hierarchical institutions, have not been so good at providing alternative ways of helping those with mental illness.

Swedlow draws explicitly upon the concept of social construction in arguing that health and illness are not givens but social constructions that stem from preferred patterns of social relationships. In recent years, this idea of social construction has captured the imagination of a growing number of social scientists.[23] This is a salutary development in many ways, but too often the idea of social construction is harnessed to a stultifying, hegemonic conception of culture. Such analyses typically unmask the myriad ways in which the dominant culture (whether capitalism, consumerism, liberalism, patriarchy, etc.) perpetuates itself, usually at the service of some privileged elite. Social construction, in this conception, often becomes merely another word for the old Marxist concept of mystification. Swedlow, as well as Hendriks and Coyle, posits contesting social constructions in place of hegemonic dominance. Especially in liberal democracies, cultures are actively debated and negotiated, not merely passively imbibed or forcibly imposed.

Cultural theory seeks to make sense not just of contemporary political alignments but of past political behavior as well. Unlike some social theorists who spurn history as inherently unscientific, cultural theorists embrace history as one of the fields upon which theory can be tested, created, refined, reformulated, confirmed, or rejected.[24] Good history makes for more powerful theories, and more powerful theories enhance our understanding of the past as well our ability to predict the future. Part 2 shows that cultural theory is as relevant to the past as it is to contemporary society by illuminating three episodes in American history: Puritanism, slavery, and populism.

In the first of the historical chapters, Gary Lee Malecha explores the Populist movement in Kansas and Nebraska in the closing decades of the nineteenth century. Malecha uses primary sources to measure not only Populist values but also the social dimensions of grid and group. Malecha matches cultural theory against other leading schools of interpretation and shows that conceiving of populism as an egalitarian social movement provides a superior explanation of central elements of Populist ideology and behavior, particularly its Manichaean worldview and its ambivalent view of state power.

Richard Ellis explores the ways in which contemporary scholars of American slavery exhibit the characteristic egalitarian tendency to romanticize the oppressed, to see in the "other" a reflection of their own preference for a tightly bounded, loving, and egalitarian community. These interpretations of slavery fail to appreciate adequately the atomized and highly prescribed nature of the social relations of slavery and the accompanying fatalistic cultural bias that these social relations generated and reinforced. Ellis also shows that fatalism was greatest when the slaves' social relations were the most constrained and arbitrary and that other cultural biases had more room to develop when slaves had relatively greater control over their lives.

Dean Hammer's study of the development of town and church in Puritanism contributes to our understanding of cultural change. Hammer shows that egalitarianism, viable as an opposition ideology in England, proved ill-suited to creating an establishment in America. As the Puritans moved from challenging established authority in the Old World to creating institutions in the New World, they rapidly found egalitarian organizing principles to be inadequate. Only by defending authority and building up hierarchical institutions could the Puritans counteract the problem of exit and hold together their newly created communities.

These historical case studies advance our understanding not only of the American past but also of egalitarianism as a cultural phenomenon. Malecha and Hammer both show how egalitarians define themselves in opposition to the establishment cultures of individualism and hierarchy. If, as in the case of the Puritans, egalitarians find themselves without an establishment to oppose, the basis of their social organization can quickly unravel. They may, as the Populists evidently tried to do, use the instrumentality of the state to achieve their ends, but this type of alliance with the system threatens the purity of their movement. The egalitarian ally of choice, as Ellis shows, is the downtrodden, in whose everyday lives the egalitarian sees a noble struggle against an unfair system. By joining forces with the ill-treated and neglected, egalitarians hope to transform an inequitable system and to maintain their purity.

The authors of the final section, Part 3, take up a number of important conceptual problems and theoretical challenges that face cultural theorists. Sun-Ki Chai and Aaron Wildavsky open a much-needed dialogue between cultural explanation and rational choice explanation.[25] Rational choice explanations, Chai and Wildavsky maintain, can be greatly strengthened by including culture. Far from subverting rationality, cultural theory provides the conceptual tools for explaining phenomena that have appeared anomalous from the perspective of rational choice.

They mount their case for cultural theory's contributions to a theory of rational choices in the specific context of explanations of political violence. Rational choice explanations of political violence falter when it seems irrational for self-interested individuals to participate in violent, high-risk collective activity because those individuals will receive the benefit of that collective action whether they participate or not. There have been some ingenious attempts to extricate rational choice models from this and other paradoxes relating to collective violence, but none have been completely satisfactory. What is necessary to resolve the paradox, Chai and Wildavsky show, is a cultural theory that discriminates between different patterns of social organization and supporting values. Of particular interest is their contention that egalitarian and hierarchical cultures shape their adherents' preferences in such a way as to make sacrifice of the individual for the collectivity eminently rational. What actions are rational, Chai and Wildavsky teach us, depends on the culture one inhabits.

If rational actions vary by cultures, how can cultural theory keep off the slippery slopes of relativism? Charles Lockhart and Gregg Franzwa confront the specter of relativism that seems to haunt cultural theories of all sorts. If the world is socially constructed, does that mean the world can be any way we wish it to be? Does social construction mean that there is no such thing as truth, that there is no way to decide between competing claims or cultures? Not necessarily. As Lockhart and Franzwa correctly point out, cultural theory is a theory of *constrained relativism*. Reality may be socially constructed, but the world sets limits upon these constructions. Cultural allegiances are not carved in stone, impervious to social experience, but rather are constantly tested in light of experience. Culture is a prism, not a prison.[26]

Culture may teach us to shut out the perception of some dangers, but these blind spots can lead to unpleasant surprises and unexpected outcomes. The cumulative mismatch between expectation and result produces first surprise, then doubt, and finally defection.[27] It is precisely because people defend their preferred pattern of social relations by making all sorts of empirical claims and promises to others that the real world can intrude and shake people's confidence in those preferred relationships. Free-market capitalism, for instance, is promoted by individualists for its ability to generate economic growth and create wealth and material well-being. Were capitalist systems to cease to deliver on their promises, many people would begin casting around for alternative ways to organize their lives, as indeed occurred during the Great Depression of the 1930s. Similarly, communist systems in Eastern Europe promised that they would be able both to create wealth and to share that wealth more equitably so that everyone would be better off. When such systems instead produced economic stagnation and gross inequalities, they became plagued by self-doubt and defections and ultimately collapsed.

Does cultural theory tell us whether one culture is preferable or better than another? In one sense, no. The grid-group approach is, after all, primarily an attempt to explain and describe patterns of preferences and organization rather than prescribe them. Its primary aims are to understand why people behave as they do or hold certain preferences and to specify the consequences of those actions and aspirations, not to tell people how they should behave or what they should want. It is, in this sense, an empirical rather than a normative theory. Yet cultural theory leaves plenty of room for the communication and criticism of values. Cultural theory helps us evaluate the desirability of preferences by examining the unintended consequences of the way people choose to live.[28] To those who value hierarchy, cultural theory can point to the ways in which such systems, when things go wrong, blame deviants or quash investigations. To those who value individualism, cultural theory can point to the ways in which such systems teach individuals to blame themselves for failures that may be beyond their control. To those who value egalitarianism, cultural theory can show how such a culture may exaggerate fears about the "establishment."[29] Knowledge of the unintended and often unsavory consequences of their favored culture may lead people to reconsider their preferences. Cultural theory thus offers what Dankwart Rustow terms "social self-knowledge."[30]

Lockhart and Franzwa contribute to our store of social self-knowledge by showing how a standard of "societal viability" can be used to judge rival values. Each culture, Lockhart and Franzwa posit, produces distinctive social goods—roughly, personal rights and productivity in individualist cultures, expertise and social order in hierarchical cultures, and social solidarity and equity in egalitarian groups—that contribute to a society's viability. To eliminate or greatly weaken any one culture would be to threaten the viability and adaptability of the society as a whole. The metaethical imperative is thus to find a balance between these rival moral goods that best suits the particular historical circumstance. Lockhart and Franzwa help us appreciate, much as Hendriks does, the importance and value of cultural pluralism in creating the good life for all.

Richard Boyle and Richard Coughlin vet the methodological problems in operationalizing cultural theory's categories. Their careful discussion of the conceptual issues involved in measuring grid and group as well as the results of their two studies—a mixed bag of support and anomalies—provide invaluable guidance for future researchers. Particularly instructive and encouraging is their success in operationalizing the grid dimension.[31] This chapter continues the hard, trial-and-error process necessary to obtain reliable measures of the relevant concepts, and Boyle and Coughlin are the first to concede the weaknesses in some of their measures.

In the final chapter, Dennis Coyle raises a number of conceptual issues that are important for the future of grid-group analysis. Among these are the questions of whether cultural theory is best conceptualized in terms of dichotomous categories or continuous dimensions, and what room cultural theory leaves for other, more conventional social science concepts such as self-interest. He warns against cultural theory trying to become a theory of everything. As David Lindley writes in

The End of Physics, any theory of everything "will be, in precise terms, a myth, [i.e.] a story that makes sense within its own terms, offers explanations for everything we can see around us, but can be neither tested nor disproved."[32] In addition Coyle provides useful guidance for researchers on how to conceptualize each of the four quadrants—giving particularly valuable attention to the oft-neglected category of fatalism and its relation to individualism. Coyle reconceptualizes fatalism as despotism and argues that individualism is best thought of as libertarianism, which does not require a fatalist class to oppress. Perhaps most important, Coyle encourages us to think of these types not as boxes into which individuals must be fitted but rather as the modes of argument and perspectives that individuals choose among as they justify their lives to themselves and to others. Coyle's chapter reminds us that the growth of grid-group analysis depends as much on conceptual clarification as it does on empirical application.

Much hard work remains to be done in developing and applying cultural theory. Our hope is that this volume will at least persuade readers that they cannot ignore culture if they are to explain how individuals act as they do and that they need not ignore culture for fear that it is unfathomable and incomparable, something more appropriate to art than science. Further, we think the chapters in this volume show grid-group analysis to be a promising methodology for integrating culture into social science; we invite others to try out the theory. The more people use grid, group, and the four cultures as analytic tools, the more these concepts will be refined and hopefully integrated into general social theory and political analysis. Culture, then, not only could be about idiosyncrasy and uniqueness but also could become the basis for comparisons and generalizations that cross time and space and that help us understand politics, policies, and institutions.

NOTES

1. See, for example, Aaron Wildavsky, "Choosing Preferences by Constructing Institutions: A Cultural Theory of Preference Formation," *American Political Science Review* 81(March 1987), 3–21; and Robert Putnam et al., "Institutional Performance and Political Culture: Some Puzzles About the Power of the Past," *Governance* 1(July 1988), 221–242; Harry Eckstein, "A Culturalist Theory of Political Change," *American Political Science Review* 82(September 1988), 789–804; and Ronald Inglehart, "The Renaissance of Political Culture," *American Political Science Review* 82(December 1988), 1203–1230.

2. See Herbert A. Simon, "Human Nature in Politics: The Dialogue of Psychology with Political Science," *American Political Science Review* 79(1985), 293–304; Walter W. Powell and Paul J. DiMaggio, eds., *The New Institutionalism in Organizational Analysis* (Chicago: University of Chicago Press, 1991); and Oliver E. Williamson, "The Economics of Organizations: The Transaction Cost Approach," *American Journal of Sociology* 87(1981), 548–577.

3. See, for example, Alasdair MacIntyre, *After Virtue* (Notre Dame, Ind.: University of Notre Dame Press, 1981); Michael J. Sandel, *Liberalism and the Limits of Justice* (New York: Cambridge University Press, 1982); Frank I. Michelman, "Law's Republic," *Yale*

Law Journal 97(1988), 1493–1537; Cass R. Sunstein, "Beyond the Republican Revival," *Yale Law Journal* 97(1988), 1539–1590; Joyce Appleby, *Liberalism and Republicanism in the Historical Imagination* (Cambridge, Mass.: Harvard University Press, 1992); and J.G.A. Pocock, *The Machiavellian Moment: Florentine Political Thought and the Atlantic Republican Tradition* (Princeton: Princeton University Press, 1975). Some of this "communitarian" literature conflates criticism of methodological individualism with an attack on individualism as a way of life. As will become clear in the course of this introduction, we reject this conflation, believing that individualism as a culture is as much a social way of life as any other culture. Instructive on the need to separate out "ontological issues" from "advocacy issues" on this specific question is Charles Taylor, "Cross-Purposes: The Liberal-Communitarian Debate," in Nancy L. Rosenblum, ed., *Liberalism and the Moral Life* (Cambridge, Mass.: Harvard University Press, 1989), 159–182.

4. On the empirical inadequacy of rational choice theory, for example, see Donald P. Green and Ian Shapiro, "Pathologies of Rational Choice Theory: A Critique of Applications in Political Science," Working Paper 1043, Institute for Social and Policy Studies, Yale University, Spring 1993.

5. John Harsanyi, "Rational-Choice Models of Political Behavior vs. Functionalist and Conformist Theories," *World Politics* (July 1969), 515. In many cases, rational and public choice theorists have delivered on this promise, using simple assumptions of economic self-interest to build sophisticated models of political behavior, law, and social action. See James E. Alt and Kenneth A. Shepsle, eds., *Perspectives on Positive Political Economy* (Cambridge: Cambridge University Press, 1990); Kristen Renwick Monroe, ed., *The Economic Approach to Politics: A Critical Reassessment of the Theory of Rational Action* (New York: HarperCollins, 1991); James M. Buchanan and Gordon Tullock, *The Calculus of Consent* (Ann Arbor: University of Michigan Press, 1962); James D. Gwartney and Richard E. Wagner, eds., *Public Choice and Constitutional Economics* (Greenwich, Conn.: JAI Press, 1988); Richard Posner, *The Economic Analysis of Law* (Boston: Little, Brown, 1973); and Daniel A. Farber and Philip P. Frickey, *Law & Public Choice: A Critical Introduction* (Chicago: University of Chicago Press, 1991).

6. Alexis de Tocqueville, *Democracy in America* (Garden City, N.Y.: Anchor, 1969), 437.

7. See John S. Dryzek, *Rational Ecology: Environment and Political Economy* (Oxford: Basil Blackwell, 1987), viii ("Taxonomy is a prerequisite to explication, explanation, and evaluation"); and Mary Douglas, "Cultural Bias," in *In the Active Voice* (London: Routledge & Kegan Paul, 1982), 200 ("Without typologizing there can be no generalizing").

8. Mary Douglas, "Introduction to Grid/Group Analysis," in Douglas, ed., *Essays in the Sociology of Perception* (London: Routledge & Kegan Paul, 1982), 2.

9. A preliminary version of the model can be found in Mary Douglas, *Natural Symbols: Explorations in Cosmology,* 1st ed. (London: Barrie & Rockliff, 1970), but the typology is best spelled out in her seminal essay "Cultural Bias." Other works in this tradition include Douglas, *Essays in the Sociology of Perception;* Mary Douglas and Aaron Wildavsky, *Risk and Culture: An Essay on the Selection of Technological and Environmental Dangers* (Berkeley: University of California Press, 1982); Jonathan Gross and Steve Rayner, *Measuring Culture: A Paradigm for the Analysis of Social Organization* (New York: Columbia University Press, 1986); Wildavsky, "Choosing Preferences by Constructing Institutions"; Michiel Schwarz and Michael Thompson, *Divided We Stand: Redefining Politics,*

Technology and Social Choice (London: Harvester Wheatsheaf, 1990); Michael Thompson, Richard Ellis, and Aaron Wildavsky, *Cultural Theory* (Boulder: Westview Press, 1990); Mary Douglas, *Risk and Blame: Essays in Cultural Theory* (London: Routledge, 1992); and Richard J. Ellis, *American Political Cultures* (New York: Oxford University Press, 1993).

10. Throughout this volume we use the term "cultural theory" to denote this theoretical model, although neither of us is particularly happy with this conventional designation of the theory. Ellis would prefer to capitalize Cultural Theory or perhaps even to use the term "Douglassian theory" in order to distinguish the particular theory advanced here from the general enterprise of theorizing about culture. Coyle prefers to stick with "grid-group" theory, which, though perhaps less felicitous, is more precise and less presumptuous than the other terms.

11. Dryzek, *Rational Ecology,* 247.

12. Peter Hall, *Governing the Economy: The Politics of State Intervention in Britain and France* (New York: Oxford University Press, 1986), 34.

13. Douglas, "Cultural Bias," 202.

14. Ibid., 192.

15. Coyle prefers to label the individualistic culture "libertarianism" and the fatalistic culture "despotism," for reasons he discusses in Chapter 12. Douglas has sometimes referred to fatalists as "isolates" ("Governability: A Cultural Question," paper presented to the Centre for the Study of Global Governance, London School of Economics, London, England, April 30–May 2, 1993) or described the high-grid, low-group social environment as one of "atomized subordination" ("Introduction to Grid/Group Analysis," 4). Individualism has often been designated by cultural theorists as "competitive individualism." And egalitarianism was referred to as "sectarianism" (Douglas and Wildavsky, *Risk and Culture*), a usage that has since been abandoned. The only uncontested usage seems to have been hierarchy.

16. Douglas, "Cultural Bias," 206.

17. Douglas makes the point more emphatically, stating that grid-group analysis "captures the wisdom of a hundred years of sociology, anthropology and psychology" ("Introduction to Grid/Group Analysis," 1).

18. See William G. Ouchi, "Markets, Bureaucracies, and Clans," *Administrative Science Quarterly* 25(March 1980), 129–141; and Oliver Williamson, *Markets and Hierarchies, Analysis and Antitrust Implications: A Study in the Economics of Internal Organization* (New York: Free Press, 1975).

19. See Thompson, Ellis, and Wildavsky, *Cultural Theory,* 13–14.

20. Ibid., xiii–xiv.

21. See Douglas and Wildavsky, *Risk and Culture*. Also see Steve Rayner, "Disagreeing About Risk: The Institutional Cultures of Risk Management and Planning for Future Generations," in Susan G. Hadden, ed., *Risk Analysis, Institutions, and Public Policy* (Port Washington, N.Y.: Associated Faculty Press, 1984), 150–169; Mary Douglas, *Risk Acceptability in the Social Sciences* (New York: Russell Sage, 1985); Michael Thompson and Paul James, "The Cultural Theory of Risk," in Jennifer Brown, ed., *Environmental Threats: Reception, Analysis and Management* (London: Belhaven, 1989), 138–150; and Mary Douglas, *Risk and Blame*.

22. Also important in this respect is Karl Dake and Aaron Wildavsky, "Theories of Risk Perception: Who Fears What and Why?" *Daedalus* 119(1990), 41–60.

23. See, for example, Donileen R. Loseke, *The Battered Woman and Shelters: The Social Construction of Wife Abuse* (Albany: State University of New York Press, 1992); Bert Klandermans, "The Social Construction of Protest and Multiorganizational Fields," in Aldon D. Morris and Carol McClurg Mueller, eds., *Frontiers in Social Movement Theory* (New Haven: Yale University Press, 1992), 77–103; Richard Whitley, "The Social Construction of Organizations and Markets: The Comparative Analyses of Business Recipes," in Michael Reed and Michael Hughes, eds., *Rethinking Organization: New Directions in Organization Theory and Analysis* (London: Sage, 1992), 120–143; Owen M. Lynch, *Divine Passions: The Social Construction of Emotion in India* (Berkeley: University of California Press, 1990); Charles W. Smith, *Auctions: The Social Construction of Value* (Berkeley: University of California Press, 1989); Wiebe E. Bijker, Thomas P. Hughes, and Trevor J. Pinch, eds., *The Social Construction of Technological Systems: New Directions in the Sociology and History of Technology* (Cambridge, Mass: MIT Press, 1987); Celia Kitzinger, *The Social Construction of Lesbianism* (London: Sage, 1987); and Chris Phillipson, *Capitalism and the Construction of Old Age* (London: Macmillan, 1982).

24. This claim is elaborated in Richard J. Ellis, "The Case for Cultural Theory: Reply to Friedman," *Critical Review* 7(Winter 1993), 541–588.

25. Also see Aaron Wildavsky, "Why Self-Interest Means Less Outside of a Social Context: Cultural Contributions to a Theory of Rational Choices," *Journal of Theoretical Politics* (forthcoming); and Wildavsky, "Can Norms Rescue Self-Interest or Macro-Explanation Be Joined to Micro-Explanation?" *Critical Review* 5(Spring 1991), 301–323.

26. Ellis, *American Political Cultures,* 174–175.

27. On the importance of surprise (and for a typology of surprises) see Thompson, Ellis, and Wildavsky, *Cultural Theory,* chap. 4.

28. This claim is elaborated in Ellis, "The Case for Cultural Theory."

29. See Thompson, Ellis, and Wildavsky, *Cultural Theory,* 59–60.

30. Samuel H. Beer, "Political Science and History," in Melvin Richter, ed., *Essays in Theory and History* (Cambridge, Mass.: Harvard University Press, 1970), 68.

31. See Douglas, "Cultural Bias," 202, for the conceptual problems that grid has posed for cultural theorists.

32. David Lindley, *The End of Physics: The Myth of a Unified Theory* (New York: Basic Books, 1993), 255.

PART ONE

PUBLIC POLICY

CHAPTER 1

Ideology, Culture, and Risk Perception

Hank C. Jenkins-Smith
and Walter K. Smith

Explanations of attitudes about nuclear policy have placed great emphasis on the role of political ideology[1] and trust in political actors.[2] The highly polarized political battles over development of the Yucca Mountain high-level radioactive waste repository in Nevada[3] and testing at the Waste Isolation Pilot Plant (WIPP) transuranic waste facility in New Mexico[4] serve to underline the importance of ideology and trust as critical factors that constrain nuclear policies.

In this chapter we seek to place the concepts of trust and ideology in a broader political context, which we hope will prove more useful for understanding the dynamics of policy disputes over nuclear facility siting. In part, our dissatisfaction with current explanations stems from the fact that specific variables (e.g., ideology) are often treated as isolated contributors to perceived risk when they may in fact be part of a larger, interactive tapestry of causal relationships. Whom one chooses to trust may well be related to ideological predispositions after all. And what one fears may well be grounded in more general political constructs such as cultural worldview. We are concerned that the primary focus on the particular linkages among trust, ideology, and nuclear policy attitudes may impoverish our understanding of the political nature of attitudes about nuclear risk. We will argue that it is essential to place the issues of trust and fear in the broader context of one's sense of control over policymaking (or political efficacy) and—more generally—in the context of one's worldview, or cultural bias.

Using data from a 1991 nationwide telephone survey of citizens from randomly selected households, we present an analysis of the relationships among measures of nuclear risk perception, trust in prominent policy actors, cultural bias, and political efficacy. Our intent is to show how citizens' judgments about nuclear risk are grounded in an array of factors that characterize their general perceptions of politics. Most prominent among these factors is political culture.

CONCEPTS AND HYPOTHESES

The existing research clearly shows the importance of ideology and trust as factors that shape attitudes about nuclear policies, but relatively little effort has been made to place ideology and trust within a broader framework of individuals' political characteristics. For example, to what degree might ideology channel trust? Would it be implausible to argue that citizens who identify themselves as extremely liberal have less trust in the major agencies responsible for nuclear weapons or more trust in environmental groups than would those who identify themselves as extremely conservative? If not, the link between attitudes about nuclear policies and trust may be partially a function of political ideology.

At the same time, we question the primary emphasis given to ideology as a determinant of attitudes and risk perceptions in nuclear policy issues.[5] An alternative line of scholarship has suggested that perceptions of risk, and hence attitudes about nuclear policies, can best be explained by the cultural biases of the groups and individuals involved. Cultural theorists argue that individuals' assessments of which kinds of risks (e.g., social, economic, or environmental) are most pressing are based on very general values and beliefs—or cultural biases—that justify patterns of social relationships.[6]

One particularly useful variant of cultural theory, as specified by Mary Douglas and Aaron Wildavsky,[7] can be taken as suggesting that preferences for patterns of social relationships, and the biases that flow from these preferences, will influence both who is trusted and attitudes toward nuclear policies.[8] Placement on two dimensions—one reflecting the degree to which individuals define themselves as part of a group (the "group" dimension), and another reflecting perceptions of the appropriate extent and variety of rules governing relations among people (the "grid" dimension)—determines one's cultural type.

Hierarchs perceive themselves as group members (high group) and accept substantial differentiation among the rules that apply to different members of the group (high grid). This placement predisposes these individuals to trust experts and those in authority, to have faith in (and relatively little fear of) technologies that are sanctioned and managed by experts, and to be chiefly concerned about threats to order and security.

Egalitarians are also high group, but low grid: For these individuals, rule differentiation among group members violates a fundamental principle of equality. For egalitarians, experts and those in positions of authority are suspect, particularly those in large centralized and secretive organizations. These individuals distrust and fear concentrations of power—particularly by those not readily held accountable for their actions. Potentially hazardous technologies and the environmental risks that flow from organizations seen as having concentrated, unaccountable power (such as nuclear utilities or corporations) are singled out as particular threats.

Individualists are low grid and low group, perceiving themselves to be involved in bidding and bargaining with other individuals to transact their own terms for social relations. Intrusions upon such individual transactions (such as the regulation of private business or imposition of standards of "political correctness" within organizations) are perceived as threats to individuals' abilities to make their own way in life. Such intrusions are seen as one of the chief risks confronting society.

Finally, fatalists are individuals who are low group (they tend to see themselves as excluded outsiders) and high grid (their world is shot through with social distinctions). As the name fatalist implies, these individuals tend to see the occurrence of events and their outcomes as arbitrary and beyond their control; the world might produce a cornucopia of wealth, health, and safety, but it might just as readily produce disaster. Fatalists see themselves as having little ability to shape such outcomes.

According to this formulation of cultural theory, an egalitarian might hold a particularly negative view of the nuclear industry (and those who support it) because nuclear technologies are seen to be the outgrowth of large corporations and central governments—both of which are held by egalitarians to be exemplars of unresponsive and concentrated power. Both those who operate and regulate nuclear facilities are likely to be distrusted. At the other extreme, a hierarch would likely find nuclear facilities to be far less salient and fearsome (because they have faith in the experts that run and regulate them). Cultural theorists would therefore argue that hierarchs will have greater trust in those who operate and regulate nuclear facilities than would those of an egalitarian stripe. Thus the link between attitudes toward the nuclear industry and trust may be driven by a third variable—culture.

Furthermore, both trust in political actors and cultural biases are likely to be associated with individuals' sense of "political efficacy"—that is, their belief that (1) they can understand and participate in the political process and that (2) the political system will respond.[9] A deep sense of political inefficacy may well spill over into distrust of the actors involved in nuclear policy. Distrust, in turn, may operate in several distinct ways to affect more specific policy beliefs and positions. First, distrust of those policy elites who act as "reference groups" within key policy areas may lead to rejection of the substantive claims and policy positions taken by that group. Second, distrust of elites or organizations that are charged with implementing policies may generate opposition to those policies due to the perception that those who run the organizations are nefarious or incompetent. Thus a systemwide inefficacy may be conflated with more specific distrust in those groups and elites who are prominently engaged in nuclear policy debates.

Beyond its implications for trust, the link between efficacy and cultural bias may be of considerable import. In particular, political efficacy concerns how individuals understand the workings of the political process and may thereby influence the ways in which centralized, high-technology policies are perceived. Less "internally efficacious" individuals (i.e., those who believe that they cannot understand and effectively participate in the political process) may be more deferential to, and willing to rely upon, hierarchical, centralized systems in which they can have less direct policy influence and may therefore have more faith in the policy outcomes of those systems. Thus we would expect those who are less internally efficacious to be more likely to share the hierarch's cultural biases. Less "externally efficacious" individuals (i.e., those who sense that existing political structures are unlikely to respond to their wants and needs) may have less faith in the policy outcomes of centralized, hierarchical systems and may therefore be more fearful of policies that emanate from such systems. In this case, we would expect those with a low sense of external efficacy to share the cultural biases of the egalitarian.[10]

These considerations guide our specific hypotheses. We will begin by retesting the standard hypotheses that perceptions of political risks are related to ideology and trust. Specifically, we hypothesize that

H_1:   Those respondents who classify themselves as political liberals will tend to perceive greater risk, and those who identify themselves as more conservative will perceive less risk.

H_2:   The greater the trust in environmental interest groups, the more likely it is that the respondent will take a position on risk advocated by that group (greater perceived risk of things nuclear).

H_3:   The greater the trust in organizations responsible for implementation of nuclear policy (the Nuclear Regulatory Commission [NRC] and the nuclear industry), the less the perceived risk of things nuclear.

Next, we will test hypotheses regarding the relationships between cultural biases and risk perception. We hypothesize that

H_4:   Respondents who lean more toward egalitarian cultural biases will tend to perceive greater nuclear risks than will those who lean toward hierarchical or individualistic cultural biases.

Regarding political efficacy, we hypothesize an indirect link, via cultural bias, in which political efficacy is associated with a particular cultural bias that, in turn, influences the perceived risks of nuclear policies (via H_4). In essence, we expect individuals with less *internal* efficacy (all other things being equal) to be more deferential and reliant on extant political and social structures and hence to be more inclined toward hierarchical cultural biases. Those who are less *externally* efficacious, in contrast, will be less willing to accept the outcomes of existing social and political structures and will be inclined more toward egalitarian cultural biases. Therefore we hypothesize that

H_5: The lower the level of external political efficacy, the greater the tendency toward egalitarian cultural biases.

H_6: The lower the level of internal political efficacy, the greater the tendency toward hierarchical cultural biases.

Finally, we hypothesize that levels of trust in prominent policy elites will be influenced by external political efficacy, ideology, and cultural bias. All other things being equal, those who believe that they can influence the actions of policy elites are more likely to trust them. Those of a politically conservative bent will be less likely to trust environmentalists and more likely to trust the NRC and the nuclear industry. And—for reasons discussed previously—those who share the egalitarian's cultural predispositions are more likely to trust environmental groups, and hierarchists are more likely to trust the NRC and the nuclear industry. Trust, in turn, will affect perceived risks (via H_2 and H_3). Specifically,

H_7: The greater the level of external efficacy, the greater the level of trust in all policy elites.

H_8: The more politically conservative the respondent, the greater the trust in those charged with implementing nuclear policies.

H_9: The more politically liberal the respondent, the greater the trust in national environmental groups.

H_{10}: The greater the tendency toward the hierarch's cultural bias, the more trust in those charged with implementing nuclear policies.

H_{11}: The greater the tendency toward the egalitarian cultural bias, the more trust in national environmental groups.

For each hypothesis, we control for possible confounding influences of basic demographic variables such as sex, age, income, education, and ethnicity. In addition, we test the hypotheses as systems of relationships in order to control for indirect effects and to assess the relative strength of potentially rival explanations for perceived risk.

DATA AND METHOD

The data for this study were taken from telephone interviews of a nationwide random sample of households, conducted in June and July 1991. The interviews were conducted with 1,234 respondents using the University of New Mexico Survey Research Center's computer-aided telephone interviewing system. The sample frame was obtained from Survey Sampling Inc., of Fairfield, Connecticut. From among all of the working telephone numbers used (that is, those that were not disconnected), we obtained responses from 23 percent.[11]

In order to test our hypotheses, we employed a subset of the questions, and several constructed variables derived from combinations of questions, taken from the survey. A brief description of each variable is provided in the text, and full question wordings are included in the notes or are available from the authors.

Perceptions of nuclear risk were operationalized by asking respondents to indicate how risky they perceive various stages of nuclear waste production and management to be, including the production of nuclear waste, temporary storage of nuclear waste, transportation of nuclear waste, and permanent storage of nuclear waste. The five-point Likert-type scale included the response categories "no risk," "slight risk," "some risk," "a lot of risk," and "extreme risk."[12]

Political ideology was measured by asking respondents to place themselves on a standard seven-point scale ranging from extremely liberal to extremely conservative.

Cultural biases, including those for the egalitarian, hierarchical, and individualist cultural types, were operationalized by using the average of three response values, each derived from a set of questions that asked respondents to agree strongly, agree, disagree, or disagree strongly with statements such as "One of the problems with people today is that they challenge authority too often." The specific items were modifications of questions employed by Karl Dake and Aaron Wildavsky.[13] These three average measures (named egalitarian, hierarch, and individualist) have values ranging from o to 3.[14]

Trust was measured by asking respondents how much trust they would place in the statements made by spokespersons for each of three prominent organizations regarding a controversial decision on nuclear waste management. The scale is an eleven-point scale ranging from o ("not at all trustworthy") to 10 ("completely trustworthy"). The organizations rated were the nuclear power industry, the NRC, and national environmental interest groups.

Political efficacy was operationalized in two separate scales representing internal and external efficacy. A measure of internal efficacy was obtained by using three standard questions that measured the degree to which respondents felt they could understand and participate in the political process. External efficacy was measured using three questions that tapped the degree to which respondents felt the government was responsive to their needs and wishes. Using principal components factor analysis, we generated factor scores for each type of efficacy.[15] These factor scores were employed as indicators of political efficacy in the analysis.

Demographic control variables included in each of the hypothesis tests included measures of age, education, income, gender, and ethnicity. The latter two variables were included as dummies, with values of 1 representing "female" and "minority," respectively. These were included to help ensure that the measures of association among the modeled variables reflect genuine associations rather than spurious associations resulting from excluded demographic characteristics.

ANALYSIS

Our three sets of hypotheses were tested using multiple linear regression analysis, including each (potentially competing) explanatory variable in one composite model to avoid the possibility of spurious or indirect attributions of influence among the specified variables. The results of tests for hypotheses 1 through 5 are presented in Table 1.1, in which the estimated effects of ideology, trust, worldview and the demographic controls on perceived risks in each of four stages of nuclear waste management are shown. Explanatory variables that had no statistically discernible effect (at the 0.10 level or beyond) on any of the four measures of perceived risk were dropped from Table 1.1 (and subsequent tables) in the interest of clarity of presentation.

First note that the overall explanatory power of the models is moderate (for individual-level survey data), with R^2s indicating that each of the models explained 15 to 17 percent of the variation in perceived risk. H_1, testing for a direct link between ideology and perceived risks, was confirmed by the analysis. For all measures of perceived nuclear risk, those respondents who identified themselves as more conservative perceived significantly *less* risk. Thus, as expected, our analysis confirms this basic finding of prior research.

H_2 was also confirmed, showing that for *all* measures of perceived risk, greater trust in national environmental groups was associated with larger perceived risks. Note that for each of the kinds of perceived risk, the direct effects of trust in environmental groups appear to be greater than those of political ideology, as shown by the magnitudes of the standardized coefficients. H_3, testing for linkages between perceived risks and trust in organizations responsible for management of nuclear facilities, was also confirmed. Trust in the nuclear industry was a particularly strong predictor of perceived risk, with the largest standardized coefficients of *any* of the explanatory variables for all four kinds of perceived risks. Trust in the NRC was significantly related to perceived risks of nuclear waste production, temporary storage, and transport of nuclear wastes. As hypothesized, wherever a significant relationship was detected, greater trust in the nuclear industry and the NRC was associated with the perception of less risk. Thus, these results are consistent with two distinct kinds of relationships between trust and perceived risks: Trust may operate via individuals' trust in the assertions of policy reference groups (such as environmental groups) or through trust in those actually charged with implementation of the relevant policy (such as the NRC and nuclear industry).

H_4 specified the expected relationships between cultural bias and perceived risk. The hypotheses were confirmed by the analysis. The greater the individuals' propensity to agree with egalitarian cultural biases, the greater the perceived risk for each of the different nuclear risk measures. Furthermore, note that for each kind of risk, the magnitudes of the standardized coefficients for the egalitarian worldview are substantially larger than those for political ideology—in some

TABLE 1.1 Explaining Nuclear Risk Perception (standardized coefficients; p-values for two-tailed test)

Dependent Variable	R^2	Explanatory Variables					Demographic Controls		
		Conservative (ideology)	Nuc. Ind.	Trust Env. Gps.	NRC	Egalitarian (worldview)	Gender (female)	Education	Income
NW production	0.172	−.086 (.006)	−.164 (<.001)	.129 (<.001)	−.112 (.005)	.146 (<.001)	.099 (.001)	−.067 (.042)	−.082 (.012)
Temp. NW storage	0.168	−.109 (.001)	−.189 (<.001)	.133 (<.001)	−.070 (<.077)	.111 (.001)	.113 (<.001)	NS	−.083 (−.083)
NW transport	0.162	−.063 (.044)	−.150 (<.001)	.131 (<.001)	−.092 (.020)	.134 (<.001)	.178 (<.001)	NS	NS
Perm. NW storage	0.154	−.071 (.023)	−.219 (<.001)	.101 (.001)	NS	.130 (<.001)	.175 (<.001)	NS	NS

Note: NW: nuclear waste; NS: estimated coefficient not statistically significant at the 0.1 level.

cases more than twice as large. Thus it appears that cultural bias is a substantially better predictor of nuclear risk perception than is self-identified political ideology, at least as measured here.[16] In addition, as hypothesized, individuals' placement on the hierarch and individualist scales was not statistically significantly related to any of the perceived risk measures. Thus, once the effects of one's propensity to egalitarian cultural biases is taken into account, affinities to the other cultural predispositions appear to be unrelated to perceived risks of nuclear wastes.

Finally, note that several of the basic demographic variables are significantly associated with perceived risk. As has been found elsewhere,[17] sex differences matter, with women perceiving significantly more risk than men. In addition, higher levels of income and education are associated with the perception of less risk. Although not the focus of this analysis, the pattern of relationships among the demographic variables suggests that nuclear risk perception may be affected by social class, with individuals of higher socioeconomic status perceiving less risk than those at the lower end of the socioeconomic ladder.

Our third set of hypotheses concerns possible indirect linkages of political efficacy to perceived risk, via cultural biases. Having established that cultural bias is a significant (and relatively large) predictor of perceived nuclear risks, we now ask to what degree levels of political efficacy may be related to these biases. Our hypotheses are that, ceteris paribus, lower external political efficacy will be associated with a greater propensity to adopt egalitarian cultural biases (H_5), and lower internal efficacy will be linked to more affinity with the hierarch's cultural biases (H_6). The results of the analysis, predicting placement on the cultural bias scales using the political efficacy measures as independent variables and controlling for basic demographic attributes, are shown in Table 1.2.

First note that the R^2s for these models are relatively modest, with none exceeding 12 percent, and one (individualist) falling below 4 percent. This is to be expected, since we specified the models with only a few of the many possible correlates of cultural bias. Nevertheless, both of our hypothesized linkages proved to be statistically significant and in the direction specified. The less externally efficacious one is, the greater the propensity to agree with the cultural bias of the egalitarian. And the less internally efficacious one is, the greater the tendency to accept the hierarch's cultural biases. Note that efficacy was unrelated to the measure of individualist worldview, partly explaining the small R^2 for that model. Note also that for the hierarch model, the internal efficacy measure was the single most influential predictor (exceeding education, gender, and age), as indicated by the magnitude of the standardized coefficient. For the egalitarian model, external efficacy was the strongest single predictor. The relative importance of the efficacy measures in these models indicates that general perceptions of one's relationship to the political process, and societywide changes in these perceptions, are important ingredients in cultural biases. And as we have shown in Table 1.1, cultural biases contribute in significant ways to the perceptions of nuclear risks.

TABLE 1.2 Explaining Cultural Bias (standardized coefficients; p-values for two-tailed test)

Dependent Variable	R^2	Explanatory Variables		Demographic Controls				
		External Efficacy	Internal Efficacy	Gender (female)	Education	Income	Age	Minority (Black, Hispanic)
Hierarch	0.070	NS	-.140 (<.001)	.076 (.013)	-.108 (.001)	NS	.131 (<.001)	NS
Egalitarian	0.114	-.174 (<.001)	NS	.090 (.003)	-.152 (<.001)	-.098 (.002)	-.055 (.059)	.079 (.007)
Individualist	0.035	NS	NS	-.084 (.007)	-.185 (<.001)	.060 (.068)	NS	NS

Note: NS: estimated coefficient not statistically significant at the 0.1 level.

Table 1.2 also shows some interesting relationships between the demographic attributes of individuals and cultural biases. The higher the education level, the lower the score on *any* of the cultural bias measures. In part this reflects a greater reluctance on the part of the more sophisticated respondents to strongly agree with any of the cultural bias items.[18] The effect of higher income was (not surprisingly) to increase agreement with the individualist cultural bias and decrease agreement with the bias of the egalitarian. Older respondents were more likely to be hierarchs and less likely to be egalitarians. And minority respondents were significantly more likely to agree with the egalitarian cultural biases.

Finally, our third set of hypotheses concerns possible effects of political efficacy, ideology, and cultural biases on trust. The import of these hypotheses concerns the *indirect* effects of the independent variables on perceived risks through their effects on trust. Focusing on trust in those groups that were significant predictors of perceived risks (the nuclear industry, the NRC, and national environmental groups), we ran linear multiple regression models with the hypothesized explanatory variables and a set of demographic control variables. The results are shown in Table 1.3.

As we hypothesized (H_8), external political efficacy was a strong predictor of trust in all policy elites. Across the board, the greater the sense of external political efficacy, the greater the level of trust. Internal efficacy measures were unrelated to trust in the policy elites.

Regarding political ideology (H_9), our hypothesis was also confirmed. The more liberal respondents were significantly more likely to trust environmental groups and less likely to trust the NRC or the nuclear industry. As indicated by the size of the standardized coefficients in Table 1.3, the link between ideology and trust for environmental groups is substantially stronger than it is for the nuclear industry or the NRC. It appears that the indirect link between ideology and perceived risk operates primarily via reference groups (such as environmental groups) and less so for those charged with implementation of specific policies.

The associations between cultural predispositions and trust in policy elites were fully consistent with our hypotheses. Agreement with the hierarch's positions was significantly associated with *greater* trust in the NRC and the nuclear industry (H_{10}), whereas agreement with the egalitarian positions was associated with greater trust for the national environmental groups (H_{11}). In contrast, individualists tended to have *less* trust in the national environmental groups.

DISCUSSION AND CONCLUSIONS

This analysis has tested an array of hypotheses regarding the potential direct and indirect linkages between cultural biases, political ideology, trust, and perceptions of nuclear risk. The intent was to use data from a national survey to assess the degree to which perceptions of nuclear risk were imbedded in patterns of relationships among more general political attitudes and constructs. The findings pre-

TABLE 1.3 Explaining Variations in Trust for Nuclear Policy Actors (standardized coefficients; p-values for two-tailed test)

| Dependent Variable | R^2 | Explanatory Variables | | | | | Demographic Controls | | |
		Conservative (ideology)	Egalitarian	Hierarch	Individualist	External Efficacy	Age	Minority (Black, Hispanic)
Trust in nuc. ind.	0.071	.064 (.045)	−.108 (<.001)	.139 (<.001)	NS	.133 (<.001)	NS	.082 (.010)
Trust in env. gps.	0.081	−.101 (.001)	.153 (<.001)	NS	−.062 (.052)	.116 (.001)	−.132 (<.001)	NS
Trust in NRC	0.072	.060 (.063)	−.100 (.003)	.114 (<.001)	NS	.162 (<.001)	NS	NS

Note: NS: estimated coefficient not statistically significant at the 0.1 level.

sented here indicate that nuclear risk perceptions, like attitudes and preferences about policies more generally, are indeed directly and indirectly entangled with political attitudes that characterize a more general political context. In particular, these results point to the importance of the direct and indirect roles of cultural bias in shaping perceived nuclear risks.

Confirming findings from prior studies, we found political ideology and trust in political elites to be significant predictors of perceived nuclear risks. In general the more politically liberal the individual, the greater the perceived risks. Also in accord with prior research, trust was a significant contributor to perceived nuclear risks. The direct affects of trust on risk perception appear to operate through two distinct routes; trust in reference groups (such as environmental groups) appears to incline one toward the stated position of that group, whereas trust in those who implement the policy (such as the NRC and the nuclear industry) is associated with less perceived risk in the outcomes of that policy.

However, we also found that cultural biases are significant direct contributors to perceptions of risk. Indeed, worldview is a substantially more powerful predictor of perceived nuclear risk than is political ideology. As suggested by the literature on cultural theory, those who opt for the egalitarian worldview perceived the greatest nuclear risk.

It was the indirect pathways by which political attitudes and beliefs affect risk perceptions that proved most interesting, however. Political efficacy is tied to perceived nuclear risk along two distinct routes. Greater external efficacy uniformly increases trust in political elites, which in turn refracts into competing influences on perceived risk (via trust in reference groups and policy implementors). External efficacy is also significantly correlated with cultural bias, with less external efficacy linked to an egalitarian worldview; those who have little faith that the political system will respond to their wants and needs appear to prefer a pattern of social relations that equalizes political (and economic) power, permitting more direct and immediate participation in shaping public policy. Those who have less internal efficacy tend to opt for a hierarchical bias; those with little sense of their own capabilities to understand and participate in politics appear to prefer a pattern of social relations that relies on tradition, role differentiation, and responsiveness to authority. Thus political efficacy appears to be intimately related to cultural bias, which in turn affects perceptions of nuclear risk.

The role of cultural bias is compounded through its own indirect influences on risk perception via its connection to trust in policy elites. Hierarchs tend to place greater trust in the NRC and the nuclear industry, which is not surprising given the centralized, expert-dependent nature of these entities. And, as noted earlier, trust in the NRC and the nuclear industry is associated with the perception of less nuclear risk. Egalitarians have less trust in both the NRC and the nuclear industry and *more* trust in national environmental groups. Individualists have less trust in environmental groups, which makes considerable sense given the individualists' abhorrence of the type of fetters on private industry that environmentalists tend to favor. Thus cultural biases have a relatively powerful direct effect on perceived nuclear risk and significant indirect effects through the pattern of linkages between culture and trust in policy elites.

In sum, individuals' perceptions of nuclear risk should not be taken out of political context. Perceived nuclear risks, and the more general controversies over nuclear technologies, are significantly influenced by cultural predispositions, ideology, trust, and political efficacy. These data make clear that risk perceptions should not be seen as driven primarily by citizens' understanding (or lack thereof) of the safety attributes of a particular policy proposal, nor should they be seen as the exclusive result of abstract psychological forces (such as risk "acceptance" or "aversion"). Rather, nuclear risk perception is subject to the full gamut of mental linkages that characterize the more standard run of policy positions, such as those regarding welfare, taxes, and environmental issues. Nuclear risk perception has deep roots in the political orientations—and particularly in the political culture—of the American public, and it is not immune to the kinds of reasoning and reacting that apply to other political issues.

NOTES

1. J. Kuklinski, D. Metlay, and W. Kay, "Citizen Knowledge and Choices in the Complex Issue of Nuclear Energy," *American Journal of Political Science* 26(1982), 615–642. Stanley Rothman and S. Robert Lichter, "Elite Ideology and Risk Perception in Nuclear Energy Policy," *American Political Science Review* 81(June 1987), 383–404.

2. Luther Carter, "Nuclear Imperatives and Public Trust: Dealing with Radioactive Waste," *Issues in Science and Technology* (Winter 1987), 46–61. Leo Gomez, Hank Jenkins-Smith, and Kenneth Miller, "Changes in Perceptions of Nuclear Risk over Time," paper presented at the annual meeting of the American Association for the Advancement of Science, Chicago, Ill., 1992.

3. Paul Slovic, James Flynn, and Mark Layman, "Perceived Risk, Trust, and the Politics of Nuclear Waste," *Science* 254(1991), 1603–1607.

4. Hank Jenkins-Smith, Jennifer Espey, Amelia Rouse, and Douglas Moland, *Perceptions of Risk in the Management of Nuclear Waste: Mapping Elite and Mass Beliefs and Attitudes* (Albuquerque, N.M.: Sandia National Laboratories, SAND90-7002, 1991). Hank Jenkins-Smith, "Alternative Theories of the Policy Process: Reflections of a Research Strategy for the Study of Nuclear Waste Policy," *Political Science and Politics* 24(June 1991), 157–166.

5. See, for example, Kuklinski et al., "Citizen Knowledge and Choices"; and Rothman and Lichter, "Elite Ideology and Risk Perception."

6. Mary Douglas and Aaron Wildavsky, *Risk and Culture: An Essay on the Selection of Technical and Environmental Dangers* (Berkeley: University of California Press, 1982). Karl Dake and Aaron Wildavsky, "Theories of Risk Perception: Who Fears What and Why?" *Daedalus* (Spring 1990), 41–60. Karl Dake, "Orienting Dispositions in the Perception of Risk: An Analysis of Contemporary Worldviews and Cultural Biases," *Journal of Cross-Cultural Psychology* 22(1991), 61–82. Michael Thompson, Richard Ellis, and Aaron Wildavsky, *Cultural Theory* (Boulder: Westview Press, 1990).

7. Douglas and Wildavsky, *Risk and Culture.*

8. Cultural theory as described here is, of course, not the only operationalization of "culture" as an explanation of attitudes about risk and environmental issues. Ronald Inglehart, for example ("Post Materialism in an Environment of Insecurity," *American Political Science Review* 75[June 1981], 880–900; *Culture Shift in Advanced Industrial Society* [Princeton: Princeton University Press, 1990]), has specified a quite different model. For a comparison of the role of the two different models of culture in shaping nuclear images, see Hank Jenkins-Smith, *Testing Rival Hypotheses About the Effects of Negative Nuclear Imagery on Regional Stigmatization* (Albuquerque, N.M.: UNM Institute for Public Policy, 1993).

9. Stephen Craig, Richard Niemi, and Glenn Silver, "Political Efficacy and Trust: A Report on the NES Pilot Study Items," *Political Behavior* 12(1990), 289–314. It is unclear to us which way the causal relationship would run between cultural bias and political efficacy: On the one hand, culture might determine one's sense of political efficacy; on the other hand, one's sense of political efficacy might very well contribute to one's cultural bias. For purposes of this analysis, however, our concern is with the pattern of associations between cultural bias and efficacy, and we leave the question of causal direction to a later analysis.

10. We would also expect those with a low sense of *both* internal and external efficacy to hold the cultural biases of the fatalist. Unfortunately, the data set employed here does not contain an operationalization of the fatalist worldview.

11. The response rate was calculated as the number of completed interviews divided by the sum of the working telephone numbers tried. Note that this calculation is much more conservative than the response rates usually reported; usually the response rate is calculated as the percentage of eligible respondents who completed the survey. In our view, that method of calculating response rates is misleading in that it lumps many potentially eligible respondents (e.g., those who were away from home during the survey or who hung up before eligibility could be ascertained) as ineligibles. For that reason, we opt for the more conservative—though admittedly less impressive—calculation used here.

12. The exact wording of the question was, "Next, we would like you to evaluate the risk involved in a number of situations. Would you say that the following situations pose extreme risk, a lot of risk, some risk, slight risk, or no risk? (1) The production of nuclear energy. (2) Temporary storage of nuclear waste in the facilities where it was produced. (3) The transportation of nuclear waste. (4) The permanent storage of nuclear waste."

13. Dake and Wildavsky, "Theories of Risk Perception."

14. Respondents were asked to "please indicate whether you would agree strongly, agree, disagree, or disagree strongly with the following statements."

Hierarchist: (1) I think I am much stricter about obeying rules than most people. (2) One of the problems with people today is that they challenge authority too often. (3) The best way to provide for future generations is to preserve our customs and heritage.

Competitive Individualist: (1) People who are successful in business have a right to enjoy their wealth as they see fit. (2) Everyone should have an equal chance to succeed or fail *without* government interference. (3) Our laws should not create special advantages or disadvantages for anyone *for any reason.*

Egalitarian: (1) Big corporations are responsible for most of the evil in the world. (2) What our country needs is a fairness revolution to make the distribution of wealth more equal. (3) Decisions in business and government should rely more heavily on popular participation.

15. For a discussion of the validity of this approach see Craig, Niemi, and Silver, "Political Efficacy and Trust."

16. It is quite possible that use of a different operationalization of political ideology (e.g., a multi-item index) would provide a stronger predictor of nuclear risk perceptions. We plan to test for such a possibility in future research.

17. See, for example, Alvin Mushkatel, J. Nigg, and D. Pijawka, "The Urban Risk Survey: Public Response, Perception, and Intended Behavior of Las Vegas Metropolitan Residents to the Proposed High-Level Nuclear Waste Repository" (Mountain West Research, for the State of Nevada Nuclear Waste Project Office, Carson City, Nev., 1989).

18. Apparently a higher level of education makes it easier to disagree with any of the cultural bias items; for eight of the nine items, education was significantly ($p < .05$) associated with greater disagreement. On the remaining item, the slope was negative (more education, greater disagreement), but it was not statistically significant.

CHAPTER 2

"This Land Is Your Land, This Land Is My Land": Cultural Conflict in Environmental and Land-Use Regulation

Dennis J. Coyle

Environmental and land-use regulation can be complex, tedious, and dry. It can seem excessively technical and far removed from the great questions of social and political life. But the questions of how the earth shall be used, and who shall decide this, are inexorably tied up with issues about the nature of society and with issues of freedom and responsibility, community and democracy. David Bloor puts it aptly: "Nature becomes a code for talking about society, a language in which justifications and challenges can be expressed. It is a medium of social interaction."[1] Environmental regulation is contentious not because the world is full of aspiring soil and water engineers but because regulation directly affects the social choices of individuals. Ordering the uses of land orders the users. As laboratories for finding everyday people grappling with the great questions of social life, a hearing at the local land-use commission or environmental review board is hard to beat. As Eric Steele has observed in regard to zoning, environmental regulation "provides a forum, frames the issues, and provides a vocabulary for communicating about normative conflict."[2]

The arguments for or against environmental and land-use regulation, arguments heard in legislative chambers and town meetings, at academic conferences and in court opinions, can be categorized according to three basic beliefs: A well-ordered society is desirable and is promoted by regulatory controls; regulation violates the basic freedoms of the individual; and greater equality is desirable, and regulation should be used to redistribute resources and power in society. The language of environmental disputes mirrors the debate over the comparative merits of social arrangements, or cultures, based on three fundamental values: liberty, equality, and order.

A culture, as I use the term, is composed of shared social practices and the values and beliefs that legitimate them. Culture, then, incorporates both ideas and practice. It is both more and less than ideology. More in that the mundane aspects of life, such as eating and gardening habits, are as much a part of culture as the ideological theories of elites. And perhaps less if anchoring thought in the details of day-to-day living is perceived as less elevating than the rarefied pursuit of pure ideology. Many participants in environmental and land-use disputes are not rigidly or even consistently ideological, but everybody has ideas about how they wish to live. Environmental and land-use disputes raise basic questions of personal freedom and social responsibility, but they are more accurately characterized as cultural disputes, in which ideas and values are implicit in different patterns of resource use, than as consciously ideological disputes.

I will show how the three major categories of the grid-group approach—hierarchy, libertarianism, and egalitarianism—help us understand the political and social conflicts embedded in environmental and land-use disputes. Table 2.1 summarizes these competing perspectives. When I say environmentalism is largely about social and political values and beliefs, I do not intend to denigrate it but rather to point out an essential element that makes it all the more fascinating. When I refer to a person as a libertarian, egalitarian, or hierarchist, I do not intend the label to be pejorative, implying excessive rigidity. It only suggests that a particular culture best characterizes her arguments and preferences.

ENVIRONMENT AND HIERARCHY

Egalitarianism and hierarchy share an appreciation of the group, and it is in these cultures that environmentalism is most at home. Environmentalism fundamentally expands the group to incorporate the natural world. As Aldo Leopold said, "The land ethic simply enlarges the boundaries of the community to include soils, waters, plants, and animals, or collectively, the land."[3]

Egalitarianism and hierarchy differ, however, in their preferred relations between nature and humanity. In egalitarian environmentalism, the natural world has intrinsic value, and efforts may be made to put it on an equal footing with people. To the hierarchist, people may have an obligation to use natural resources responsibly, but they are clearly superior to nature and may employ it in the service of the good society. This acceptance of humans' domination over nature can be seen in the early conservation movement, the predecessor of modern environmentalism.[4] For example, Lester Ward, an employee of the United States Geological Survey who worked with John Wesley Powell, rejected laissez-faire but also saw waste and inefficiency in nature.[5] Powell himself decried the inefficiency of nature, urging, for example, that engineers harness rivers that would otherwise "run to waste."[6]

Conservationists such as Ward and Bernhard Fernow saw care for the environment as an extension of the developing welfare-state ethic, what Fernow called

TABLE 2.1   Environmental and Land-Use Cultures

	Hierarchical	Egalitarian	Libertarian
Key value	Order	Equality	Liberty
Planning arena	Public, closed	Public, open	Private
Key actors	Specialists	Citizens	Owners
Response to uncertainty	Centralize, Expertise	Decentralize, Simplify	Market discovery
Environmental theory	Conservation	Deep ecology	Free market
Attitude toward environment	Homeocentric	Ecocentric	Egocentric
Ideal community	Everything in its place	Self-sufficient	Prosperous
Ideal variation among communities	Great, Predictable	Small	Not predictable
Best land-use control	Euclidean zoning	Consensual planning	Private covenants
Desired zoning reform	Tighten variances	Inclusionary zoning	End zoning
Housing solution for poor	Multifamily zone or city	Fair share requirements	Filtering
Constitutional doctrine	Police power	Equal protection	Takings
Illustrative case	Euclid	Mt. Laurel	National Land

"providential government."[7] Both the natural and the social worlds required restructuring and central direction to be efficient and harmonious. Ward's prescription was a national commission of wise elites, otherwise known as social scientists, to identify social problems and recommend solutions. According to Tim O'Riordan, early conservationists "believed that they were competent to allocate resources without political interference. They felt that politics confused matters, created inefficiencies, and thus frustrated rational and efficient decisions. The idea that the 'lay' public should in any way be involved in conservationist principles was anathema to them: the management of resources was a matter for experts."[8]

The conservationists of the Progressive Era were fighting a holy war against the libertarian sins of nineteenth-century development. Control over resources and land use would be removed from the amoral hand of the market and entrusted to expert elites who could rise above the self-interest of politics and profits. The very basis of economic and political relations must be changed; "The laissez faire theory of government is no longer tenable," asserted Newman Baker, an attorney prominent in the creation of zoning.[9] The antidote to the excesses of individualism was to be "a system of regulation which established a hierarchy of uses ... a community whose planned and orderly development provided a place for everything, and kept everything in its place."[10]

Modern land-use controls in the United States began with the development of zoning in the early 1900s. Zoning was just one product of the progressive impulse for order and predictability. The pressure for zoning, particularly in New York, followed decades of rapid growth that were accompanied by the influx of millions of immigrants. Early zoning advocates justified their measures as necessary to avoid the social ills of urban ethnic neighborhoods inhabited by the new arrivals.[11] Constance Perin has argued that zoning was a barely disguised tool of class and ethnic discrimination.[12] In effect, the hierarchists of America were having trouble finding a room in their house for the new groups. In the South, zoning was a tool for explicitly preserving racial segregation. Atlanta's zoning law divided residential areas into "three race districts, white, colored, and undetermined."[13] Robert Whitten, the author of the Atlanta racial zoning ordinance, also led the development of zoning laws in the North,[14] although they were not explicitly racial.

The Supreme Court ratified the new environmental hierarchy when in 1926 it upheld the constitutionality of zoning in *Euclid v. Ambler Realty Co.*[15] A lower federal court had invalidated the ordinance, and the judge assailed the imposition of what we term hierachy through regulation: "The purpose," he wrote, "is really to regulate the mode of living of persons. ... The result to be accomplished is to classify population and segregate them according to their income or situation in life."[16] Ambler Realty argued that, in cultural terms, liberty trumps hierarchy: "That our cities should be made beautiful and orderly is, of course, in the highest degree desirable," the company argued in its brief, "but it is even more important that our people should remain free."[17]

On appeal to the high court, Justice Sutherland reasoned that zoning was in the public interest because it was essentially an extension of the common law that prohibits nuisances: "A nuisance may be merely a right thing in the wrong place—like a pig in the parlor instead of the barnyard."[18] This is a curious analogy, because we don't know who owns the pig and who the parlor, and thus whether any nuisance exists at all. If I keep my own pig in my parlor, it is not a nuisance. Indeed, a pig in a parlor is a rather fashionable pet these days. If my pig prefers *your* parlor, but you do *not* prefer my pig in your parlor, then it is a nuisance. But offending the new hierarchy of land use was sufficient to be condemned as a nuisance; pigs, factories, and homes would now be required to stay where they belonged. The analogy of environmental degradation to the traditional notion of nuisance remains today the central underpinning of the constitutionality of regulation.

Modern mainstream environmentalism with its reliance on expertise and the anticipation and regulation of all environmental effects of human actions is also rich with the language and the logic of hierarchy.[19] Many environmentalists echo the progressive notion that nature can serve humans through enlightened management. The ecologist Eugene Odum, for example, recommends that environmental policy be based on the "esthetic and recreational as well as product needs" of society and seek to "ensure a continuous yield of useful plants, animals, and materials by establishing a balanced cycle of harvest and renewal."[20]

Hierarchy often connotes conservatism, a reverence for the established order, and environmentalism has a strong preservationist ethic. Robert Paehlke acknowledged the similarity to political conservativism when he said: "Environmentalists must heed the wisdom of Edmund Burke and build on the past rather than seek to destroy it."[21] The American past he seeks to preserve is not liberal individualism but the ideals of socialism, which he seeks to merge with environmentalism to reinvigorate progressive politics. And the social welfare state does evoke the hierarchical culture, with its elevation of the common interest and reliance on expertise and planning.

Hierarchical and libertarian environmentalists, unlike their egalitarian brethren, share a utilitarian concern for the social welfare. They agree that nature should serve humans but disagree fundamentally about how that should be done. Hierarchy presumes that centralized organization will produce essential knowledge, such as what the public interest is and how it can be obtained, and that society can fully anticipate the consequences of human action. One group of land-use scholars, for example, argues that "the full impact of any specific proposal for development on the natural, social and economic environment of a community can, and must, be evaluated."[22] Hierarchy requires convergence on values as well as on facts. Ian McHarg asserts that "we can identify social [and natural] values and rank them from high to low. ... Wildlife habitats, scenic quality, the importance of historic buildings, recreational facilities can all be ranked."[23]

Proponents of hierarchy put their faith in the expertise and centralized control of science and planning. An unelected body of specialized experts is frequently advocated to diagnose environmental ills and prescribe cures. Robert Linowes and Don Allensworth, for example, advocate creating a "court of ecology" composed of elites "from various walks of life—including lawyers, architects, engineers, hydrologists, geologists, urbanologists, conservationists, and planners." The purpose of this panel would be to "control the environment in the public interest."[24] Alvin Weinberg recommends creation of a permanent "priesthood" of nuclear technologists to secure safe operation of centralized energy systems.[25] William Ophuls speaks of a "class of ecological mandarins."[26]

Although the growth of national, state, and regional environmental regulation reflects increasing reliance on hierarchical nostrums of comprehensive planning, prediction, and control, the regulatory process in the United States is hardly the hierarchical ideal. Richard Babcock, an attorney and scholar, has described the planning utopia as "a bunch of happy, well-informed people with a social IQ of 150 sit[ting] around making decisions in complete freedom from outside pressure."[27] As any exasperated planner will tell you, reality does not match the ideal. In a nation with strong traditions of democracy, localism, and individual autonomy, environmental and land-use regulation has been more subject to political control and less comprehensive than planners often think wise. Reflecting the frustration of the profession, planner Melvin Levin says, "Planners are bringing bad news to the unheeding; we resemble killjoy adults among frolicking children."[28] But "frolicking children" frustrated by the constraints of regulation, such as an owner seeking to use her property, may look to the low-grid culture of libertarianism for an alternative vision of environment and society, and it is to that perspective that we now turn.

LAND AND LIBERTY

The libertarian conception of social good and evil is virtually a mirror image of the hierarchical (as we would expect of a culture that lies at the opposite end of the grid and group poles). For the founders of conservation, central control was a way to replace the nightmare of unregulated development with the serenity of order. For libertarians, it is the coercive power of the state that destroys community and individual satisfaction. From this perspective, the best way to serve the public is to promote the private. Libertarians such as Ellen Frankel Paul and Richard Epstein argue that justice and the Constitution require a substantial retraction of the government tentacles reaching over private property.[29] Their agenda calls for a sweeping rollback of the welfare state. "It will be said," Epstein has concluded, "that my position invalidates much of the twentieth century legislation, and so it does."[30] Among the modern governmental powers that would fail Epstein's standard are wealth redistribution, estate and gift taxes, urban renewal, rent control, most zoning, and minimum-wage and maximum-hour regulations.[31] Why must the current century be rolled back to meet the demands of justice? Just what is so sacrosanct about private property, anyway? In the libertarian ideal, property is the coinage of freedom. It is the medium for personal development and expression and for social exchange, and the guarantor of political liberty.

Critics charge that individualism results in wasteful competition and leaves social needs unmet. The libertarian response is that freedom benefits society as well as individuals. As people pursue profits through the market, they produce goods and services valued by others, thus inadvertently serving social needs. A role for planning remains in the libertarian ideal; the key distinction is that no one has the exclusive power to plan. Unlike hierarchy, which implies fact and value agreement, libertarianism implies conflict and uncertainty. Through markets, individuals, groups, and companies can not only pursue their own ends but also test their own hypotheses. Competition, Friedrich Hayek argues, is a "discovery procedure" that allows simultaneous pursuit of different strategies for meeting social needs.[32] Decentralization of planning ensures that the mistakes of any single person or business will have limited effect and increases the likelihood of beneficial discoveries.

The Pennsylvania Supreme Court ushered in the modern era of concern with the social consequences of land-use regulation when in 1965 it invalidated large-lot zoning in *National Land & Investment Co. v. Easttown Board of Adjustment*,[33] and the opinion is rich with libertarian language.

"Zoning is a means by which a governmental body can plan for the future," wrote Justice Roberts. "It may not be used as a means to deny the future."[34] Local governments must shoulder the responsibilities that "time and natural growth invariably bring" and cannot "stand in the way of the natural forces which send our growing population into hitherto undeveloped areas in search of a comfortable place to live."[35] Contrast this openness to unregulated growth with the hostility of the New Jersey court, in its later cases attacking zoning, to "uncontrolled migration to anywhere anyone wants to settle, roads leading to places they should never be."[36] Whereas the New Jersey court has sought to bend hierarchical planning to its social preferences, the tendency in Pennsylvania has been to trust the market.

"There is no doubt that many of the residents of this area are highly desirous of keeping it the way it is," wrote Justice Roberts. "These desires, however, do not rise to the level of public welfare. This is purely a matter of private desire which zoning regulations may not be employed to effectuate."[37] An asserted need for large lots is "purely a matter of private desire" only if we assume libertarian premises. From the more group-oriented perspectives of hierarchy or egalitarianism, it might well be appropriate to expect individuals to defer to deeply felt preferences of their neighbors.

The libertarian tolerates exclusive communities, but not with a boost from government. Quoting an earlier opinion, Roberts said in *National Land* that "an owner of land may constitutionally make his property as large and as private or secluded or exclusive as he desires and his purse can afford."[38] If forced to bargain in the private market, according to the libertarian argument, people will have to face the social costs of their exclusionary predilections and decide whether they are willing to literally pay the price. Government regulation, the libertarian argues, masks the social costs and thus skews land-use development patterns toward socially inefficient uses.

Libertarians regard resource exploitation as a desirable consequence of individual initiative and creativity because the pursuit of personal preferences creates social wealth. They agree with John Locke that if God gave the earth to humankind, he gave it for "the use of the industrious."[39] Nature provides a bounty for human prosperity that is limited only by our imaginations.

Libertarians may be pessimistic about human nature in that they see selfishness as unavoidable and distrust plans for mass social action, but they brim with optimism about the environment, assuming that nature will be as tolerant as our neighbors should be. The libertarian rejects Malthusian warnings of impending ecological catastrophe[40] and assumes either that no human mistakes will prove fatal to the environment or that if they might, we cannot accurately anticipate these effects. Julian Simon and Herman Kahn argue, for example, that there's no reason to stop the party and turn out the lights. They assert that technological and geological discovery will expand energy supplies "at least until our sun ceases to shine."[41]

Engaging in a futile pursuit of perfect knowledge brings only paralysis; better to rely on spontaneous responses to unanticipated problems.[42] Jerry Taylor, a policy analyst at the libertarian Cato Institute, turns the tables on hierarchy, arguing that centrally planned societies "eventually experience the very collapse feared by conservationists. Liberal societies, built on free markets and open inquiry, create resources and expand the possibilities of mankind."[43]

"Environmentalism" is not a part of the libertarian culture, if by that we mean an obligation to consider what is "good" for nature separate from our own preferences. The "free market environmentalism" school argues that there is nothing so unique about the environment that it cannot best be protected through the market pursuit of self-interest, as long as property rights incorporate the natural environment.[44] Trees don't have property rights, but their owners do, and people who value trees will pay for them, such as by banding together to purchase a nature preserve. An alternative to purchase is to negotiate covenants restricting the use of private property, which for decades have been the primary means of controlling land use in Houston. Even for pollution, a market solution is asserted: I might pay an industry owner to stop his pollution, or the owner might pay me for permission to pollute my property. As an alternative to buying out the neighborhood polluter, I might take him to court. Pollution is a physical nuisance, and most libertarians, such as Murray Rothbard, would recognize a property right protecting against such intrusions.[45]

Even the housing needs of the poor can arguably best be met without governmental control. The poor, the libertarian argument goes, need housing, but not necessarily new housing. Communities should permit the unrestrained development of housing in response to market demand. As qualified homebuyers move into new homes, they will move out of their old ones, and the housing opportunities will "filter down" to those most in need. Imposition of government coercion, such as rent control, is argued to be not only unjust but also foolish, as it will only discourage the production of new housing and the maintenance of existing housing.[46]

The unpredictable society preferred by the libertarian is not for the risk-averse. Many will be the mistakes, but, it is argued, greater will be the social rewards. The claims of the libertarian purist are rather grandiose: "Only we," writes Rothbard, "offer technology without technocracy, growth without pollution, liberty without chaos, law without tyranny."[47] In this shining utopia, preferences are known, and information and opportunities are plentiful. There are no transaction costs to impede voluntary bargaining and efficient exchange, no resource deprivations severe enough to subvert personal freedom.

THE PURSUIT OF SOCIAL
AND ENVIRONMENTAL EQUALITY

Egalitarianism, the third and final of the cultures I will discuss, seeks to reconcile the libertarian concern for the individual with the hierarchical acceptance of public control (to combine, in other words, the low grid of libertarianism with the high group of hierarchy). In doing so, it creates an alternative social vision, rooted in the pursuit of equality, that is fundamentally at odds with both libertarianism and hierarchy. Frederick Thayer's book, for example, is entitled *An End to Hierarchy and Competition.*[48]

Traditional planning and conservation are troublesome to the egalitarian for three reasons: First, they place control in the hands of specialized experts, divorcing the common citizen from control over her environment. Second, they can perpetuate, intentionally or not, social inequality. And third, they take a paternalistic attitude toward nature. All three offenses are, in the language of cultural theory, aspects of grid, the imposition of constraints (external to the individual) that limit opportunities. These criticisms mirror the complaints of libertarians, with whom egalitarians share a disdain for high-grid cultures.

Yet egalitarians also decry the libertarian indifference to the larger group, to the social consequences of individual actions and to the inequalities that can arise in the absence of centralized control. They seek to combine the social responsibility of hierarchy with the freedom of libertarianism, to be both high group and low grid.

Egalitarians are an eclectic bunch, but they share a commitment to two fundamental goals: broad participation in decisionmaking, such as in regulatory procedures, and greater substantive equality of resources, including land. Disagreement over how those goals are to be reached, and which goal should take precedence, divides egalitarians into two camps: the social and ecological idealists, best represented by the "deep ecology" proponents, and the pragmatic egalitarians who emphasize using the power of the state, in essence a bargain with hierarchy, to restructure society.

Environmental protection is to a large degree inescapably hierarchical; trees and toads cannot speak for themselves.[49] But an egalitarian rationale for environmentalism emphasizes the injustice of humans' domination over nature.[50] This is Green ecology with a capital G, also known in its many modest variations as deep ecology, ecocentrism, or ecologism.[51]

Both man and nature can be liberated through the proper intentional community,[52] according to the "deep ecologists."[53] As the journalist David Gancher describes it, "'Deep Ecology' ... reduces ... to two basic premises: 1) self-realization by humans will bring us into harmony with Nature, and 2) 'Biocentric Equality,' the belief that all Nature—including worms, germs and rocks—have equal value."[54] According to Arne Naess, a Norwegian philosopher who first used the term "deep ecology,"[55] self-realization and biocentric equality are "ultimate norms which are themselves not derivable from other principles or intuitions."[56] These are the bedrock principles, precisely what we would expect in the low-grid, low-group box of the cultural model: the belief that humans (and nature) can and should be both free and equal.

In this view, social and environmental justice become inseparable. "A Green concern for the environment," Andrew Dobson admonishes, "leads not (only) to the care of country houses or the saving of the whale, but to the desire to restructure the whole of political, social and economic life."[57] According to Naess, "Ecologically responsible parties are concerned only in part with pollution and resource depletion. There are deeper concerns which touch upon principles of diversity, complexity, autonomy, decentralization, symbiosis, egalitarianism, and classlessness."[58] The compatibility of social and environmental equality is not always apparent. Those who are socioeconomically deprived may put a higher priority on food and housing than on communing with nature. As Lawrence Chickering asked rhetorically, "Why are there no Poor People in the Sierra Club?"[59] Murray Bookchin has criticized deep ecologists for getting more excited about the perils of slugs than the poverty of the inner cities. "I'm a social ecologist," he said. "I put human beings first."[60] "There is a powerful almost existential urge," notes O'Riordan, who is sympathetic to egalitarian environmentalism, "to safeguard objects of physical and environmental meaning regardless of the distributive consequences."[61] Extensive environmental protection can raise the costs of economic development, shrinking the pie that must feed the poor as well as the rich. But to the ecocentrist, the poor often are locked in the same mindless pursuit of materialism as the capitalists; they are just less successful at it. The egalitarian environmentalist argues that a viable community, although more frugal in resource use, would provide greater equality and richer lives for all its citizens.

Solutions that might prove beneficial for the environment are therefore seen as inadequate unless they also promote social equality, autonomy, and community. For example, Devall and Sessions reject the free-market approach (turning natural resources over to private owners and fully defining property rights), even though they acknowledge it might eliminate the "tragedy of the commons"[62] because it is "human-centered."[63] Similarly, technological solutions are appropriate only if they are "compatible with the growth of autonomous, self-determining individuals in nonhierarchical communities."[64]

The ideal, in O'Riordan's words, is "the 'human-scale' self-reliant community connected to, but not dependent on, thousands like it scattered across the face of the land ... living in harmony with [its] natural surroundings in a classless society."[65] Egalitarianism echoes the classical republican preference for the small, self-sufficient community in which virtue—the voluntary embrace of the common interest—is more readily encouraged through mutual dependence and affection. In such a community, inequalities will be more apparent and easier to rectify. And, ecocentric theorists suggest, so will environmental problems.[66] "Local autonomy," according to John Dryzek, "provides a way of 'mapping' ecological feedback signals onto social choice. ... Local residents are forced to heed negative feedback signals from their natural environment."[67]

The egalitarian ideal is an "ongoing dialogue in a community of equals"[68] instead of hierarchical reliance on specialized expertise. Certainly some of the changes in administrative law, such as the broadening of legal standing to intervene in suits, the public funding of adversarial groups, the expansion of notice and hearing requirements, and the requirement of administrative responses to public comments, have progressed in this direction.[69] A major consequence of the National Environmental Act has been the expansion of participation in regulation. Regulatory procedings in recent years have gotten increasingly drawn out and complex, in part because everyone with a claim to be affected by a decision has a say. As Jerry Mashaw writes, "The demands for participation begin to look like a demand that the administrative state be dismantled, and that all decisions instead be made by some combination of popular referendum, adversary adjudication, and negotiation to consensus."[70] In such a climate, the voice of the property owner can be drowned out by other claimants. "This ideology," according to Patrick McAuslan, a British scholar of land-use regulation, "denies the property-owner any special place in participation; such an interest is merely one of a great number to be considered in the democratic process of decision-making and by no means the most important."[71] If there are no rights tied to ownership that merit special protection, this is not troublesome. If land uses should reflect group preferences, there is no reason to vest an owner with privileges just because his name is on the deed.

At its best, the process allows an informed deliberation about preferences and produces a decision accurately reflecting community sentiment. But decision-making by consensus can be time-consuming and tedious as disparate opinions are gradually molded into a common view. Not surprisingly, it works best in small groups that already share basic values, such as the Green Party and antinuclear "affinity groups" used for antinuclear protests. The Greens seek to practice what they preach, rooting their environmentalism in a consensual, egalitarian process. According to a platform published by a Green group in California, "We conduct all our meetings according to the principles of consensus democracy, emphasizing unanimous or near-unanimous agreement on all decisions. No representative may make decisions on behalf of the Greens without the approval of the entire membership. We encourage the use of consensus democracy in all social, economic and political institutions."[72]

How the ideal society is to be created is a bit mysterious. How persons corrupted by institutions and degraded by self-interest can make the transition to socially and ecologically responsible free citizens has been a challenge to egalitarian movements since Rousseau and the French Revolution.[73] Allowing individuals to live freely, paradoxically, may first entail requiring them to live equally. In the practical world of policy disputes, egalitarians may advocate using private coercion and the power of the state to force change. And so Greenpeace boats block whalers and monkeywrenchers spike redwoods, and the Natural Resources Defense Council favors aggressive litigation.

The leading example of the push for equality in land use is the demand for an end to "exclusionary" zoning. Egalitarians seek to disassociate themselves from broader libertarian attacks on regulation and focus their critique on its inegalitarian aspects. "Exclusionary zoning," according to Paul and Linda Davidoff, "may be defined as the complex of zoning practices which results in closing suburban housing and land markets to low- and moderate-income families. All regulations," they admit, "are, in a sense, exclusionary. For example, they are exclusive in that they restrict degrees of individual freedom." But such coercion is "not of concern here."[74] Similarly, Norman Williams and Thomas Norman have argued that only limits on the rights of the poor should be termed "exclusionary"; other groups may be only "highly restricted."[75]

The first step in breaking down exclusionary barriers is to remove regulations such as minimum lot-size and floor-size requirements that make it difficult to erect inexpensive housing. But equality can demand more: Municipalities can be required to accommodate their "fair share" of the region's poor by building housing, subsidizing rents, and requiring builders to sell units at designated prices. In the *Mount Laurel* decisions,[76] the New Jersey Supreme Court led the way in requiring that each "developing" municipality incorporate its "fair share" of low-income housing. If housing choices were left to an unrestricted market, inequalities between communities could still result.

Equality at the community level is important because it provides more equal education, economic, and social opportunities and makes remaining inequalities more local and thus visible rather than insulating them in islands of exclusion. In *Mount Laurel II* (1983), the New Jersey court acknowledged that reducing regulation might allow affordable housing to "filter down" to the poor but rejected this solution because it would "exacerbate the economic segregation of our cities and suburbs."[77] The fundamental policy issue for the court was not simply the lack of housing for the poor and working class but also the unequal distribution of such housing between communities.

The New Jersey court made clear its rejection of market approaches. "The lessons of history are clear, even if rarely learned," Justice Wilentz declared (although he did not explain why his "lessons" are so difficult for other mortals to learn, if indeed they are clear).

One of those lessons is that unplanned growth has a price: natural resources are destroyed, open spaces are despoiled, agricultural land is rendered forever unproductive, and people settle without regard to the enormous cost of the public facilities needed to support them. Cities decay; established infrastructures deteriorate for lack of funds; and taxpayers shudder under a financial burden of public expenditures resulting in part from uncontrolled migration to anywhere anyone wants to settle, roads leading to places they should never be—a pattern of total neglect of sensible conservation of resources, funds, prior public investment, and just plain common sense.[78]

Hierarchical land-use control was not fundamentally flawed, in the opinion of the court, but only needed to better serve substantive equality. The Pennsylvania court has looked to the market to correct government-created inequities; the New Jersey court has adopted the hierarchical strategies of prediction, distinction, and control. "The specific location of such [affordable] housing will of course continue to depend on sound municipal land-use planning."[79] Once a court had defined the appropriate region, Justice Hall wrote in *Mount Laurel I* (1975), "through the expertise of the municipal planning adviser, the county planning boards and the state planning agency, a reasonable [fair share] figure for Mount Laurel can be determined, which can then be translated to the allocation of sufficient land therefore on the zoning map."[80]

Curiously, the Pennsylvania and New Jersey supreme courts have based their contrasting rationales and prescriptions on nearly identical constitutional language that protects property rights.[81] The Pennsylvania rhetoric has echoed the libertarian sentiment of these clauses; the New Jersey approach more accurately reflects equal-protection concerns closer to egalitarianism. "The basis for the constitutional obligation is simple: the State controls the use of land, *all* of the land," declared Wilentz in *Mount Laurel II.* "In exercising that control, it cannot favor rich over poor."[82]

Egalitarianism is ambivalent toward property rights. Jennifer Nedelsky, for example, criticizes private property as an impediment to participatory democracy yet also values individual autonomy.[83] Egalitarians seek to distinguish property rights that contribute to autonomy from those that impede the freedom of others. Property rights that protect rights such as free expression or privacy are valued; rights to exclusive control of material resources are not. Margaret Jane Radin would protect only those property rights that she perceives as promoting "personhood."[84] Leonard Levy, although disclaiming any intent to resurrect property or economic rights in general, has advocated elevating the right to pursue an occupation of one's choice to a fundamental right because he sees it as essential to personal identity. The double standard of rights that has dominated constitutional doctrine since the New Deal is the epitome of egalitarian jurisprudence in that it seeks to do what libertarians claim is impossible: protect personal rights while leaving economic interests subject to public control.

Reconciling freedom with order through an egalitarian community can be a difficult balancing act. And ecocentrism also says little about how self-sufficient communities are to be coordinated to deal with broader ecological problems without reintroducing hierarchy.[85] But the cultural idealism of the Green philosophers and the deep ecologists, the ecocentrists and the ecofeminists,[86] is an animating force for a large segment of the environmental movement today, even if the reality of lobbying, litigating, and civil disobedience is a far cry from Utopia.

THE FUTURE OF
ENVIRONMENTAL POLICY

Culture affects policy, and policy affects culture. Libertarians like liberty, hierarchists like order, and egalitarians like equality; and they tend to favor environmental prescriptions that are compatible with their values and beliefs and preferences. But the cultural approach emphasizes that people form their preferences through social interaction, not through abstract reflection. People tend to prefer the institutions and processes to which they are accustomed, especially when they seem to produce an adequate level of satisfaction. Environmental policy and land-use regulation, as part of this context, help shape our perceptions, our social relations, and our politics. The environment is fruitful terrain for political science for three reasons: First, broader political and social issues are embedded in policy debates; second, environmental policy has social and political consequences; and third, the policies and institutions of environmental regulation contribute to the context of preference formation. Grid-group analysis helps illuminate all three of these phenomena.

The strength of all three political cultures in the environmental policy arena ensures that issues of regulation will continue to be important and contentious, creating a wonderland of opportunities for academic research. It is a time of ferment. Reliance on regulation continues to grow at the same time that egalitarian and libertarian attacks grow sharper. These changes provide marvelous opportunities for studying the relations between policy, ideas, and culture and for considering the direct effects that technical regulatory policy and arcane procedures can have on the character of communities and the larger society, on individual opportunity, and on the balance between the cultures of liberty, equality, and order.

NOTES

This chapter includes substantial material reprinted with permission from Dennis Coyle, *Property Rights and the Constitution: Shaping Society Through Land Use Regulation* (Albany: State University of New York Press, 1993).

1. David Bloor, "Polyhedra and the Abominations of Leviticus: Cognitive Styles in Mathematics," in Mary Douglas, ed., *Essays in the Sociology of Perception* (Boston: Routledge and Kegan Paul, 1982), 198.

2. Eric H. Steele, "Community Participation and the Function of Rules: The Case of Urban Zoning Boards," *Law & Policy* 9(1987), 279, 281.

3. Aldo Leopold, *The Land Ethic* (Oxford: Oxford University Press, 1949), 204.

4. On the early history of conservationism, see Samuel P. Hays, *Conservation and the Gospel of Efficiency: The Progressive Conservation Movement, 1890–1920* (Cambridge, Mass.: Harvard University Press, 1959); and Donald Worster, ed., *American Environmentalism: The Formative Period, 1860–1915* (New York: John Wiley).

5. See Lester Ward, *The Psychic Factors of Civilization* (Boston, 1893), 240–262.

6. John Wesley Powell, "The Lesson of Conemaugh," *North American Review* (August 1889), 12.

7. Bernhard E. Fernow, *Economics of Forestry* (New York, 1902), 1–20.

8. T. O'Riordan, "Environmental Ideologies," *Environmental Planning A* 9(1977), 6–7.

9. Newman Baker, *Legal Aspects of Zoning* (Chicago: University of Chicago Press, 1927), 35.

10. Robert M. Anderson, "Introduction to Symposium on Exclusionary Zoning," *Syracuse Law Review* 22(1971), 465.

11. See James Metzenbaum, *The Law of Zoning* (New York: Baker, Voorhis, 1930), 128.

12. Constance Perin, *Everything in Its Place: Social Order and Land Use in America* (Princeton: Princeton University Press, 1977).

13. Bruno Lasker, "The Atlanta Zoning Plan," *Survey* 48(April 22, 1922), 114.

14. See William M. Randle, "Professors, Reformers, Bureaucrats, and Cronies: The Players in *Euclid v. Ambler*," in Charles M. Haar and Jerold S. Kayden, eds., *Zoning and the American Dream: Promises Still to Keep* (Chicago: Planners Press, 1989), 31.

15. 272 U.S. 365 (1926).

16. 297 F. 307, 318.

17. 272 U.S. at 379.

18. 272 U.S. at 388.

19. On the role of elites in environmental policy, see Samuel P. Hays, *Beauty, Health and Permanence: Environmental Politics in the United States, 1955–1985* (New York: Cambridge University Press, 1987).

20. Eugene P. Odum, *Fundamentals of Ecology,* 3rd ed. (Philadelphia: Saunders, 1971), 408.

21. Robert C. Paehlke, *Environmentalism and the Future of Progressive Politics* (New Haven: Yale University Press, 1989), 9.

22. Victor John Yannacone, Jr., John Rahenkamp, and Angelo I. Cerchione, "Impact Zoning: Alternative to Exclusion in the Suburbs," in Robert H. Frielich and Eric O. Stuhler, eds., *The Land Use Awakening: Zoning Law in the Seventies* (Chicago: American Bar Association Press, 1981), 154.

23. Ian L. McHarg, *Design with Nature* (Garden City, N.Y.: Natural History Press, 1969), 32–33.

24. Robert R. Linowes and Don T. Allensworth, *The Politics of Land Use: Planning, Zoning and the Private Developer* (New York: Praeger, 1973), 149.

25. Alvin M. Weinberg, "Social Institutions and Nuclear Energy," *Science* 177(1972), 27–34.

26. William Ophuls, *Ecology and the Politics of Scarcity: Prologue to a Political Theory of the Steady State* (San Francisco: W. H. Freeman, 1977), 163.

27. Richard F. Babcock, *The Zoning Game: Municipal Practices and Policies* (Madison: University of Wisconsin Press, 1966), 19.

28. Melvin R. Levin, "Introduction," in *The Best of Planning* (American Planning Association) (Chicago: Planners Press, 1989), xii.

29. See Ellen Frankel Paul, *Property Rights and Eminent Domain* (New Brunswick, N.J.: Transaction Books, 1987); and Richard A. Epstein, *Takings: Private Property and the Power of Eminent Domain* (Cambridge, Mass.: Harvard University Press, 1985).

30. Epstein, *Takings,* 281.

31. Ibid., 314–324, 303–305, 178–181, 186–188, 263–273, 279–280.

32. Friedrich A. Hayek, "The Discipline of Freedom," in *The Political Order of a Free People* (Chicago: University of Chicago Press, 1979), 163.

33. 419 Pa. 504, 215 A.2d 597 (1965).

34. 215 A.2d at 610.

35. 215 A.2d at 612.

36. *Mount Laurel II,* 456 A.2d at 429.

37. 215 A.2d at 611.

38. 215 A.2d at 612.

39. John Locke, *The Second Treatise of Government* (Indianapolis: Bobbs-Merrill, 1952), 21.

40. See Julian L. Simon, *The Ultimate Resource* (Princeton: Princeton University Press, 1981).

41. Julian L. Simon and Herman Kahn, *The Resourceful Earth* (Oxford: Basil Blackwell, 1984), 25.

42. See Aaron Wildavsky, *Searching for Safety* (New Brunswick, N.J.: Transaction Press, 1988).

43. Jerry Taylor, "The Growing Abundance of Natural Resources," in *Market Liberalism: A Paradigm for the 21st Century* (Washington, D.C.: Cato Institute, 1993), 363–378, 378.

44. See Terry Anderson and Donald Leal, *Free Market Environmentalism* (San Francisco: Pacific Research Institute, 1990); and Fred L. Smith, Jr., and Kent Jeffreys, "A Free-Market Environmental Vision," in *Market Liberalism* 389.

45. See Murray N. Rothbard, *For a New Liberty: The Libertarian Manifesto,* rev. ed. (New York: Collier Books, 1978), 254–262.

46. See William Tucker, *The Excluded Americans* (Washington, D.C.: Regnery Gateway, 1990).

47. Rothbard, *For a New Liberty,* 320.

48. Frederick C. Thayer, *An End to Hierarchy and Competition* (New York: New Viewpoints, 1981).

49. But see Christopher D. Stone, *Should Trees Have Standing? Toward Legal Rights for Natural Objects* (Los Angeles: William Kaufman, 1974), for a discussion of how courts might act *as if* nature had a voice.

50. See Mary Douglas and Aaron Wildavsky, *Risk and Culture: An Essay on the Selection of Technical and Environmental Dangers* (Berkeley: University of California Press, 1982) for a discussion of the relation between "sectarianism," essentially egalitarianism, and environmentalism.

51. See Andrew Dobson, *Green Political Thought: An Introduction* (London: Unwin Hyman, 1990); and Robyn Eckersley, *Environmentalism and Political Theory: Toward an Ecocentric Approach* (Albany: State University of New York, 1992).

52. See Arne Naess, "Self-Realization in Mixed Communities of Humans, Bears, Sheep and Wolves," *Inquiry,* 22(1979), 231.

53. See Bill Devall and George Sessions, *Deep Ecology* (Salt Lake City: Peregrine Smith Books, 1985); and Michael Tobias, ed., *Deep Ecology* (San Diego: Avant Books, 1985).

54. David Gancher, "When Is Ecology Deep/Shallow?" *San Francisco Sunday Chronicle & Examiner Book Review* (April 28, 1985), 1.

55. See Arne Naess, "The Shallow and the Deep, Long-Range Ecology Movements: A Summary," *Inquiry* 16(1973), 95–100.

56. Devall and Sessions, *Deep Ecology,* 66.

57. Dobson, *Green Political Thought,* 3.

58. Naess, "The Shallow and the Deep, Long-Range Ecology Movements," 95.

59. A. Lawrence Chickering, "Land Use Controls and Low Income Groups: Why Are There No Poor People in the Sierra Club?" in *No Land Is an Island* (San Francisco: Institute for Contemporary Studies, 1975).

60. Quoted in Harold Gilliam, "Shades of Green," *This World, San Francisco Sunday Chronicle & Examiner* (July 24, 1988), 18.

61. O'Riordan, "Environmental Ideologies," 5.

62. See Garrett Hardin, "The Tragedy of the Commons," *Science* 162(1968), 1243.

63. Devall and Sessions, *Deep Ecology,* 7.

64. Ibid., 35.

65. O'Riordan, "Environmental Ideologies," 4. See also E. F. Schumacher, *Small Is Beautiful: Economics As If People Really Mattered* (New York: Harper and Row, 1973).

66. See William R. Catton, Jr., *Overshoot: The Ecological Basis of Revolutionary Change* (Urbana: University of Illinois Press, 1980).

67. John S. Dryzek, *Rational Ecology: Environment and Political Economy* (Oxford: Basil Blackwell, 1987), 216.

68. Jerry L. Mashaw, "Administrative Due Process: The Quest for a Dignitary Theory," *Boston University Law Review* 61(1981), 930.

69. For a classic analysis of these changes, see Richard Stewart, "The Reformation of American Administrative Law," *Harvard Law Review* 88(1975), 1689–1813.

70. Mashaw, "Administrative Due Process," 904.

71. Patrick McAuslan, *The Ideologies of Planning Law* (New York: Pergamon Press, 1980), 5.

72. Quoted in Devall and Sessions, *Deep Ecology,* 37.

73. On this point, see Peter J. Steinberger, *Ideology and the Urban Crisis* (Albany: State University of New York Press, 1985).

74. Paul Davidoff and Linda Davidoff, "Opening Up the Suburbs: Toward Inclusionary Land Use Controls," *Syracuse Law Review* 22(1971), 519.

75. Norman Williams, Jr., and Thomas Norman, "Exclusionary Land Use Controls: The Case of North-Eastern New Jersey," *Syracuse Law Review* 22(1971), 475, 479.

76. *Southern Burlington County NAACP v. Township of Mount Laurel (Mount Laurel I),* 67 N.J. 151, 336 A.2d 713 (1975); and *Southern Burlington County NAACP v. Mount Laurel (Mount Laurel II),* 92 N.J. 158, 456 A.2d 390 (1983).

77. 456 A.2d at 451.

78. 456 A.2d at 429.

79. 456 A.2d at 416.

80. 336 A.2d at 733.

81. Art. 1, Sec. 1, of the Pennsylvania Constitution reads: "All men are born equally free and independent, and have certain inherent and inalienable rights, among which are those of enjoying and defending life and liberty, of acquiring, possessing and protecting property and reputation, and of pursuing their own happiness." Art. 1, Sec. 1, of the New Jersey Constitution states: "All persons are by nature free and independent, and have certain natural and unalienable rights, among which are enjoying and defending life and liberty, of acquiring, possessing and protecting property, and of pursuing and obtaining safety and happiness."

82. 456 A.2d at 415.

83. See Jennifer Nedelsky, *Private Property and the Limits of American Constitutionalism: The Madisonian Framework and Its Legacy* (Chicago: University of Chicago Press, 1990).

84. Margaret Jane Radin, "Property and Person," *Stanford Law Review* 34(1982), 957.

85. For attempts to grapple with this problem, see Dryzek, *Rational Ecology;* and Thayer, *An End to Hierarchy and Competition.*

86. On ecofeminism, see Irene Diamond and Gloria Feman Orenstein, eds., *Reweaving the World: The Emergence of Ecofeminism* (San Francisco: Sierra Club, 1990); Judith Plant, ed., *Healing the Wounds: The Promise of Ecofeminism* (Philadelphia: New Society Publishers, 1989), 18–28; and Karen J. Warren, "Feminism and Ecology: Making Connections," *Environmental Ethics* 11(Spring 1989), 17.

CHAPTER 3

Cars and Culture in Munich and Birmingham: The Case for Cultural Pluralism

Frank Hendriks

The motorcar is a defining feature of modern society. It is omnipresent in the lives of millions, especially those in the industrialized West. Attitudes toward the automobile, however, vary tremendously. The motorcar has been described as liberator, extended living room, pack donkey, status symbol, ego-tripper, and killing machine. In addition, people differ over what government should do about traffic. The variety of policy options is large, including carpooling, intelligent highway systems, road pricing, traffic-guidance systems, parking pricing, "park and ride," car-free pedestrian zones, free public transport, and free public bicycles.

Behind these diverse opinions and policy options, however, it is possible to distinguish a much smaller set of internally consistent "policy cultures." The first section of this chapter draws upon cultural theory's grid-group typology to derive four distinct policy cultures, each of which manifests a distinctive cultural bias and a distinctive approach to dealing with urban traffic problems. In interaction these four policy cultures produce a cultural regime that can be classified on a scale running from monocultural hegemony to multicultural pluralism. In the second section the case is made for a pluralistic regime characterized by cultural checks and balances. Pluralism offers favorable conditions for correcting project blindness and for achieving greater *Lebensqualität*—quality of life. Empirical support for these arguments is offered in the subsequent two sections, analyses of postwar traffic policy projects in Birmingham, England, and Munich, Germany. The different ways in which the Inner Ring Road in Birmingham and the Altstadtring in Munich have been planned and implemented is shown to be related to the different cultural regimes of these cities. The relative success of the multicultural policymaking process in Munich and the failure of the monocultural process in Birmingham demonstrate the value of cultural pluralism in creating sustainable and livable public policies.

51

THE FOUR POLICY CULTURES

"Do we have too many cars or do we have too little space?" This question, posed by a Dutch journalist regarding motoring in Amsterdam, neatly summarizes the present debate. Using more arcane social science jargon, one could pose the issue as a tension between "the streams" of traffic versus a "bed" of public space and infrastructure. The question would then be, Does the stream fit within the bed? And, if not, which of the two should be adjusted? The answers to these questions will vary depending upon one's appreciation of cars and traffic streams on the one hand and the evaluation of public space and infrastructure on the other hand. The merit of cultural theory is that the variety of evaluations and answers can be narrowed down to a mutually exclusive and exhaustive set of ideal types that can be used to categorize the numerous policy actors involved in this field. Cultural theory distinguishes four ideal types, three of which come to the fore in this policy field: the individualist, the hierarchist, and the egalitarian. This chapter focuses on these three active types, their core values, their characteristic ways of defining the policy problem, and their preferred ways of managing the problem. The preferred management styles of each cultural type can be explained in terms of Anthony Downs's distinction between supply-side strategies, aimed at the capacity of infrastructures to carry cars, and demand-side strategies, aimed at people's preferences to use their automobiles. Both the demand-side and the supply-side strategies can be further subdivided into either market-regulation strategies, based on price mechanisms, or administrative regulation strategies, based on administrative prohibitions or mandates.[1]

The core values of the individualist as they relate to traffic policy are self-determination and accessiblity. Also highly valued are privacy and speed. Compared with other modes of transportation—walking, cycling, public transportation—the car best promotes these values, and so it is not strange that the calculating individualist feels attracted to the automobile. The individualist's love affair with the car is supported by the low-group–low-grid characteristics of car traffic. The motorist decides for herself where to go, and in this process she is only marginally guided by traffic rules.

Nature in general and the urban environment in particular is benign in the eyes of the individualist.[2] Against that background, the individualist is not prone to see the increase in automobiles in recent decades as a fundamental problem. On the contrary, individual mobility is seen as fundamentally good. For the individualist it is common sense that people want to take the motorcar to all possible places, and the individualist strongly believes that as long as people use their ingenuity and creativity, there is always a way to the chosen destination. As long as she believes she can personally find a way out of a traffic jam and into a vacant parking space, the individualist is not going to worry about traffic. It is not until she is confronted with impediments to her mobility—and thus to her way of life—that the individualist is willing to come into the discussion about the problem of traffic.

Then, it is most likely that the individualist will define the problem in terms of a shortage of parking space, passable roads, and useful traffic information and thus as a loss of valuable time and opportunities.

An individualistic bias gives rise to two divergent—though equally rational—management styles. First, there is a pragmatic standpoint that arises from the wish not to pay more than has been customary. It is common in urban areas that the use of the public road is free for all. This means that the motorist has to pay only for operating his own car and not for the external effects that his operational choices have on other users of the public space in terms of congestion and inconvenience.[3] These effects are desired by no one individually, but they are nevertheless the aggregate result of all the individual choices taken together. In its extreme form, this result resembles Garrett Hardin's "tragedy of the commons."[4] Road capacity is different from the classic commons scenario in the sense that capacity can be expanded by widening existing roads or building new ones. The pragmatic individualist favors this approach. She prefers that government take care of this, which will give her the feeling that she gets something in return for her taxes. When road construction leads to higher taxes, the pain of paying more money will be relieved by the knowledge that the costs are being shared by all taxpayers and that the resulting road space will be freely available in the near future.

Second, there is a principle that every individual should carry the consequences (and the costs) of his choices. This principle is inspired by the market model, which implies an easy solution to the problem of capacity—as the motoring problem tends to be defined by individualists. If the demand rises faster than the supply, then the supply becomes increasingly scarce and thus costly. As roads become more congested, peak-hour tolls or parking taxes might be increased, discouraging use. Motorists would still be free to go wherever they wanted as long as they paid a fair price for their choices. Although this approach is consistent with the individualistic culture, many individualists may have second thoughts about it, since the price mechanism applied to road use means paying for something that has always been free.[5]

The typical hierarchist places the most value on orderliness (the existence of stable and predictable systematic relations), synopsis (the possibility of keeping track of all changes in the system), and control (the capacity to keep the traffic flows going within the infrastructural bed). We find these values expressed in large technocratic organizations such as city engineering departments or national departments of transportation. In contrast to the individualist and the egalitarian, the hierarchist is involved less in the generation of demand than in the production of adequate supply in light of a given demand. This is consistent with the hierarchical myth of nature, in which the boundary line between the "normal" state of tolerance and the "abnormal" state of perversity comes to the fore. In the hierarchical policy culture, everything hinges upon mapping and managing the boundary line between these two states. In this policy field, the "stream" of cars is continually threatening to overflow the "bed" of existing infrastructure. It is the hierarchist's task to keep the stream within the bed, so that the whole traffic system remains orderly and controllable.

In principle, the hierarchist has little problem with car mobility. If many people want to drive cars, then there is a lot to be arranged and interfered with, which calls for a hierarchical way of thinking and acting. Car traffic will become a problem in the eyes of the hierarchist only when so many people become mobile at the same time that either total chaos or complete stagnation threatens to develop. This problem has two sides, as we have seen before: a demand side (the need for mobility) and a supply side (the infrastructural capacity). Like the individualist, the hierarchist is prone to define the problem in terms of supply. There is either too little capacity or this capacity is inefficiently used. These are problems that can be handled in a technocratic way. Only when the limits of what is technically possible cannot be stretched further is the hierarchist ready to say that demand is too high. Until that point is reached, the hierarchist will accept existing demands and will address the lack of capacity.

Which management strategy best fits hierarchy? Referring back to Downs's theory, we would expect a hierarchist to prefer an interventionist approach over a market approach and to prefer a supply-directed approach over a demand-directed approach. The essence of administrative intervention is the existence of a regulating and controlling authority, which suits the hierarchical purpose. Central to the market approach is the idea of self-regulation helped by an invisible hand, an idea that is foreign to the hierarchist. The market approach is only interesting to the hierarchist as far as it entails technocratic or bureaucratic assistance. That is why hierarchists have been involved in the development of road-pricing systems, which rely upon ingenious devices for measuring road use and on bureaucratic means for passing costs on to motorists.

The expectation that hierarchists would rather enlarge capacity than reduce demand can be derived from their definition of the problem. Those who are involved in the issue of car traffic are predominantly experts: road engineers, traffic planners, traffic forecasters, and the like. As specialists, they are motivated to find more and more ingenious answers in the form of bridges, tunnels, rails, traffic-guidance systems, and so on. The hierarchist would much rather show his technical power and knowledge than admit that some things cannot be done. Only when there is no technical way of enlarging capacity is the hierarchist willing to reduce demand. He will then typically suggest external ways of regulating demand, preferably through prohibitions or mandates, that are most familiar to and supportive of his own way of life.

The egalitarian approach to traffic policy emphasizes the values of equal access, sustainability, and livability, values that egalitarians contend are gravely neglected in modern, technologically advanced societies. Egalitarians wish to create understanding and appreciation for an alternative way of life based on solidarity and simplicity. They feel it is only fair that all people—residents, pedestrians, cyclists, motorists, and users of public transport—have equal access to the public space and that users leave the common heritage in a condition no worse than they found it. This means that users of the public space, including motorists, must take into account future as well as present livability. A way of life and a style of traveling is only good in the eyes of the egalitarian when it is sustainable, that is, when it can be maintained for all future generations equally. Individual travel by car is at odds with the egalitarian policy culture that is advocated by, for example, anticar action groups, ecological protest groups, and other "new social movements."[6]

Egalitarians challenge the establishment's definition of the dominant problem, the establishment in their view consisting of a coalition of individualists and hierarchists. Egalitarians feel that the problem is not a lack of road capacity but an excessive demand for car mobility. The infrastructure, egalitarians believe, is much too big, not too small. The problem is that government takes a docile, technocratic attitude toward the growing number of cars, which in turn leads to an erosion of the public space and a deterioration of the environment of present and future generations. The more fundamental problem is materialistic individualism, which encourages more people to satisfy more and more personal needs, including the constant need to be somewhere else and to go there by car. Measured by egalitarian standards, the motorist is selfish, shifting the negative effects of his freedom onto others and the defenseless environment. Car driving is equated with ego-tripping.

The typical solutions that follow from the egalitarian approach diverge dramatically from the individualistic and hierarchical solutions. What egalitarians want to achieve above all is that people tone down their need for mobility and get around in ways that conserve the scarce public space. In descending order of preference these ways are walking, cycling, using public transport, and—as a last resort—carpooling. The pure egalitarian prefers to see people driven by inner conviction rather than by external incentives to cast aside their cars. Ecologically sound behavior should ideally be the result of environmental consciousness, which should be stimulated by education, discussion, and the good example. Pricing policy and bureaucratic regulation are clearly second and third best in the eyes of the egalitarian. From the egalitarian perspective, market mechanisms do have the advantage of ensuring that the consequences of personal choices are directly passed on to the individual, which stimulates the internalization of environmental costs. The great disadvantage of such a pricing policy, however, is that it hits the poor harder than the rich. In this respect bureaucratic rules are more fair. In principle they do not discriminate between the haves and the have-nots. However, strong rules run counter to the noncoercive way in which egalitarians want to live together.

Egalitarians do not approve of the capacity-enlarging strategies of hierarchists and individualists. Extending infrastructures in cities is taboo because it diminishes the size of enjoyable public space. Making more efficient use of road capacity—by using "intelligent" systems to allocate traffic to roads, for example—is not as bad but still not good because it facilitates more traffic and thus greater pollution per road. Egalitarians prefer that a lowering of supply would follow a lowering of demand, that people would say, "We do not want that road anymore because we do not need to drive so much anymore." More pragmatic egalitarians would also accept the reverse, that is, discouraging the use of cars through decreasing the supply of efficient roads. If road conditions get worse for the car, then the competitive position of the other modes of traffic will get better—which means greater justice in the eyes of egalitarians.[7]

THE CASE FOR A
PLURALISTIC CULTURAL REGIME

Policy cultures can be analyzed at three levels: first, the microlevel of the individual; second, the mesolevel of the social organization; and third, the macrolevel at which distinctive policy cultures interact to produce a cultural regime.[8] The interaction at the macrolevel results in the formation of policy networks or policy communities[9] composed of networking individualists, representatives of hierarchical organizations, and, to a lesser extent, representatives of egalitarian-bounded groups.

A policy network characterized by interdependent, exchange-based relations[10] is the preferred setting for individualists. Those in hierarchical organizations usually participate on account of their roles or functions in a policy network and try to control other actors in the field. In contrast to individualists, hierarchists tend to perceive relations in the policy network in more vertical terms. Yet despite these differences, hierarchists and individualists with an interest in traffic-policy tend to maintain working relations that are mutually satisfying. Individualists need hierarchists to plan and control infrastructures with analytical rigor and operational vigor, whereas hierarchists need individualists to use these infrastructures and to instigate more ingenious projects.

Egalitarians detest a passive attitude toward the issue of traffic and do not want to be marginalized in the same way that fatalists are. Nevertheless, they have an ambivalent attitude toward participating in the traffic-policy network. On the one hand, they want to protest against the traffic policy of the establishment and bear witness to their faith in an alternative way of getting around. On the other hand, they want to defend the egalitarian-bounded group against the terror of the outside world. Egalitarians often shrink from cooperation with the establishment, which in their view is characterized by abuse and exploitation as well as by instrumentalism and authoritarianism. Egalitarians want to cooperate on an equal footing and operate in complete openness. Decisions, they feel, should be reached unanimously, which is often difficult, since they are also adamant about not compromising their principles.

As a result, the integration of egalitarians into the traffic-policy network is often limited. The constraints stem not only from the logic of the egalitarian-bounded group but also from the establishment's tendency to exclude rivals in order to maintain a mutually beneficial coalition between the individualistic and the hierarchical cultures. Fatalists are not represented in the process, though they certainly bear many of the hazards and inconveniences of public policies. These unequal positions of power in the policy network raise normative problems, since each policy culture holds different views of the good life, the good city, and the good way of getting around. In this chapter, however, I wish to focus on the empirical or functional arguments that can be made in favor of cultural pluralism.

Each cultural bias contains blind spots. Because each way of seeing is also a way of not seeing, every cultural bias has problems it fails to detect, underplays, pigeonholes, or ignores. These blind spots, if left uncorrected, can lead to policy failures, particularly when these blind spots are combined with a huge investment of resources and with dramatic intervention, both of which are common to infrastructural projects.[11] Because these projects tend to take up a huge amount of resources and change the city's structure and appearance for a long time, project blindness can have serious consequences and may be regretted very deeply.[12] Cultural theory posits that rival cultures may compensate for each other's blind spots by looking at the same issue through different cultural lenses.

Consider the hypothetical case of a planned road that would connect the center of a city to an outlying highway network by cutting through an old neighborhood. What are the likely contributions to the policy debate of the three active cultures and in what ways are they likely to correct each other?

The individualist is most likely to be optimistic and to see the new road in terms of increased opportunities: More shoppers and tourists could be lured to the city, members of the business community and products could more easily get out of the city, and new offices could be developed along the road. The disadvantages and negative externalities, to which the individualist tends to be blind, are likely to be unveiled and exposed by the egalitarian. She would point to the houses, the trees, and the communities that would be destroyed. She would argue that other modes of transport are going to suffer and that the road will only attract more cars, which will result in more noise, stench, air pollution, and visual degradation. The egalitarian, however, also has her blind spots. In general, she tends to play down the necessity of technological development and economic growth for the city as a whole. The egalitarian assumes that growth is good only for the establishment, often not seeing that the economic surplus could be used to finance things egalitarians would value, such as redistribution or strict environmental measures.

The strength and the weakness of the hierarchist in the policymaking process is the tendency to think and act systematically. The hierarchist is able to translate the preferences of the individualist and the egalitarian into precise consequences for the system as a whole, using traffic-flow models and other complex calculations. He can tell the individualist how much money his desired road is going to cost and what this could mean in terms of taxes. He can tell the egalitarian how much traffic may accumulate if the road is not built and what this could mean for traffic on the smaller streets in the surrounding neighborhoods. When a decision is finally reached, the hierarchist has the legal authority to implement it on behalf of the public interest. The problem is that the hierarchist tends to be blind to the values that are outside the parameters of his particular calculations, which are typically colored by the functional mission of his organization. A road-engineering department is expected to keep traffic flowing on roads; preserving the visual appearance of the city and stimulating motorists to switch over to public transport are not its task. That is what the architectural department or the public transport authority does, again with its own institutional blind spots. Individualists and egalitarians would criticize the hierarchists' way of analyzing a subject and could compensate for it by continously asking what the combined policy effects would mean for ordinary people.

Pluralism is functional not only in terms of preventing project blindness but also in terms of achieving "quality of life," a term that has become especially popular among town-planning experts. In most town-planning literature, quality of life is connected to the existence of variety and multifunctionality in contrast to monotony and monofunctionality, which were associated with modernist planning and architecture in the early postwar period. With the rise of postmodernity, the argument goes, people are no longer satisfied with a city that functions with the precision, efficiency, and drabness of a machine.[13] It is generally recognized that the city is used not only by motorists who want to go as quickly as possible from A to B but also by people who want to cycle, stroll, or simply sit down, who want to enjoy the cityscape, meet strangers, be surprised, or simply relax. The expected benefits of diversity and multifunctionality can be found not only in improvements in leisure and recreation time but also in a strengthened economy.

There is, of course, no guarantee that a pluralistic cultural regime will produce satisfying policy. Pluralism is, however, a favorable condition for minimizing the regret that results from project blindness and from monofunctionality. Pluralism can also be seen as upgrading the quality of policy-oriented learning.[14] Representatives of a single culture tend to be restricted to "single-loop learning"; that is, they are able to detect and correct error in relation to a given set of operational norms. When representatives of different policy cultures communicate with each other, they encounter other norms and other ways of defining and solving problems. This is a necessary requirement for "double-loop learning," which implies the ability to take a second look at the situation by questioning the relevance and importance of operating norms.[15] Single-loop learning tends to restrict policymaking to a single-problem–single-solution approach. Double-loop learning can push policymaking up to a multiple-problem–multiple-solution approach, characterized by sensitivity to more than one way of defining and tackling a policy problem.[16]

The different qualities of these policymaking approaches are illustrated in the subsequent sections by looking at the cases of the Inner Ring Road in Birmingham and the Altstadtring in Munich. The Birmingham case demonstrates what can happen if the cultural bias of a dominant policy community goes unchecked and the corresponding project blindness goes uncorrected. In the Munich case, by contrast, establishment policymakers have learned on the job that listening to other points of view is a valuable way of compensating for cultural bias and producing a traffic policy that better serves the needs and interests of all its citizens.

BIRMINGHAM'S INNER RING ROAD: THE COSTS OF PROJECT BLINDNESS

At the end of World War II, the chairman of the Public Works Committee and the city engineer of Birmingham proposed an Inner Ring Road around the Victorian heart of the city. It would take twenty-five years and a great deal of destruction in Birmingham's city center to build the road. Another twenty years would pass before leading decisionmakers opened their eyes to the disadvantages of this project for the city.

The Inner Ring Road (IRR) was the core element of a planning philosophy aimed at turning a congested Victorian city into a modern, functional city. The modernist planning philosophy, which propagated a clear division between urban functions (living, working, shopping, recreation) and the development of spacious suburbs, was already popular before the war. Indeed, the idea for an IRR even went back as far as 1917, when the city engineer of the day proposed to build "a kind of loop round the city center, which should be widened for both ordinary and tramway purposes."[17] After World War II a policy window seemed to open, partly because the German Luftwaffe had left some holes in the cityscape, but above all because policymakers felt that Birmingham should be prepared for a new era in which the car was expected to be the principal means of transportation.

Thus, the trams anticipated in the IRR proposal of 1917 were dropped in the IRR proposal of 1944—in itself a remarkable decision as the Public Transport Department developed into the most profitable city undertaking before the war and witnessed a growing patronage until at least the end of the 1940s.[18] Trams as well as trolley buses and bicycles simply did not fit into the modernist vision of a sound traffic policy. Members of the City Engineer's Department and of the Public Works Committee were preoccupied by one problem (how to keep traffic going with a growing number of cars) and one solution (building an Inner Ring Road). They were so focused on the solution that they ignored, for example, the point of view of a traffic advisory panel arguing that "a north-south tunnel would be much more effective than a ring road in diverting traffic from the centre."[19] The same goes for the city council as a whole, which rejected an amendment that called for a second opinion of planning experts.

The IRR scheme was consistent with the core values of the hierarchical policy culture and with its characteristic way of defining problems and solutions in this policy field. Hierarchists such as Herbert Manzoni, the city engineer and surveyor, and his subordinate traffic engineers played a dominant role in this period. Individualists supported the plan, most of them silently as (soon to be) car owners and drivers, but some of them vocally, as in the case of the Birmingham Chamber of Commerce.[20] The support of individualists appeared to be important in the acquisition of funds to build the road, which was no easy task. In the middle of the 1950s the Ministry of Transport had still not granted its standard subsidy of 75 percent of the construction costs. In 1955 a delegation of public officials and private business leaders visited the minister in London in order to convince him of the necessity and economic advantages of the IRR. Finally, Alderman Price, the Conservative chairman of the Public Works Committee, who was a local businessman as well, persuaded the new minister of transport, Harold Wilkinson, in 1957. The decisive argument of Birmingham's roads lobby was that the Ring Road would be the logical complement of the national highway network.

An unintended effect of the indecisive attitude of the Ministry of Transport over the years was the strengthening of the single-problem–single-solution approach on the part of Birmingham. Anthony Sutcliffe and Roger Smith clarify why policymakers were so preoccupied by the Inner Ring Road: "Any suggestion by the City Council that the road might not provide a complete solution to Birmingham's current traffic problems could well have given the Minister of Transport an excuse to postpone the work still further." In 1945 a conference of interested council members confirmed once more that "it wanted the road and nothing but the road."[21] Birmingham City became entrapped in its single-problem–single-solution approach. Illustrative of this entrapment was the series of decisions about rapid public transport. In 1948 as well as in 1950, the Public Works Committee rejected schemes for underground railways, being convinced that rapid transit would never pay its way in Birmingham. This conviction was, however, tightly connected to a policy in which urban highways, with the Inner Ring Road as showpiece, and suburban life, characterized by low population densities, were the core elements. The prophecy that the car had a brilliant future in store and that rapid transit could never become a success was bound to become self-fulfilling. In the mid-1950s, Alderman Bowen drew a blank on two occasions with a proposal for a partly tunneled electric railway. First, the scheme was discarded at the advice of city engineer Manzoni, who minimized its effect on traffic congestion and warned that it might slow down progress on the IRR, which was his life's work. On the second occasion, the city council decided to postpone further discussions on rapid transit "until it became clear what sort of traffic problem would remain after the ring road's completion,"[22] indicating that expectations ran high regarding the city's traffic policy. Tram services were dismantled in the 1950s, and further into the 1960s, city buses and suburban rail lines fell into a negative spiral of decreasing patronage, decreasing payoff, and disinvestments. In 1968 a plea for rapid transport was again peremptorily dismissed. In contrast to plans for rapid transport, road schemes continued to be adopted in the 1950s and 1960s. Besides the IRR, the plans envisaged the building of a middle ring road, an outer ring road, a motorway ring, and several arterial roads, some of which are now urban highways (the Aston Expressway and the Coventry Road, for example). It is typical for Birmingham that these roads were not only planned but also realized with great vigor.

From 1953 until 1972 the center of Birmingham was one big building site. Plans for the IRR and the arterial roads feeding into it were fixed; the lots around the city center stood open for project developers who had good relationships with the Public Works Committee and who were willing and able to build quickly. Patrick Dunleavy has described how tight relations were among a small group of public officials and private developers in Birmingham and how close the linkage of interests came to outright corruption.[23] During the reign of this coalition of hierarchists and individualists, the Inner Ring Road was imposed upon the city center without much differentiation between hated slums and precious landmarks. "The change was not achieved painlessly and part of the cost of redevelopment included the demolition of many fine old buildings, seemingly recklessly demolished by the urge to erect something more modern. ... Some said that the heart had been taken out of Birmingham."[24] In this period, the egalitarian counterweight in the policy process was weak. Egalitarian groups, which popped up in many European cities in the 1960s, were virtually nonexistent in Birmingham's traffic-policy network. Some individual architects and planning experts criticized the monotony and drabness of the center, but they did not challenge the establishment coalition. The Birmingham Civic society, founded in 1918, advised the city several times not to pull down buildings of historic interest, advice that was ignored in almost all cases. Like many of the other traditional conservation and civic societies, this society was too familiar with the establishment to protest loudly and radically against it. "Accustomed to work with the Corporation, not against it, it made almost no effort to stir up public opinion in favour of better planning, and by 1970 it was almost moribund."[25]

The physical product of Birmingham's cultural regime of the day—characterized by a strong coalition of hierarchists and individualists and the weak position of egalitarians—was officially displayed in 1971 when the queen opened the Inner Ring Road. The result was impressive: 3.5 miles of roadway to take traffic from incoming arterial roads around the central area, with roundabouts at seven huge junctions and no less than fifty-two pedestrian subways. The predominant characteristic of the Inner Ring Road was its monofunctionality, its complete dedication to the single function of moving cars around. The IRR was a typical engineer's plan, "giving greater priority to the needs of traffic than pedestrians, who were channelled in subterranean warrens below street level ... the road broke up old street patterns and vistas and often exposed the backside of buildings to the view of traffic passing around the city centre."[26]

During the 1970s the chorus of opposition to the monofunctional city center grew more vocal, but it was too late in many respects. The IRR was already there to stay—at least for another twenty years—and the demolished Victorian and Edwardian buildings were not going to return despite the establishment of the Conservation Areas Advisory Committee—consisting of representatives of the Public

Works Committee and of various conservation and civic societies—and the Conservation Trust. In the same period groups with more egalitarian outlooks were on the rise. Friends of the Earth Birmingham (FoEB) was established in the beginning of the 1970s, and neighborhood-focused action groups against traffic plans were formed. However, communication between the established policy community and the new groups, which promoted egalitarian values such as livability, sustainability, and equal access, was sporadic and strained. In 1973 Birmingham experimented with a public participation exercise that was meant to provide input and feedback on the new structure plan, but real participation and communication was not achieved.[27] Cheap access by public transport was given higher priority in the 1970s, but it remained difficult for the bus to compete with the car, since travel by the latter had been facilitated for so many years. In the 1980s Birmingham could still be called "the biggest European city without a metro."

Not until the middle of the 1980s did egalitarian values such as livability, sustainability, and equal access find broad acceptance in the policy community concerned with car traffic in Birmingham. In 1984 a City Center Study Team set up to foster the economic prosperity of the central area advised the city council to improve the appearance of the center and pay more attention to quality-of-life values. The new way of looking at the city center culminated in the City Center Symposium, held in 1988. British and foreign observers unanimously concluded that the IRR had become a physical and psychological barrier that had created a hostile pedestrian environment and that restricted economic progress. At the beginning of the 1990s it was generally acknowledged that the Inner Ring Road had endangered the livability and the prosperity of Birmingham. It was decided that the "stranglehold" of the Inner Ring Road on the city center should be relieved, and that the "concrete collar" around the city's neck should be taken off.[28]

The decisive force behind this shift in policy was the economy. The decline of Birmingham's basic industries, which was thought to be just a cyclical problem in the 1970s, appeared to be a permanent phenomenon in the 1980s. It became clear that Birmingham had to diversify its production and improve its physical appearance if it was to survive in the postindustrial era. Much later than in many cities on the Continent, leading policymakers in Birmingham discovered the benefits of cultural diversity and multifunctionality. Because its dominant establishment coalition has been blind to these qualities for so long, Birmingham has had to put in a tremendous amount of effort just to catch up with cities such as Munich, in which project blindness was corrected at a much earlier stage of policymaking.

MUNICH'S ALTSTADTRING:
LEARNING ON THE JOB

At the end of World War II the city center of Munich—once proclaimed the capital of the Fascist movement by Adolf Hitler—was almost totally in ruins. As in most devasted German cities, the idea of making a brand-new start was prominent in the public mind and in the proposals of city planners. The wish to leave dictatorial collectivism behind and to liberate the individual ran parallel to the wish to leave maximum room for cars within a neutral, modern, and functional urban environment. In Munich's postwar policy the first wish would largely be realized, the second wish largely not.

Postwar Munich offered a unique opportunity for tabula rasa planning—much more so than postwar Birmingham—but the leading policymakers of the day decided to rebuild the historic city center along the traditional street pattern rather than drastically transforming it. In 1946 Karl Meitinger, who had been city engineer since 1937, presented his plan for "das neue München," in which he tried to find a compromise between the needs of modern society and the traditional "spirit and measure" of Munich. On the one hand he envisaged three concentric ringroads: the Altstadtring, the Mittlerer Ring, and the Autobahnring. On the other hand he emphasized that the city center should be accessible by rail (U-Bahn and S-Bahn) and that the Altstadt should be safeguarded against through-traffic and parked cars.[29] Some of these ideas went back to the National-Socialists,[30] who had been skeptical about unrestricted mobility of automobiles in the traditional German city centers and who had displayed a keen interest in collectivist modes of transport.[31]

Many city planners and traffic engineers criticized the Meitinger plan as too conservative and as too restrictive regarding cars. Throughout the 1940s and 1950s Munich witnessed a stream of reports that recommended restructuring Munich as a functional "autogerechten Stadt," that is, a city in which conditions for car traffic would be optimal.[32] All these plans, however, which implied large-scale destruction, could count on the skeptical reaction of Thomas Wimmer, mayor from 1948 until 1960 (and vice-mayor from 1945 until 1948). Wimmer was a former carpenter and trade unionist who had strong roots in the small-scale, traditional Munich, and the door of this mayor's office was always open to the grass roots of Munich. Although he did not offer any alternatives himself, he kept the agenda open for alternative approaches.[33] In this way he nurtured a multiple-problem–multiple-solution approach and this, in turn, stimulated learning by variation and selection.[34]

Meitinger and Wimmer contributed to the cultivation of a cultural regime that was sensitive not only to car traffic but also to other modes of transportation. In contrast to Birmingham, Munich maintained its trams and welcomed ideas for rapid rail, which was getting increasingly serious attention in the 1950s. This culminated in Munich's Development Plan and General Traffic Plan of 1963, in which car traffic and public transport received about equal attention. The implementation of these plans was stimulated by the 1972 Olympic Games. Many in Munich were anxious to show the world a revived German city that would appear to be well-organized, reliable to trade with, and pleasant to visit. Hierarchists and individualists within the city were particularly enthusiastic about this project. The door was wide open for the construction of the U-Bahn and for the acquisition of a car-free pedestrian zone in the center of town—although the latter was frowned upon by most of the shopowners at the time.

Another project the city wanted to have completed before the Olympic Games started was the Altstadtring—the first of the three conceived ringroads.[35] The western part was relatively easy to build because it followed the line of old fortifications. The biggest difficulties arose in the northwestern and northeastern parts, where the planned road cut through old neighborhoods—Maxvorstadt and Lehel—and where two important cultural institutions would have been affected: The House of Art would lose the monumental stairs in front of the building and the Prince Carl Palace would lose its basement. Many people opposed these plans and—in contrast to in Birmingham at that time—many of them got together in "Bürgerinitiativen" (citizen initiatives), which were egalitarian groups. A famous example is the Münchner Bauforum, a collective of critical architects who succeeded in reducing some of the negative effects on the Prince Carl Palace and the House of Art, although they could not completely block the implementation of this part of the road plans. Much the same was true of the egalitarian citizen initiatives in Maxvorstadt and Lehel, which succeeded in gaining some concessions even though they could not prevent the Altstadtring from being built in this part of the city.

The initial egalitarian opposition against parts of the Altstadtring inspired other citizen initiatives. After the popular outcry in Maxvorstadt and Lehel, the opposition became increasingly vocal and experienced in organizing protest campaigns, so much so that the southern and southwestern parts of the Altstadtring were never upgraded to the standard level. Also, the widening of the road along the river Isar—which was planned in close connection with the Altstadtring—was axed under popular pressure. Moreover, the city "learned on the job" to involve societal groups and concerned citizens in the decisionmaking process. In 1968, the Planning Department and the Münchner Bauforum agreed to constitute the Münchner Forum, which still serves as a clearinghouse for action groups and a platform for discussions between action groups, other interests, and the city. The intensified communication between the established policy community and the egalitarian counterculture stimulated double-loop learning, which can be illustrated by the experience of Hans-Jochen Vogel. Vogel started as a progressive Social-Democratic mayor in 1960 and seemed to welcome "creative destruction" in the service of material progress. By the end of the 1960s, however, he had learned to take a "double look" at the situation, questioning the traditional traffic policy. He wrote a famous column titled "The Car Is Killing Our Cities," and he made the oft-cited statement: "With every million more that one puts into urban road construction, one is taking the city closer to its death."[36]

In 1971 the queen of England opened the massive Inner Ring Road in Birmingham, surrounded by a monofunctional urban environment in which people could work but for the most part wanted to pass through as quickly as possible. One year later the Olympic Games opened in Munich, showing the world a multifunctional city with a colorful pedestrian zone where traditional Bavarians as well as bohemians and hippies seemed to feel at ease; an efficient public transport system consisting of buses, trams, and metros; and also an Altstadtring.[37] Compared with Birmingham's Inner Ring Road, however, the Altstadtring was relatively modest, permeable, and not fully completed. The Altstadtring could be crossed at street level at various spots (although there were some pedestrian subways), it did not not prevent trams from going into the city (on the western part cars and trams even shared road space), and it was on the whole not such a visual, psychological, and physical barrier as the IRR in Birmingham. Whereas the IRR made Birmingham highly dependent upon a single way of traveling (by car) that was consistent with a particular way of life (suburban), the Altstadtring accommodated various traffic modes and ways of life.

In the 1970s representatives of the different policy cultures continued to exchange arguments concerning the area within and around the Altstadtring. The initial clash of cultures was gradually transformed into a relatively consensual and cooperative communication between cultures. This resulted in the city's Second Development Plan of 1974, which emphasized that the interests of all citizens—pedestrians as well as motorists and have-nots as well as haves—should be furthered. The central concern of this plan was to consolidate growth in such a way that the quality of life and the traditional spirit of Munich would be guaranteed. In addition, a restrictive attitude toward the growth of car traffic was taken. This implied extending pedestrianization in the city center and slowing traffic in the central residential areas. The general idea was to reduce traffic from and to the city center by creating multifunctional suburban centers within a polycentric structure. With respect to the remaining traffic, public transport was given priority.[38]

Nevertheless, car traffic continued to grow in the course of the 1970s as in most European cities, which inspired some action groups in central Munich to propose more drastic measures. Egalitarian citizen initiatives from five central wards got together with members of the five Bezirksausschüsse (ward committees with representatives of the various political parties, who are supposed to communicate local needs to their colleagues in the city council) and with members of the planning and engineering departments to develop a traffic plan that was presented to the city council in 1982. Many of the ideas that were developed in this way were integrated into the Third Development Plan of 1983. This plan was developed very much in line with the prime objectives of the 1974 plan, which had to be redefined, however, in the context of tighter spatial and financial limitations. The intensive communication between city planners and representatives of societal groups was also continued. Münchner Forum organized a discussion among experts and a hearing with representatives from the city and the metropolitan region and published a critical analysis of the Development Plan and a statement containing the final conclusions of the public examination. The forum was most critical of the envisaged downgrading of the tram services. After years of the forum's campaigning for the continuation of the tram services, which culminated in the presentation of a petition to the city council, traffic policy was changed in favor of the trams.

Thus, the center of Munich has remained accessible by various modes of transportation: car, bus, train, metro, tram, bicycle, and foot. No particular piece of infrastructure such as the Altstadtring has been all important. Consequently it did not take a radical conversion and a complete change of policy, as in Birmingham, to make Munich's city council decide to downgrade the Altstadtring. This decision was instead a logical consequence of Munich's policy, which since the beginning of the 1970s has been aimed at reducing car traffic within and around the Altstadtring.[39] The Altstadtring has already been narrowed from the eastern part to the northeast, and there are plans to extend this narrowing further.

It is typical of Munich's cultural regime that hierarchists as well as egalitarians and individualists have played an active role in the current debate about the Altstadtring. A remarkable result of the intensive communication between policy cultures over the years is that the representatives of these cultures are sensitive to the arguments of others and try to make their own arguments acceptable and understandable to the other policy cultures. For example, the car manufacturer BMW, which has its headquarters in Munich, has launched the concept of the Blue Zone, a zone demarcated by the present Altstadtring.[40] In the BMW concept, the Altstadtring will be changed into a green, parklike environment in which motorists will find a series of huge parking garages. From there on, the individual can take only the tram or the bus into an almost completely pedestrianized city center. The case for a pedestrian city center and for the greening of the Altstadtring is made with arguments that come very close to those of the egalitarian policy culture. BMW has also tried to make the concept acceptable to those with a hierarchical bias. An ingenious traffic-guidance system is envisaged in order to lead the motorist along the least-congested corridor—thus in the most efficient way—to his parking lot along the Blue Zone. One must, of course, not overlook that BMW developed this concept above all to maintain an individual way of traveling by car as far as possible given the current political climate. To take another example, the Green Party, the most egalitarian party in Munich's city council, has suggested turning half of the western part of the Altstadtring into a boulevard and a bicycle path. Besides the typical egalitarian arguments—referring to the equal treatment of traffic modes and the preservation of the environment—the Greens also try to make their case acceptable to individualists by arguing that the public space will provide more freedom, opportunity, satisfaction, and fun and to hierarchists by using sophisticated traffic models to argue that their suggestions do not lead to, but instead solve, traffic congestion.

When different policy cultures interact intensively and even reach out to each other, the chance of a planning disaster is minimized and the chance of creative combinations in policymaking is maximized. Both advantages are related to the multiple-problem–multiple-solution approach, an approach that has flourished in

Munich since the 1960s. The positive results of this variegated and flexible approach are not confined to the Altstadtring. They can be experienced in Munich's city center as a whole, which offers diversity, multifunctionality, and, as a consequence, quality of life for different ways of life.

CULTURAL THEORY AND POLICY-ORIENTED LEARNING

The two cases present divergent patterns and levels of policy-oriented learning. Learning in Birmingham's policy community has been limited to detecting and correcting error in relation to the traditional assumption that more cars call for more roads. Munich has surpassed Birmingham not so much at this level of "single-loop learning." Leading policymakers in Munich have been able to take a "double look" at the traditional policy theory and, by doing so, have become sensitive to more than one way of managing the motoring issue. The case studies strongly support the hypothesis, derived from cultural theory, that it is the level of cultural pluralism that makes the difference. The more rival policy cultures penetrate into the policy community, the more likely it is that the blind spots in an otherwise taken-for-granted policy will be detected and corrected.

NOTES

I am especially indebted to Marco Verweij and Richard Ellis for comments and suggestions on earlier drafts of this chapter.

1. Anthony Downs, *Stuck in Traffic: Coping with Peak-Hour Traffic Congestion* (Washington, D.C.: Brookings, 1992), 23–24.

2. On the views of nature that are characteristic of each cultural type, see Michael Thompson, Richard Ellis, and Aaron Wildavsky, *Cultural Theory* (Boulder: Westview Press, 1990), 26–28.

3. Downs, *Stuck in Traffic,* 14.

4. Garrett Hardin, "The Tragedy of the Commons," *Science* 162(December 13, 1968), 1243–1248. Also see Elinor Ostrom, "Institutional Arrangements and the Commons Dilemma," in Vincent Ostrom, David Feeny, and Hartmut Picht, eds., *Rethinking Institutional Analysis and Development, Issues, Alternatives and Choices* (San Francisco: Institute for Contemporary Studies, 1988).

5. Downs, *Stuck in Traffic,* 14.

6. For a good overview of the values of the ecological movement, see Robert E. Goodin, *Green Political Theory* (Cambridge, Mass.: Polity Press, 1992). On the new social movements, see Russell J. Dalton and Manfred Küchler, eds., *Challenging the Political Order, New Social and Political Movements in Western Democracies* (New York: Oxford University Press, 1990).

7. The fatalistic attitude toward car traffic is passive and reactive. The fatalist is not apt to contribute to the definition of the traffic problem and the selection of alternative solutions, being convinced that such actions would not make any difference. He is more in-

clined to wait for the policies of others and to follow them, though with plenty of grumbling. Transport is typically organized for, not by, the fatalist. Of all traffic modes, mass transport fits best with the fatalistic worldview: Time of departure, route, speed, and stops are determined by others. Whatever their preferred mode of transport, adherents of the fatalistic culture are not inclined to propose or organize in behalf of any of the possible policy options. Instead, they usually acquiesce in whatever the powers that be decide.

8. Michael Thompson, "Among the Energy Tribes: A Cultural Framework for the Analysis and Design of Energy Policy," *Policy Sciences* 17(May 1984), 329.

9. Policy community and policy network are related concepts. The former highlights the actors and the latter the relationships among actors at the mesolevel. See Michael M. Atkinson and William D. Coleman, "Policy Networks, Policy Communities and the Problems of Governance," *Governance: An International Journal of Policy and Administration* 5(February 1992), 158.

10. See Kenneth Hanf and Fritz Scharpf, eds., *Interorganisational Policymaking: Limits to Coordination and Central Control* (London-Beverly Hills: Sage, 1978); and Volker Schneider, "The Structure of Policy Networks," *European Journal of Political Research* 21(February 1992), 110.

11. See Thompson, Ellis, and Wildavsky, *Cultural Theory*, 91.

12. On project blindness, see Michael Thompson and Michael Warburton, "Decisionmaking Under Contradictory Certainties: How to Save the Himalayas When You Can't Find What Is Wrong with Them," *Journal of Applied Systems Analysis* 12(December 1985), 26.

13. See Charles Jencks, *The Language of Postmodern Architecture* (London: Academy Edition, 1977, 1991); and David Harvey, *The Condition of Postmodernity* (Oxford: Basil Blackwell, 1990).

14. See Paul Sabatier, "Knowledge, Policy-Oriented Learning, and Policy Change: An Advocacy Coalition Framework," in *Knowledge: Creation, Diffusion, Utilization* 8(June 1987), 649–692.

15. Chris Argyris and Donald Schön, *Organizational Learning: A Theory of Action Perspective* (Reading, Mass.: Addison Wesley, 1978), 18–29. Gareth Morgan, *Images of Organization* (London-Beverly Hills: Sage, 1986), 88.

16. See Thompson and Warburton, "Decisionmaking Under Contradictory Certainties," 11.

17. James L. Macmorran, *Municipal Public Works and Planning in Birmingham, 1852–1972* (Birmingham: Everyware-Oscott, 1973), 26.

18. Anthony Sutcliffe and Roger Smith, *History of Birmingham: Birmingham 1939–1970*, vol. 3 (London: Oxford University Press, 1974), 412.

19. Ibid., 401.

20. Ibid., 404.

21. Ibid., 407.

22. Ibid., 406.

23. Patrick Dunleavy, *The Politics of Mass Housing in Britain, 1945–1975* (Oxford: Clarendon Press, 1981), 293.

24. I. Heard, *Developing Birmingham 1889 to 1989: 100 years of City Planning* (Birmingham: Studio Press Print Group, 1989), 97.

25. Sutcliffe and Smith, *History of Birmingham*, 287.

26. Heard, *Developing Birmingham*, 90.

27. See Barry Fusijhin, *Styles of Advocacy, The Role of Voluntary Organizations in the Birmingham Planning Process* (University of Birmingham Press, 1975), 104.

28. Birmingham City Council, Department of Planning and Architecture, "The Inner Ring Road: Making Changes," 1991.

29. Otto Meitinger, "Grundzüge der Münchner Stadtplanung nach 1945," in Peter M. Bode, *München in den 50er Jahren* (Munich: Buchendorfer Verlag, 1992), 18.

30. The Nazis had actually started tunneling the Lindwurm Strasse for U-Bahn purposes in 1938 and had developed measures for traffic reduction in the Altstadt of Munich. See Peter Hall and Carmen Hass-Klau, *Can Rail Save the City?: The Impact of Rail Rapid Transit and Pedestrianisation on British and German Cities* (Aldershot: Gower, 1985), 26.

31. The Nazis' rejection of the enlightenment project and their critical attitude toward modern technologies parallels in some ways the egalitarian critique of modernity and technological progress. Ecophilosophers are particularly likely to subscribe to the antimodern cultural critique of philosophers such as Martin Heidegger and Arnold Gehlen, who have been accused of sympathizing with the Nazis. See Hans Achterhuis, *De maat van de techniek* (Baarn, The Netherlands: Ambo, 1992), 93, 201.

32. Kurt Seeberger and Gerhard Rauchwetter, *München, 1945 bis Heute: Chronik eines Aufstiegs* (Munich: Hugendubel, 1970), 236.

33. Richard Bauer, "Grosstadtverkehr," in Richard Bauer, ed., *Thomas Wimmer und sein München, Eine Stadt im Afbaum 1948–1960* (Munich: Hugendubel, 1989), 30.

34. Herman R. Van Gunsteren, "Het Leervermogen van de Overheid," in Mark Bovens and Willem Witteveen, eds., *Het Schip van Staat* (Zwolle, The Netherlands: Tjeenk Willink, 1985), 53–74.

35. Landeshauptstadt München, Baureferat, *Bauen in München 1960 bis 1970* (1970), 80.

36. Hans-Jochen Vogel, *Die Amtskette, Meine 12 Jahre, Ein Erlebnisbericht* (Munich: Süddeutscher Verlag), 133–140.

37. For facts and figures, see Hall and Hass-Klau, *Can Rail Save the City?* 195–199.

38. Landeshauptstadt München, Presse-und Informationsamt, *Stadtentwicklungsplan 1974, Grundlage für die öffentliche Diskussion* (1974), 57.

39. Joachim Lorenz, "Oekologische Verkehrspolitik in München, Einstieg in dem Unstieg," *Verkehrszeichen* 7(January 1992), 24.

40. L. Janssen, "City-Konzept Blaue Zone München, Die Zukunft der Stadtmitte," *Internationales Verkehrswesen* 45(April 1993), 196–203.

CHAPTER 4

Cultural Influences on Policies Concerning Mental Illness

Brendon Swedlow

When scientists consider culture and mental illness together they usually intend to show how culture contributes to variations in the types and frequencies of mental illnesses. In these investigations, culture is often synonymous with country, as in "Obsessive-Compulsive Disorders in Chinese Culture." But almost any human aggregation can be considered a culture; for instance, tribes—"Psychogenic Disorder and Social Conflict Among the Zulu"; ethnic groups—"Cultural Differences in Mental Disorders: An Italian and Irish Contrast in the Schizophrenias—U.S.A."; or a group of islands—"Culture and Individual Personality Integration on Truk."[1]

One literature review identified no less than eleven ways that culture conditions the expression of mental illnesses.[2] Culture may supply the beliefs that become the substance for individual delusions, as when an Ojibwa Indian believes he is possessed by the Witiko, a cannibalistic spirit, and consequently kills and eats his family members. Culture influences child-rearing practices such as toilet training, breast-feeding, nurturing, and weaning, which in turn may produce disorders of the kind Freud identified as linked to these practices. Cultures not only teach what is right and wrong but how the right are to be rewarded and the wrong punished, which has implications for mental health. Some cultures, for example, may encourage hysterical, frenzied behavior by bestowing the role of medicine man or holy man on persons who express themselves in this way. Cultures that make the individual responsible for his deviance may produce more depressed, self-abusing persons than those that hold the group accountable for wayward members. Cultural appraisal of roles may also create stress and mental disorders, as among the Tanala, where second-born sons and childless wives are devalued and consequently suffer disproportionately from a condition called "tromba." Cultural changes that affect role rewards and responsibilities can also produce psychic troubles, as when slaves were freed or when women were expected to have husbands, children, and careers. Culturally instilled feelings of fear, jealousy, or unrealistic aspiration may have similar effects. Culture can also influence the expression of genetic causes of mental disease, as when a self-segregated elite repeatedly intermarries. Then there are cultural influences on physical health that can have mental health consequences, as when a culturally determined diet causes vitamin deficiency or malnutrition, affecting the nervous system. Finally, culture itself may inherently cause some amount of mental illness, since cultures everywhere regulate human urges and channel, if not repress, human sexual and aggressive impulses.

Culture and mental illness are also jointly investigated by scientists who want to understand how culture influences ideas about mental illness or affects actions taken toward those designated mentally ill. In these studies, cultures are countries. U.S. and German high school students, mental hospital staff and patients, for example, are compared with respect to their conceptions of mental illness.[3] Or American and British psychiatrists are asked to diagnose the mental afflictions of the same set of videotaped patients, with surprising diagnostic differences emerging.[4] But culture is not retained as an organizing and analytical concept at the subnational or subsocietal level. What one does find are particular psychiatrists criticizing their profession from positions clearly embedded in a complex of other commitments—to particular people, to distinct values, to a certain cosmology.[5] What one also finds are other scientists analyzing the politics and policies of these antipsychiatry psychiatrists.[6] These political analyses contain much of what might be included in a subcultural analysis: They include discussions of beliefs and values and descriptions of the followers of these antipsychiatry leaders. Yet these analyses are so freighted with the idiosyncrasies of antipsychiatry positions or their authors are so taken with recounting the peculiar configuration of interests that pushed through a certain piece of legislation or faced off over a particular legal standard in court that larger commonalities and differences are obscured.

This chapter draws on the writings of psychiatrists and "antipsychiatrists" and on secondary accounts of their politics and policies. I will try to make central what in these materials is too often peripheral: a subcultural level of analysis. That is, I will look for evidence of the defense and proselytization of a particular culture or way of life. This evidence can be found in details and in nuances that demonstrate basic values, beliefs, and behaviors that define a life-space, or way of being in the world. When we run these various writings through a subcultural filter, three mutually exclusive sets of beliefs, values, and preferences regarding relations with others emerge: the hierarchical, the egalitarian, and the individualistic or libertarian. This subcultural analysis provides two immediate analytic payoffs. It allows the reader to see connections among personalities and policies more often considered separately. And for these same personalities and policies, the reader is also able to see cleavages that in other discussions are disguised by lumping, for example, all antipsychiatrists together.

ALAN A. STONE AND THE DEFENSE OF
HIERARCHICAL DOCTOR-PATIENT RELATIONS

Historians of mental health policy often speak of waves of reform, three or four of them.[7] The second of these involved a shift from a policy of collecting all undesirables in asylum warehouses, the first reform, to a policy of psychiatric treatment in state hospitals. This change in policy was the result of a shift in human capacities for dealing with mental illness, through the rise of the psychiatric profession, and of a shift in public attitudes supporting both the idea of treatment and psychiatrists as treaters.[8] Although this was certainly a big policy change, it does not represent as great a change in cultural influences as occurred in the third wave of reform (the community mental health movement) or as are represented in debates about specific policies in our time, such as involuntary or civil commitment.

From a cultural perspective, moving mentally ill persons from asylums to state hospitals does not reflect a significant alteration of attitudes toward these people because the belief persisted that some of us can decide that some others are different and therefore deserve to be treated differently. Psychiatrists replaced wardens as the new custodians of these others' welfare. The hierarchical doctor-patient relationship was substituted for the hierarchical keeper-kept relationship, and both sets of relationships were sanctioned by the wider public. What changed is where the public placed itself in relation to these other parties. Whereas society had once stood above both the wardens and their wards, it now perceived itself as superior only to the patients, paying deference to the expertise of the doctors.

In our time the right of persons who accredit themselves as "doctors" who can identify others "in need of treatment" has been most vigorously defended by professor of law and psychiatry Alan A. Stone, in what his students describe as the "thank-you theory of paternalistic intervention."[9] "Its basic premise," Stone maintains, "is that in the area of civil confinement the only justification for abrogating procedural safeguards is the provision of benefits which ameliorate human suffering."[10] Stone believes that those who are so mentally ill as to be incompetent to seek out or consent to psychiatric treatment will thank him once they become sane for forcing that treatment upon them. In other words, he is confident that his patients will retroactively approve of his belief that some have the power to decide what is in the best interests of others. By making the sick well, he will therefore also have gained converts to his hierarchical worldview.

Stone's genuflection to "procedural safeguards" represents a considerable concession to those who do not see the world the way he does, that is, to egalitarians and libertarians. In his five-step procedure for deciding what is in another's best interest, he makes every effort to ensure that "only someone who is irrational, treatable, and incidentally dangerous would be confined in the mental health system."[11] Yet at every step along the way to the mental hospital, his civil commitment procedure calls on some particular professionals to make decisions for the rest of us. Courts relying on the opinions of psychiatrists must decide whether a person is "severely mentally ill"; whether his "immediate prognosis involves major distress"; whether treatment is "available"; whether this diagnosable, very distressful yet treatable, severe mental illness "impaired the person's ability to accept treatment"; and whether "a reasonable man might reject such treatment."[12]

That this whole scheme ultimately rests on the belief that some can legitimately decide for others is most evident in the identification of those too "impaired" to accept treatment. The "impaired" person, Stone writes, is one who was "either too disturbed to communicate, or because of incapacity arising from the illness such as delusions and hallucinations, the person was unable to comprehend the possibility of treatment."[13] Someone other than the impaired person obviously makes the decision that he is impaired. The impaired are "volunteered" for treatment.

Stone formulates the last step in his process for involuntary commitment as a "balancing test," which of course implies that some are "the balanced" and others "the balancers." Judges and psychiatrists in fact are the ones applying the test to those whose behavior has gotten them as far as the courtroom. The parenthetical statements I have inserted in Stone's proposed test are intended to reveal the hidden hierarchical relations imbedded in this suggested legal standard: "Would a reasonable man," (as determined by the court) "given the patient's serious illness and suffering," (as determined by the court's confidence in the testifying psychiatrist) "be willing to give up a certain amount of freedom in that particular institution in exchange for a treatment that" (according to the psychiatrist) "in similar cases produces a specific range of results?"[14]

Stone's perception of his relationship to others, his belief in his own ability (and that of the psychiatric profession generally) to act in others' interests, fits the hierarchical worldview. Hierarchs look for human variation and believe that differences among individuals justify their different treatment. They tend to believe that human differences are innate, or at least the product of such intensive social conditioning as to be intractable. A related tendency is to view people not as individuals but as types. One feature of a person has to be emphasized so that she can be properly categorized and elsewise properly treated by the hierarchical community. Hierarchs are very concerned about two things: the maintenance of the community and the preservation of its various parts in proper relation and proportion to one another. Stone's balancing test may profitably be viewed as one hierarch's attempt to keep some sort of order in the community. Judges and psychiatrists retain their unique, well-delineated place in the society Stone envisions, in part by being able to make certain sorts of decisions for other people, which of course also "helps" those people retain their "mentally ill" roles or positions.

THE RISE OF ANTIPSYCHIATRY, OR THE EGALITARIAN AND LIBERTARIAN ASSAULT ON STONE'S HIERARCHICAL CULTURE

The third wave of mental health reform was driven, as already indicated, by a basic cultural shift in attitudes toward doctors. The legitimacy of the notion that one set of people could decide what was best for another came under attack, with two heretics, psychiatrists Ronald D. Laing and Thomas S. Szasz, leading the charge.[15] "Much of Laing's appeal lay in his use of psychiatric credentials to define the establishment as insane," write Rael Isaac and Virginia Armat, authors of *Madness in the Streets,* a recent analysis of the politics of deinstitutionalization.[16] "If you want a perfect example of schizophrenia, just read a psychiatric text," Laing writes, citing several, "and you will see manifested in the mentality of the psychiatrist the very disease, the very psychopathology, that is projected onto the person who is supposed to be the patient."[17] Szasz, for his part, does not invert the relationship between doctors and patients but maintains that there are patients only because there are doctors: "The identity of an individual as schizophrenic depends on the existence of the social system of (institutional) psychiatry. Hence, if psychiatry is abolished, schizophrenics disappear. ... There assuredly remain persons who are incompetent, or self-absorbed, or who reject their 'real' roles, or who offend others in some other ways," Szasz concedes. "But if there is no psychiatry, none of them can be schizophrenic."[18]

The contrast between Stone's views on the doctor-patient relationship and Laing's and Szasz's views is striking. All three men are psychiatrists. Yet they see their relationships with the people they call their patients so differently. How can this be? How can such a variety of views be sustained in the same profession at the same time? Part of the reason for this is the powerful influence of culture on perceptions, which are selective: We find what we are looking for. Culture backgrounds certain things and foregrounds others. Culture organizes perception, gives meaning to the perceived. Some psychiatrists, such as Stone, for example, are confident that they can tell a mentally ill person from a mentally well one. Other psychiatrists, such as Laing and Szasz, have less confidence than Stone in the diagnostic capabilities of their profession. These different perceptions, I suspect, have something to do with the culturally instilled identities of these men. One, Stone, probably takes more of his personal identity from his professional identity than do the other two. If there were no mentally ill people, who or what would Stone be? Szasz, by contrast, has a stake in seeing only the infinite variety of the human condition. If mental illness really is a disease and there really is an identifiable class of mentally ill persons, then maybe he would have to carry more of the burden of being a practicing doctor. Laing averts his eyes from the categorical differences Stone sees and from a Szaszian world that is all individuality, emphasizing instead our commonalities, the community of sufferers in which each has something to teach the other. Another reason that these three psychiatrists see themselves, their patients, and what they are doing so differently is because these different perceptions are shared by their patients.[19] When beliefs and values are shared, and when shared beliefs and values reflect the way people live together, cultural theorists call the results cultures. Here, I am attempting to show the presence of three distinct doctor-patient cultures.

EGALITARIAN BY ASSOCIATION: RONALD D. LAING, KINGSLEY HALL, AND THE "NEW LEFT"

Those attacking the hierarchical "Stone Age" culture were unified in what they were against, but not in what they were for, and it is this last reality that has in particular been obscured in accounts of ideological influences on policies on mental illness. Isaac and Armat come closest to making this distinction, noting that Laing and Szasz had different views and influenced different people, but do not analyze the consequences these differences have for mental health policy. Laing is perhaps best known for establishing Kingsley Hall, a three-story building in London's East End that could comfortably house thirteen people. Over 100 psychiatrists, other mental health care workers, and patients lived there between 1965 and 1969. Morton Schatzman, a psychotherapist and year-long Kingsley resident, writes that the hall's founders "hoped to fulfill in the 'community' their seed-idea that lost souls may be cured by going mad among people who see madness as a chance to die and be reborn."[20] Kingsley was a place where people who had been "put together" or socialized in a haphazard, harmful way could "strip themselves down" or just "fall apart" without censure and then "re-assemble" themselves and be resocialized by caring cohabitants as a prelude to reentering the larger society.[21]

Most interesting for my purposes is Schatzman's account of relations among residents. A real effort was apparently made to allow them to go their own ways: maximum individual autonomy commensurate with preservation of the Kingsley "community." "Each person at Kingsley Hall may choose to assume the obligations of a reciprocal bond with another person, or other people, or the 'group.' He pledges to do so, or dissolves his pledge, by an initiative that originates in his own interior."[22]

Two residents severely tested this ethic. A woman named Mary Barnes who had been both a patient and a staff person in mental hospitals when she came to Kingsley at age forty-two went through a period of very antisocial behavior coupled with great dependency on others. She would frequently strip naked and smear herself and the walls of her next-to-the-kitchen room with her own excrement. Then she stopped eating and had to be bottle-fed by the other residents.

They found it difficult to live with her and discussed whether they should permit her to live as she chose, wondering whether a person has, as Schatzman put it, "a right to a 'smell space' that extends beyond the four walls of his or her room."[23]

Another resident, Joseph, age twenty, came to live at Kingsley after three years in a mental hospital. He heard unseen others plotting against him. To stop these voices from communicating, he cut wires to the building and disconnected the telephone receiver. He threatened to set fires and burn down the building and would have set his mattress afire on the building roof had another resident not stopped him. The other residents felt severely threatened by his behavior and met daily to discuss it. Joseph was invited to these meetings but usually would stay for only a few minutes, leaving to search for the "real" meeting he thought to be secretly under way elsewhere. Schatzman's summary of the questions considered at the residents' meetings reveals how far they were willing to go to accommodate others. "Was it possible to talk about him without making true in a sense his fantasy that 'voices' were talking about him?" they wondered. "What did his behaviour mean? Was it worth the nuisance or the risk to us to let him live with us while we tried to find out? What would happen to him if we told him to leave? If we, who wished to understand him, could not, could anyone? ... Did his behaviour serve some purpose for us? We were coming together more often to talk to each other because of him than we had been before. Had he elected himself to be our scapegoat, for our sake?"[24] Residents' questions regarding Mary and Joseph were resolved in favor of letting them live on at Kingsley in their own idiosyncratic and often threatening ways. These decisions and the inclusive, self-searching, nonjudgmental way in which they were made are, I believe, representative of how Kingsley residents lived with each other. Especially noteworthy is how concerned residents were about censuring someone, even accidentally, even at the person's own invitation. They apparently feared that group solidarity might be based on hierarchical principles of differentiation (here, scapegoating) more than they feared that an individual who behaved differently and dangerously would physically hurt them.

Another visible aspect of residents' relations was their rigorous attention to role avoidance. Schatzman reports that residents admitted newcomers with an eye toward maintaining a "balance" between those who could do the work of shopping, cooking, cleaning, and repairing the place and those who could not or would not. Still, "No one who lives at Kingsley Hall sees those who perform work upon the external material world as 'staff,' and those who do not as 'patients.' No caste system forbids people to move freely from one sub-group to another, as it does in mental hospitals. ... No organization, no ossified apparatus, imposes upon anyone the need to administrate others: to distribute communal tasks, to allocate responsibilities and to make rules."[25] Kingsley visitors, often having staff positions at mental hospitals, frequently guessed wrong about the previous status of Kingsley residents, mistaking former patients for doctors, and doctors and nurses for former patients.

In Schatzman's description of relations among residents of Kingsley Hall there seems to be little that would offend Thomas Szasz. People were allowed their idiosyncrasies and their personal developmental paths. This appears to be all that Laing wanted Kingsley to be as well. Of his stay there he recalls the lack of roles: "Among us there were no staff, no patients, no locked doors, no psychiatric treatment to stop or change states of mind." And there was promotion of individuality. "We declared a free-for-all: freedom to think, see, feel in any way whatever; freedom of biorhythm (autorhythm) for all of us." [26] Kingsley Hall and Laing's approach to mental health apparently become insufferable for Szasz in the emphasis on community, in the value placed on interaction among people. It is in this communitarian focus that one detects the greatest difference between Laing's Kingsley Hall and Szasz's libertarian utopia. In his analysis of what is wrong with human relationships, Laing repeatedly decries the lack of camaraderie, solidarity, community, and communion. [27]

The egalitarian preoccupation with power differentials and inequities is rarely explicit in Laing's writings. [28] At the core of his ideas about mental health is the thought that patients should be allowed to experience their condition completely as part of their personal growth and identity development. Laing thereby appears to share Szasz's libertarian aspirations, But Szasz values autonomy as an end in itself, and for Laing autonomy is a form of treatment that works for some people. It is Laing's communitarian values that separate him from Szasz, and his striving for a community without patients and doctors that is attractive to egalitarians. So although Laing is not preoccupied with inequality, when he feeds his egalitarian readers a passage like the following, one can almost hear them inserting their concerns between the lines:

> Whatever else was going on in psychiatry, it was, and is, one interface in the socioeconomic-political structure of our society where camaraderie, solidarity, companionship, communion is almost impossible, or completely impossible. Psychiatrists and patients were, and are, too often ranged on opposite sides. Before we meet, we are far apart. The psychiatrist-patient rift across the sane-mad line seemed to play a part in some of the misery and disorder occurring within the field of psychiatry. Maybe this loss of human camaraderie was the most important thing. Maybe its restoration was the *sine qua non* of "treatment." [29]

In *Psycho Politics,* Peter Sedgwick convincingly chronicles Laing's romance with and later rejection of the New Left. [30] Laing's writings alone never placed him squarely in its political camp. [31] But during the mid-1960s to early 1970s, [32] Laing associated with so many people whose politics were unambiguously egalitarian that any exercise in classification by affiliation would make him one of them. Or, as German folk wisdom has it, "Tell me who you hang out with, and I'll tell you who you are." Kingsley Hall hosted a sampling of Laing's admirers. "The community has been a link in a chain of 'counter culture' centres," reports

Schatzman. "Experimental-drama groups, social scientists of the 'New Left,' classes from the Antiuniversity of London, leaders of the 'commune' movement and avant-garde poets, artists, musicians, dancers and photographers, have met at Kingsley Hall with residents in the last three and a half years. The 'Free School of London' met there for the first time."[33] Laing also wrote for what Isaac and Armat call "New Left countercultural forums" such as *Peace News, New Left Review,* and Timothy Leary's *Psychedelic Review.*[34]

THOMAS S. SZASZ:
SELF-IDENTIFIED LIBERTARIAN

Szasz apparently hated these egalitarians. Isaac and Armat characterize him as an "unsparing libertarian" who "had nothing but contempt for the New Left."[35] They retell a story related to them by a former University of Michigan student who, together with other New Left sympathizers, went to applaud one of his lectures "only to find themselves roundly denounced by Szasz from the platform."[36] Szasz's main target, like Laing's, is traditional psychiatry, but it is clear that Szasz does not want to be lumped with other anti-psychiatrists. "It is true, of course, that in traditional, coercive psychiatry, the anti-psychiatrists and I face the same enemy. So did, in another context, Stalin and Churchill," he begins. "At any rate," he continues, getting more to the heart of their differences,

> anti-psychiatrists do not clearly state whether they object only to involuntary psychiatric interventions, or also to those that are voluntary; to all involuntary psychiatric interventions, or only those practiced by their political adversaries. They do not frankly acknowledge whether they support real tolerance for contractual psychiatric interventions, or only "repressive tolerance" for (against) them—because such practices occur in an "exploitative-capitalist" context of free market and free enterprise.

"Actually, as we shall see," Szasz finally concludes, what distinguishes him from them is that

> the anti-psychiatrists are all self-declared socialists, communists, or at least anti-capitalists and collectivists. As the communists seek to raise the poor above the rich, so the anti-psychiatrists seek to raise the "insane" above the "sane"; as the communists justify their aims and methods by claiming that the poor are virtuous, while the rich are wicked, so the anti-psychiatrists justify theirs by claiming that the "insane" are authentic, while the "sane" are inauthentic.[37]

In these specific analogies between communists and antipsychiatrists, Szasz does not seem to be objecting so much to the lateral constraints found in the egalitarian community of equals as against the impositions from above characteristic of hierarchical communities of unequals. He somehow believes that anti-psychiatrists are working toward the day when the formerly insane will be able to impose upon and coerce the formerly sane. In fact, his analysis of Laing's Kingsley Hall indicates that Szasz believes that that day has already arrived.[38]

Szasz does not fear an egalitarian leveling so much as an inversion of relationships. He does not fear consensus decisionmaking so much as orders from on high. He realizes that he is somehow very different from others who oppose traditional psychiatry. He fears communism and favors one-on-one contractual relations. Sedgwick says, "Szasz subordinates his many historical-analytical excursions to one propagandist and polemical task, the demolition of collectivist pretensions in psychiatry and medicine."[39] Yet the collectivism he fears is clearly more one of the hierarchical type, where there are masters and slaves, and it is this type of collectivization that he believes his antipsychiatry colleagues are planning. This reality is neatly expressed in his more-generalized political analysis. "The conflicts between those who have power and those who want to take it away from them fall into three distinct categories," Szasz informs us. "First, there are those who want to take power away from the oppressor and give it to the oppressed, as a class—as exemplified by Marx, Lenin, and the Communists. Revealingly, they dream of the 'dictatorship' of the proletariat or some other group." This sounds like Laing forcing the sane to support sufferers. "Second, there are those who want to take power away from the oppresser and give it to themselves as the protectors of the oppressed—as exemplified by Robespierre in politics; Rush in medicine; and by their liberal, radical, and medical followers. Revealingly, they dream of the incorruptibly honest or incontrovertibly sane ruler leading his happy or healthy flock." This sounds like Stone trying to retain a civil commitment alternative to criminal incarceration. "And third, there are those who want to take power away from the oppressor and give it to the oppressed as individuals, for each to do with as he pleases, but hopefully for his own self-control—as exemplified by Mill, von Mises, the free-market economists, and their libertarian followers. Revealingly, they dream of people so self-governing that need for and tolerance of rules is minimal or nil."[40] This sounds like Szasz's dream, and it is.

Szasz clearly rejects communitarian and collectivist forms of social organization. But what is he for? Freedom, liberty, and autonomy are good guesses. "Autonomy is my religion," he says. "It is freedom to develop one's self—to increase one's knowledge, improve one's skills, and achieve responsibility for one's conduct. And it is freedom to lead one's own life, to choose among alternative courses of action so long as no injury to others results."[41] Both psychiatric impositions and those of one's fellow commune dwellers are too much of a restraint on autonomy to be tolerated. "Young radicals were enthusiastic about his work," note Isaac and Armat, "but misunderstood or ignored the libertarian root of his anti-psychiatric polemics."[42] Sedgwick makes the same observation, giving the example of Phil Brown, editor of *Radical Psychology*. Brown anthologizes Szasz along with Marx, Reich, Fanon, and other left-wing writers but is puzzled by the apparent "contradiction between his political views and his condemnations of psychiatry."[43]

"Young radicals," socialist and New Left admirers, and scholars of mental health policy probably mistook Szasz for another Laing because these two men do have something in common, as do community mental health advocates and civil libertarians. All oppose the hierarchical social relationships found in Stone's thank-you theory of paternalistic intervention. But they dislike hierarchical relationships for different reasons, which is another way of saying that they are united in what they are against but divided in what they are for. Laing's association with the New Left and Szasz's accusations that Laing's followers were communists and levelers suggest that these admirers, like community mental health advocates, oppose Stone and his way of life, which is hierarchical from an egalitarian perspective. They dislike civil commitment and state hospitals and psychiatrists because of the inequities they find in those institutions and relationships. Szasz and his civil libertarian lawyer counterparts oppose hierarchical relationships and structures because of the way in which these restrict the individual's freedom to choose her relationships, her health care provider, and her lifestyle.

Given Szasz's views of the good life, it is perhaps no surprise that Isaac and Armat characterize him as "a loner by temperament." They believe that his loner tendencies combined with the fact that he offered no alternative treatment and denounced rather than played to the radical galleries were reasons that he developed little following outside of "a small circle at Syracuse." But here Isaac and Armat ignore their own evidence to the contrary. Szasz did develop a following, and it is probably much bigger and consequential than that of Laing. In the authors' words, "For Szasz mental illness is purely and simply a test case in human liberty. It is this orientation that has made Szasz such a favorite with the legal profession, which in the 1960s began to arrogate to itself the decision-making power that had belonged to psychiatrists. While Laing is rarely quoted in the precedent-setting briefs and judicial decisions that effected this transfer of power, Szasz is quoted constantly and at length."[44] Szasz's followers are lawyers either because they share his libertarian beliefs or because the legal tools of "due process" and constitutional "rights" with which they have to work are forged from such beliefs.

IDEOLOGY AND DEINSTITUTIONALIZATION: COMMUNITY MENTAL HEALTH ADVOCATES VERSUS CIVIL LIBERTIES LAWYERS

In 1955, state mental hospitals contained 560,000 chronically ill patients. Thirty years later their numbers had declined to 130,000. Some commentators question whether "deinstitutionalization" adequately characterizes this change, since many of the older of these patients were simply transferred to other institutions such as nursing homes.[45] But enough of these in-patients became out-patients to justify describing them as deinstitutionalized. New drug therapies are widely credited with facilitating their return to "the community," but many other forces were also at work.[46] Among them were the criticisms of antipsychiatrists, the cultural influences on deinstitutionalization that concern us here. As I will demonstrate, both community mental health advocates and civil liberties lawyers were all for getting and keeping patients out of state mental hospitals. But they had different ideas about what should be done with them once deinstitutionalization had been accomplished. Civil liberties lawyers were prepared to let them roam our streets untreated if they elected to do so. Community mental health advocates, by contrast, felt that it was still our responsibility to care for these people, only in a less coercive, more compassionate setting.

Nancy K. Rhoden attempts to account for the role that ideology played in deinstitutionalization and its failures. She argues that "excessive reliance upon the influential sociological theory suggesting behavior is deviant largely because society labels it as such, when combined with an idealized view of the benefits of community care, could have led adherents to underestimate both the need to establish adequate community facilities before releasing patients and the difficulty of this task."[47] Rhoden's article is titled "The Limits of Liberty: Deinstitutionalization, Homelessness, and Libertarian Theory." Yet as is apparent enough from this excerpt from that article, the ideology she associates with deinstitutionalization's difficulties is not libertarianism. Szasz does not romanticize the community, as Rhoden claims these mental health advocates do. She says they believed "that being in the community was per se therapeutic," and that in the community "the deviant mysteriously would be reconstituted."[48] Again, these are not the beliefs we have heard Szasz espousing, nor are they beliefs other libertarians share, as will be seen. But what kind of beliefs are they, and who holds them?

An answer to this question is suggested by Richard Rumer in a recent article entitled "Community Mental Health Centers: Politics and Therapy," which begins as history but ends as advocacy for an egalitarian approach to mental health care. Rumer fortunately lets the reader know where he is headed in his acknowledgments at the bottom of the first page: "A special thanks goes to the staff and volunteers of Hassle House in Durham, North Carolina, for the experience of what a community of counselors and an egalitarian approach can accomplish."[49] In his vision of community mental health centers, "Clients are left with the responsibility for changing their lives, communities have substantial control over their mental health facilities, mental health professionals are regarded as experts providing analysis and methods but sharing decision-making with their clients and the community."[50] Rumer concludes: "In essence, what is needed is an egalitarian partnership in mental health care."[51]

Egalitarians believe that illness ultimately is caused by inequalities and that the more equal people become in their conditions and power over each other, the healthier they are going to be. These beliefs certainly influenced the Kennedy administration's proposal and Congress's passage of the Community Mental Health Centers Act in 1963. "A romance with the concept of 'community' was a ... significant background element influencing the direction that the revamping of the mental health system was to take," says David A. Rochefort in his account of the origins of the act. "Eliciting the 'maximum feasible participation' of lower-class groups in the structures that governed them constituted one strategy for combating this sense of powerlessness and alienation that was believed to cause various forms of social deviancy."[52]

Psychiatrist Anthony F. Panzetta participated in and now criticizes the thinking behind the community mental health movement. In his book *Community Mental Health: Myth and Reality*, Panzetta recounts how he and his colleagues believed they could "get to the cause of mental illness" by attacking societal inequities. "If we can influence oppression, poverty and overcrowding," their thinking went, "then there will be less depression and alcoholism."[53] In 1966 Panzetta was a unit head in the Temple University Community Mental Health Center in Philadelphia, which, according to Isaac and Armat, is one of the "two most famous examples of centers that pursued mental health through political protest. ... We supported a rent escrow drive to force landlords to do better by their tenants," Panzetta remembers. "We were part of marches. ... We thought we'd prevent mental illness somehow by doing the sort of things we were doing."[54]

Cultural theorists would say that Panzetta and his fellow psychiatrists in the community mental health movement thought illness and inequality were related because egalitarian beliefs and social forms direct their adherents' attention in a way that causes them to associate bad things with inequities and good things with their leveling.[55] This is why egalitarians believe that inequalities cause crime and the symptoms psychiatrists label as mental illness. They may concede that people differ but believe that these differences are more likely to be imposed than to be naturally occurring. Whatever their cause, society has an obligation to see that any differences that exist among people do not deprive them of all the things this world has to offer. Differences are even valued by egalitarians to the extent that these do not allow one person or group of persons to impose something on others. This notion makes the community and not individuals the final arbiter of what happens to its members. Egalitarians believe that people act legitimately only when they act through the community as a community, by consensus, not individually, not autonomously.

In his 1988 presidential address to the Community Psychology Division of the American Psychological Association, Kenneth Heller looks nostalgically on the times Panzetta recounts, laments psychology's continuing focus on the individual, and advocates a "return to community." "I am sure we are all aware of the fact that community psychology developed in the 1960s as part of a paradigm shift away from an individually oriented psychology that was unresponsive to social needs," he began. "Motivating themes in community psychology at that time, involved a desire for increased equity in American life, and a belief that psychology could be enlisted as an ally in achieving this goal," he continued. Then, connecting past and present, Heller said: "The belief in social equity and the need to reverse long-standing social conditions was, and still is, a value stance among community psychologists that represents a moral and philosophical underpinning to much of what we do." "For example," he says, "my guess is that the current interest in stress, coping, and social support is in part motivated by a desire to understand and mitigate aversive social conditions."[56]

Opponents of involuntary civil commitment of the mentally ill do not by and large argue for treatment in the community as an alternative. Instead, they fight for the liberty of their clients. As indicated, Szasz has his greatest following among lawyers, and he is a libertarian, not an egalitarian. In "A Preference for Liberty: The Case Against Involuntary Commitment of the Mentally Disordered," law professor Stephen J. Morse argues against civil commitment and for freedom, barely mentioning community and not even touching on the egalitarian themes so prevalent in the arguments for community treatment of the mentally ill. Morse maintains that "a commitment to human dignity and liberty requires that all persons be allowed to decide for themselves issues as important as psychiatric hospitalization and treatment, even if the reasons that they give seem crazy and not hospitalizing them seems inhumane."[57]

Countering the anticipated claim that "freedom is illusory for some crazy persons because they lead lives of degradation and misery," Morse argues that "a great number of persons who are not crazy lead lives of degradation and misery and could probably be helped by social rehabilitation measures, but we respect their right to liberty rather than deprive them of their freedom by forcing them into rehabilitation programs in locked institutions."[58] "If involuntary commitment is abolished," he says in summation, "the mentally disordered will no longer be subject to special restraints on their right to physical liberty, freedom of speech, freedom of association, and other fundamental rights." Indicating the kind of self-directed social organization he prefers, Morse concludes that "our society should be willing to allow some preventable harms in order to increase the liberty of its citizens."[59]

The mental health bar, "or more precisely," as Isaac and Armat say, the "mental patient liberation bar," came into being dedicated to the elimination of involuntary civil commitment.[60] Bruce Ennis, its founder, tells how, fresh out of law school, he applied for a job with the New York Civil Liberties Union. They told him they were starting a special project on the rights of the mentally handicapped. "I went home," Ennis says, "and then I went to the library and I looked under 'law and psychiatry' and found some books by a man named Thomas Szasz which I found interesting from a civil liberties perspective. ... I decided it was an important enough subject to devote a lot of my time and life to, so I did."[61] That was in 1968. Today, Ennis says: "My personal goal is either to abolish involuntary commitment or to set up so many procedural roadblocks and hurdles that it will be difficult, if not impossible, for the state to commit people against their will."[62] He cannot see any health care situation in which it is right for some to substitute their wills for others, at least not where the result is a total loss of liberty. "The fact a person has a mental illness rather than a heart illness doesn't justify locking them up," he says. "It's just never really been very important to me if there is or is not a mental illness."[63] "I'm simply a civil libertarian and in my view you don't lock people up because they've got a problem."[64]

Szasz, Morse, and Ennis articulate very similar visions of the individual and his proper relation to other people. Duties and obligations are not owed to others but to oneself. Individuals, not egalitarian or hierarchical communities, give meaning to life. Individuals, not collectives, act. People should be able to choose how they want to live. This is what libertarians, or what cultural theorists call individualists, believe. People are different, yes, and the only duty society has toward them is to allow them their differences, their idiosyncrasies. This makes for mental health. Deviance is to be tolerated, even celebrated, not treated. Autonomy and the opportunity for self-definition and self-creation are of primary value. No, people don't start out equal. Nor should they end up that way. Rather, people should be allowed to do as they will with what they are given genetically and in the way of material and social resources.

CONCLUSION

These examples certainly do not qualify as a complete ethnography of mental health policymaking cultures. But the foregoing strongly suggests the influence of three rather than two sets of mutually reinforcing beliefs, values, and social relations on policies concerning mental illness. Cultural theory allows us to see that civil libertarians and community mental health advocates dislike paternalistic policies toward mentally ill persons, but they dislike them for different reasons. They agree that paternalism is coercive and that coercion is bad. But civil libertarians do not like coercion because it deprives individuals of the ability to order their lives as they choose; community mental health advocates dislike coercion because it reflects power differentials and an unequal distribution of resources.

Szasz's railing against the communism and collectivism of the New Left also suggests that if the community mental health movement had successfully entrenched itself in community mental health centers,[65] civil libertarians probably would have attacked these centers for the same reasons that they attacked state mental hospitals. The consensus sort of decisionmaking favored by egalitarians is anathema to civil libertarians for the same reason that Stone's decision to commit them is abhorred. In both cases, others are involved in choosing health care services, a choice that civil libertarians believe should be left to the individual to make. As it turned out, community mental health centers never established enough of a presence to deprive the mentally ill of the autonomy that civil libertarians value so highly. In cultural terms, egalitarian community mental health advocates triumphed over hierarchical state hospital psychiatrists only to fumble their just-acquired "policy football" to the benefit of individualistic civil libertarians.

Reanalyzing debates over mental health policy from the perspective of cultural theory is not just an academic exercise. More important than realizing that the debate over those policies has been three-sided is realizing that each "side" is in fact three-dimensional. By this I mean that what is being defended and advocated in each case is not just a position but a whole complex of ideas and relationships amounting to a way of life, or culture. Viewing the struggle over mental health policy in this way allows us to see how, for example, preferred forms of interacting with others are related to beliefs about the sources of mental illness. Individualists equate free choice and health and restraints on that choice as a source of illness. Egalitarians think equality and health are related and believe that illness is generated by inequities. Hierarchs find health with the maintenance of differentiation among people. If there are no experts, no psychiatrists, no doctors, and no patients, then we won't be able to know who is sick and who is going to cure them. The erosion of these distinctions is the ultimate cause of illness in their view. Each of these cultural perspectives taps a truth about the causes of health and illness at least some of the time, which is another reason why these views can coexist. But to the extent that mental health care policies are driven by preferences regarding our relationships with each other rather than by a good, tight fit between a well-documented problem and its proposed and well-delineated solution, these policies are likely to do more harm than good. An awareness of cultural influences on policies on mental illness, I would argue, is therefore a necessary part of improving these policies.

NOTES

1. Bingham Dai, "Obsessive-Compulsive Disorders in Chinese Culture," 243–256; J. B. Loudon, "Psychogenic Disorder and Social Conflict Among the Zulu," 351–369; Marvin K. Opler, "Cultural Differences in Mental Disorders: An Italian and Irish Contrast in the Schizophrenias—U.S.A.," 425–442; and Thomas Gladwin and Seymour B. Sarason, "Culture and Individual Personality Integration on Truk," 173–210, in Marvin K. Opler, ed., *Culture and Mental Health* (New York: Macmillan, 1959).

2. Alexander H. Leighton and Jane M. Hughes, "Cultures as Causative of Mental Disorder," *Roundtable on Causes of Mental Disorders: A Review of Epidemiological Knowledge, 1959* (New York: Milbank Memorial Fund, 1961), 341–365.

3. See John Marshall Townsend, *Cultural Conceptions and Mental Illness: A Comparison of Germany and America* (Chicago: University of Chicago Press, 1978).

4. See R. E. Kendell, J. Cooper, A. Gourley, and J. Copeland, "Diagnostic Criteria of American and British Psychiatrists," *Archives of General Psychiatry* 25(1971), 123–130.

5. See, for example, Thomas S. Szasz, *Ideology and Insanity: Essays on the Psychiatric Dehumanization of Man* (London: Marion Boyers, 1973, 1983); Ronald D. Laing, *The Politics of Experience* (New York: Ballantine, 1967); and Peter Sedgwick, *Psycho Politics: Laing, Foucault, Goffman, Szasz and the Future of Mass Psychiatry* (New York: Harper and Row, 1982).

6. See Sedgwick, *Psycho Politics;* Rael Jean Isaac and Virginia C. Armat, *Madness in the Streets: How Psychiatry and the Law Abandoned the Mentally Ill* (New York: Free Press, 1990); Diana Ralph, *Work and Madness: The Rise of Community Psychiatry* (Montreal: Black Rose, 1983); and Patricia M. Wald and Paul R. Friedman, "The Politics of Mental Health Advocacy in the United States," *International Journal of Law and Psychiatry* 1(1978), 137–152.

7. Howard H. Goldman and Joseph P. Morrissey, "The Alchemy of Mental Health Policy: Homelessness and the Fourth Cycle of Reform," *American Journal of Public Health* 75(July 1985), 727.

8. See Gerald N. Grob, "Historical Origins of Deinstitutionalization," *New Directions for Mental Health Services,* H. Richard Lamb, series editor, no. 17 (March 1983).

9. Alan A. Stone, *Mental Health and Law: A System in Transition* (U.S. Government Printing Office, 1975), 18.

10. Ibid., 18–19.

11. Ibid., 70.

12. Ibid., 66–67.

13. Ibid., 67.

14. Ibid., 69.

15. Isaac and Armat, *Madness,* 21.

16. Ibid., 31.

17. Richard I. Evans, *R. D. Laing: The Man and His Ideas* (New York: E. P. Dutton, 1976), xxiii.

18. Thomas Szasz, *Schizophrenia: The Sacred Symbol of Psychiatry* (New York: Basic Books, 1976), 136.

19. For evidence of variation in patients' views of psychiatrists' decisions to commit them, see Gail A. Edelsohn and Virgina Aldige Hiday, "Civil Commitment: A Range of Patient Attitudes," *Bulletin of the American Academy of Psychiatry and Law* 18, no. 1 (1990), 74–75.

20. Morton Schatzman, "Madness and Morals," in Robert Boyers, ed., *R. D. Laing & Anti-Psychiatry* (New York: Octagon, 1974), 253.

21. Words and phrases in quotation marks in this sentence are popular, not professional, expressions.

22. Schatzman, "Madness and Morals," 267.

23. Ibid., 257.

24. Ibid., 270.

25. Ibid., 267.

26. R. D. Laing, *Wisdom, Madness, and Folly: The Making of a Psychiatrist* (New York: McGraw-Hill, 1985), ix.

27. Ibid., 27–30.

28. Laing does say, though, that the distribution of power and control over possible treatments are core issues. Of electric shocks, for instance, Laing says that "the critical issue is the politics of the matter. Who has the power to do what to whom against whose will?" (ibid., 23).

29. Ibid., 145.

30. Sedgwick, *Psycho Politics,* 102–107.

31. "In retrospect," writes Sedgwick, "the radicalism was less an implication than an obscure insinuation. Somewhere in a forthcoming volume, we were led to believe, or at

least in an ongoing draft, or at the very least in the barest hint of a conception, Laing was going to deliver a theory encompassing and criticising within its single span every type and kind of interference by one human being with another" (ibid., 103). It is easy to see how Laing's writings could be appropriated by egalitarian admirers, because the passages quoted here, even though written after Laing had disavowed the New Left, readily fit the egalitarian worldview.

32. Ibid., 94.

33. Schatzman, "Madness and Morals," 253.

34. Isaac and Armat, *Madness,* 29.

35. Ibid., 33.

36. Ibid., 39. Sedgwick relates the same anecdote, relying on a different source (*Psycho Politics,* 158).

37. Richard E. Vatz and Lee S. Weinberg, *Thomas Szasz: Primary Values and Major Contentions* (Buffalo, N.Y.: Prometheus Books, 1983).

38. Of the psychotics at Kinglsey Hall, Szasz writes that "Laing accepts such persons as 'residents' in his 'communities' and legitimizes them as 'sufferers' who, because of their 'victimization,' are more worthy than others." He goes on to conclude that "Laing has thus replaced the coercion of the taxpayer by the government on behalf of the mental patient. Formerly, sane citizens could detain those whom they considered to be mad; now they must maintain those who undertake to 'journey' through madness." Ibid., 172–173.

39. Sedgwick, *Psycho Politics,* 169.

40. Vatz and Weinberg, *Thomas Szasz,* 117.

41. Ibid., 34.

42. Ibid., 39.

43. "But," rejoins Sedgwick, "Szasz's politics are not an aberration, and in no sense contradict positions he has taken on psychiatric issues. Politically, psychologically and philosophically his beliefs form a unified and consistent whole, a distinct ideological complex which is most succinctly labelled 'libertarian' " (*Psycho Politics,* 158).

44. Ibid., 33–34.

45. See John A. Talbott, "The Chronic Mentally Ill: What Do We Now Know, and Why Aren't We Implementing What We Know?" in W. Walter Menninger and Gerald T. Hannah, eds., *The Chronic Mental Patient/II* (Washington, D.C.: American Psychiatric Press, 1987), 4.

46. See Grob, "Historical Origins of Deinstitutionalization," for a general discussion; and also Eugene Bardach, *The Skill Factor in Politics: Repealing the Mental Commitment Laws in California* (Berkeley: University of California Press, 1972), for a detailed account of one state's experience.

47. Nancy K. Rhoden, "The Limits of Liberty: Deinstitutionalization, Homelessness, and Libertarian Theory," *Emory Law Journal* 31(1982), 375, 395.

48. Ibid., 400.

49. Richard Rumer, "Community Mental Health Centers: Politics and Therapy," *Journal of Health Politics, Policy and Law* 2, no. 4 (Winter 1978), 531.

50. Ibid., 551.

51. Ibid., 552.

52. David A. Rochefort, "Origins of the 'Third Psychiatric Revolution': The Community Mental Health Centers Act of 1963," *Journal of Health Politics, Policy and Law* 9(Spring 1984), 7.

53. Anthony F. Panzetta, *Community Mental Health: Myth and Reality* (Philadelphia: Lee & Febiger, 1971), 31.

54. Isaac and Armat, *Madness,* 87.

55. Karl Dake and Aaron Wildavsky, "Theories of Risk Perception: Who Fears What and Why?" *Daedalus* 19(Fall 1990), 41–60.

56. Kenneth Heller, "The Return to Community," *American Journal of Community Psychology* 17(1989), 1–2.

57. Stephen J. Morse, "A Preference for Liberty: The Case Against Involuntary Commitment of the Mentally Ill," *California Law Review* 70(1982), 94.

58. Ibid., 95.

59. Ibid., 98.

60. Isaac and Armat, *Madness,* 110.

61. Ibid., 110–111. See also Bruce J. Ennis, *Prisoners of Psychology* (New York: Harcourt, Brace, and Jovanovich, 1972), for more on his views, for case histories of several patients he represented in court, and for the introduction by Szasz.

62. Isaac and Armat, *Madness,* 111.

63. Ibid., 110–111.

64. Ibid., 110.

65. Two reasons community mental health centers were not successful are endemic to egalitarian forms of social organization. First, since equality is egalitarians' primary value, they try to treat all problems, or all aspects of a problem, as equally important. Prioritization implies hierarchy implies mental illness, and evil generally. So for anything to get done, everything has to be done at once. Second, since equality is their primary value, whatever gets done has to be agreed to by everyone and everyone has to participate in doing it. Acting with a lack of consensus would be to act by excluding someone's opinion, which cannot be justified where the premise is that everyone's opinion is equally valid and important. Also, a division of labor is problematic for egalitarians because this implies roles, and roles imply hierarchy. Panzetta's reflections on his four years of experience at Temple Community Mental Health Center provide evidence of both these egalitarian problematics.

PART TWO

HISTORY

CHAPTER 5

A Cultural Analysis of Populism in Late-Nineteenth-Century America

Gary Lee Malecha

Late-nineteenth-century American populism has been the object of countless scholarly analyses, yet there is still no agreement on its character and historical impact. As historian James Turner puts it, "Pushing on toward a century after Populism burned its course across the American horizon, we have yet to puzzle out what impelled that brief meteor. This is not for lack of trying. Even the historian's infinite capacity for disagreement has barely accommodated the quarrels over the Populists."[1]

This chapter joins this contentious debate by offering an interpretation of the Farmers' Alliance movement in the Great Plains states that draws upon cultural theory. After showing that the principal interpretations of the Farmers' Alliance movement have produced an inadequate understanding of the Populists' objectives, I then enlist the concepts of cultural theory to sketch an alternative account of the Populist insurgency that reconciles aspects of Populist thought and behavior that have hitherto been seen as inconsistent or anomalous. Great Plains populism, I argue, is best understood as an egalitarian response to the dominant cultures of individualism and hierarchy.

THE ELUSIVE SPIRIT OF AMERICAN POPULISM

Most of the scholarship on populism can be placed into one of three general schools of thought: progressivism, liberal exceptionalism, and New Left historiography. Each of these schools of thought presents a theoretical framework that purports to explain U.S. political development.

The Progressive Synthesis

The largest body of Populist scholarship stems from the progressive synthesis of American politics. Popularized by Vernon Louis Parrington and Charles Beard,[2] this paradigm accentuates material interests and conflict between classes over the allocation of resources.[3] Adapting Frederick Jackson Turner's "frontier thesis" to this framework, John D. Hicks provided what for a time was considered the definitive account of populism. Hicks argued that agrarian unrest marked the beginning of a protracted, apocalyptic struggle to rescue the United States from the excesses of an industrial capitalist order. In his view, populism was a harbinger of twentieth-century democratic liberalism, for it aimed to emancipate government from the plutocracy and to enlist the state in curbing the "selfish tendencies" of those who profited at the "expense of the poor and needy."[4]

Although Hicks's reliance on Turner's frontier thesis was subsequently repudiated, his conceptualization of populism as a salutary force remained influential. Scholars like C. Vann Woodward, Walter T.K. Nugent, and Gene Clanton continued, with certain qualifications, to emphasize the movement's progressive affinities.[5] As Clanton recently explained, by advocating state intervention to meliorate socioeconomic and political inequities, populism epitomized a democratic attempt to secure for individuals their transcendent and universal rights.[6]

The most complex formulation of the progressive thesis is found in the works of Norman Pollack. Initially, Pollack portrayed populism as a forward-looking, "radical" political uprising that could have transformed the United States "in a socialist direction."[7] In subsequent works, however, he modified this hypothesis, arguing that populism's "propertied consciousness" precluded judging the movement as a species of radicalism. Still, he contended that populism, by steering clear of both self-regulating market mechanisms and corporate liberalism, betrayed an intention to use a neutral, activist state to check monopoly power. What it sought was "a new synthesis of capitalism and democracy" that would retain both of these elements while "varying their proportions to ensure public sovereignty." Approaching "the border between radicalism and reform," the movement's real goal was the institution of "democratic capitalism."[8]

Liberal Exceptionalism

Markedly different interpretations were derived from the liberal exceptionalist paradigm. Formulated by Tocqueville and popularized by Louis Hartz,[9] liberal exceptionalism locates the analytic key for understanding American political development in the uncontested ascendancy of middle-class practices and ideology.[10] From this perspective, social movements that cannot be easily situated within the ideological complex of acquisitive individualism are frequently treated as irrational responses to imagined grievances or enemies. As H. Mark Roelofs explains, implicit in Hartz's argument was the claim that since liberalism had "no visible enemies" in America, "it was forced to invent invisible ones." The upshot of this is that past conflicts have at times been interpreted as "caused by a natural pugnacity inflamed by periodic bouts of hysteria, even hallucination."[11]

The most prominent exponent of the liberal exceptionalist view of populism was Richard Hofstadter. Using social psychological concepts to analyze the Populist response to modernity, he argued that this uprising was Janus-faced. Although Hofstadter acknowleged that populism was one of the first significant political movements to confront the challenges of industrial capitalism and insist that the "federal government has some responsibility for the common weal," he contended that it evinced malicious, even retrogressive, impulses. These were animated by an unfounded belief in an arcadian myth. Rooted in nostalgia for a "lost agrarian Eden," this myth invoked nature as a norm, and it stressed the convergence of interests between farmers and the petite bourgeoisie. Accompanying these conservative beliefs was the Populists' tendency to project responsibility for their economic failures on to others. This, in Hofstadter's view, accounted for populism's Manichaean cosmology and its corollary, a predisposition for conspiracy theories.[12]

Hofstadter's analysis provided the impetus for other revisionist interpretations.[13] One group of scholars, imputing to the movement such qualities as anti-Semitism, nativism, and primitivism, interpreted populism as a philosophical or historical antecedent of inchoate Fascist tendencies manifested in popular movements like Coughlinism or McCarthyism. Victor Ferkiss, for instance, argued that populism was rudimentary fascism;[14] in *The New American Right,* a volume of essays edited by Daniel Bell, scholars like Peter Viereck, Talcott Parsons, Seymour Martin Lipset, David Riesman, and Nathan Glazer followed Hofstadter's lead by interpreting the emergence of the "radical right" in the 1950s as a recrudescence of Populist ideology and temperament.[15]

The alternative interpretation that can be produced from this paradigm underscores populism's continuity with a dominant Lockean ethos. Emblematic of this view are the works of K. D. Bicha. After examining administrative and legislative behavior of Populists, he concluded that populism was animated by the "old, traditional and conservative values" of classical political economy. To Bicha, the movement was committed to realizing a market society of equal entrepreneurs unencumbered by centralized state controls.[16]

New Left Perspective

The third image of populism is derived from the New Left model of historical inquiry. Exponents of this approach reject the liberal exceptionalist synthesis, which they believe is inherently conservative. They also contend that the progressive paradigm's concentration on material interests and class conflict is too narrow. Finally, they argue that much of what passes as historical analysis is nothing more than a narration of events from an elitist vantage point. Focusing on the masses and peripheral social groups, their rendition of history emerges "from the bottom up" for the purpose of highlighting traditions critical of what they understand to be the constraints imposed on human relations by bourgeois liberalism.[17]

The most influential New Left interpretation of populism was developed by

Lawrence Goodwyn. He held that Farmers' Alliance members' participation in agricultural cooperatives provided shared experiences that transformed agrarian "political consciousness." As a result, Populists not only gained insight into the hierarchical structures that regimented American life but were also able to articulate a new conception of a social order and to conceive "new political institutions" that could give expression to that "new interpretation." This culminated in a "movement culture" that transcended economic reform. Emerging as a collective effort to transmogrify the "inherited caste structure" of "democratic hierarchy," populism was "a movement of ordinary Americans to gain control over their own lives and futures, a massive democratic effort to gain that most central component of human freedom—dignity." The movement thus envisaged was one of the last organized expressions of "what authentic political life is in a functioning democracy."[18]

Each of the interpretations presented possesses a degree of validity and captures something important about populism, but the problem, as Margaret Canovan concludes, is that "one can hardly recognize the same movement in different accounts."[19] Some have viewed Populists as humane, reform-minded farmers willing to enlist government aid for benign ends; others have stressed populism's support for an acquisitive individualist ethic. Critics have identified the movement as a regressive, intolerant social force; populism's defenders have suggested it was a noble, autonomous political movement that aimed to surmount the oppressive, hierarchical forms of American life. What understanding populism still requires is a synthesis capable of transcending anomalies in the existing scholarly literature. To offer an alternative interpretation that incorporates and explains what appears in Populist historiography as disparate, indeed seemingly incompatible, attitudes and behaviors, I enlist cultural theory.

APPLYING CULTURAL THEORY

In this chapter cultural theory is applied by examining the rhetoric and social interactions of individuals who formed the Farmers' Alliance network in Kansas and Nebraska during the latter decades of the nineteenth century. These beliefs and behaviors were ascertained through an analysis of primary materials and secondary interpretations. Although this sample limits the conclusions that may be advanced, these two states, since they were Alliance strongholds, provide important test cases for my analysis.

Alliance members were located on the group continuum by looking for indications of social incorporation. Did they, for example, betray a collective identity? Did they spend a substantial amount of their time associating with other group members? Did they act on behalf of the group? Did they rely on the collective to sustain them in different aspects of their lives? Were they subject to some form of group influence, control, or determination? Did they adhere to rules regulating admission to the group? Positive responses to the foregoing questions indicate strong group boundaries; negative answers suggest weak group commitment.

Strength of the grid variable was ascertained by assessing the scope of discretion left to Alliance members. This was done by asking questions that gauge the degree of insulation, autonomy, control, and competition in the movement.[20] For instance, were Alliance members located in an environment in which social classifications regulated and restricted interpersonal relationships and social options? Was the disposition of their time, property, and so forth heavily prescribed? Were they encumbered by authoritative controls or some form of supervision? Were they subject to highly routinized patterns of behavior? Was access to various roles contingent on ascriptive, noncompetitive criteria? Negative responses to these questions are indicative of weak grid; affirmative answers suggest that grid is strong.

My analysis suggests that Great Plains Alliance members were committed to a life of voluntary association. Also consistent with their predilection for a low-grid, strong-group social environment was a profound desire, espoused by many in the movement, to bring about greater equality of results.

The Group Dimension

There are several indicators of the strength and pervasiveness of populism's group boundedness. Primary among these are the formal and informal barriers alliances imposed to limit and regulate their memberships; the members' extensive involvement in the social activities of alliances; and the movement's use of cooperatives or Alliance-sanctioned businesses to constrain transactions of group members with outsiders.

Central to Populist economic analysis was the belief that wealth was created by labor, not capital. A derivative of Populists' acceptance of this labor theory of value was their understanding of society as bifurcated into righteous manufacturers of wealth, that is, the "common people who till the soil" and labor in the factories, and ignoble social parasites, or bankers, lawyers, railroad magnates and merchants and their "sycophantic apologists" who exploited the productive classes.[21] It was this ontological dualism that in turn determined criteria for membership in the Farmers' Alliance.

The myriad local alliances encompassed by state and national alliances were composed of the "toilers" of the earth.[22] The purposes of these organizations were communitarian, moralistic, and educative.[23] Alliances demarcated and maintained boundaries against outsiders by erecting barriers in the form of eligibility rules proscribing the membership of merchants, merchants' clerks, bankers, lawyers, and speculators as well as editors who were unaffiliated with reform presses or Alliance newspapers. Many alliances also required candidates for admission to take an oath affirming allegiance to Alliance principles.[24] Members were furthermore admonished to "know well" the "character and antecedents of every person applying for membership" in their "orders."[25] These farmers were cognizant that deviation from enunciated principles of exclusion would dilute group harmony and strength. "Nothing," declared one member, "will tend to disintegrate the Alliance so quickly and so thoroughly as the admission to membership of persons who are not eligible under the constitution."[26]

Populists believed that vigilance with regard to admission practices would not suffice to ensure collective strength. Consequently, they encouraged one another to "purge" their rolls of affiliates who set "pernicious examples" for Alliance members. Their newspapers included calls to "fire out" from their "ranks" insidious "tricksters and traitors" who provoked "dissension," discouraged attendance at meetings, or contravened the "fundamental objects" of Alliance orders. Members were also reminded that affiliates who denounced others in the movement or the "principles of the order" should be expelled. Once excommunicated, "traitors" were not to be physically harmed, for that would bring the Alliance into disrepute; instead, they were to be treated to a fate "worse than death," namely, they were to be shunned. As the *Farmers' Alliance* admonished its readers: "The man whose neighbors despise him—who meets averted eyes and no extended hands—is a living corpse. This punishment is due to a traitor."[27]

Alliances fortified their boundaries by sponsoring a wide range of activities that absorbed much of their members' lives. Local alliances, which usually included individuals who were neighbors and members of the same churches, convened frequent meetings, and members oftentimes gathered in each other's homes over dinner. Affiliates of alliances formed study groups and developed circulating libraries. They came together for picnics, torchlight parades, festivals, public lectures, summer encampments, weekend rallies, and basket lunches. Such gatherings afforded farmers opportunities to develop common bonds and purposes by sharing experiences of the difficulties they sought to surmount.[28] Through these gatherings they created an environment in which they collectively articulated, as Goodwyn has termed it, a "culture of ideas."[29]

At times, alliances even supplanted existing institutions. This was especially the case with rural churches. Many local alliances, for example, provided burial services for their members, supported members' orphans and widows, aided members who were infirm and indigent, and ministered to the spiritual needs of their people through prayer services and religious instruction. As Peter Argersinger has shown, by acting as surrogate religious communities, alliances reinforced group identity and cohesion. Local alliances performed an "integrative function" by creating, through the quasi-religious activities they sponsored, a community of interests out of otherwise dissociated individuals. Alliances also engaged in an "interpretative function" by disseminating information through newspapers, meetings, and grass-roots lecturing. Last, by inculcating agrarian values in their members, alliances "reestablished the integrity" of farmers' existence, thus reasserting through "ritual and symbol the essential morality of their world."[30]

Also indicative of Populists' social incorporation was the role assigned to cooperatives and Alliance-supported stores. Some local alliances instituted cooperatives that procured seeds and supplies and sold agricultural products, and a few of them even established "mutual insurance associations," loan agencies, and grain elevators. Oftentimes these were the only economic enterprises with which members would do business.[31] Farmers who circumvented boycotts of sellers not affiliated with alliances were stigmatized as "traitors."[32] And when boycotts were not arranged and cooperatives were not available, members entreated their "brothers" and "sisters" to curtail their transactions with those outside their circles, exhorting them to come together to establish their own "savings banks" and stores.[33]

The presence of these different indicators of social incorporation suggests the extent of Populists' concerns about group boundaries. Not only did they set themselves apart from the rest of society by imposing barriers to membership in their associations, but they also reinforced group boundedness by using alliances to sponsor social activities that increased the frequency of their interpersonal transactions. At the same time, as alliances came to perform a broad range of educative, religious, and economic functions, they displaced competing social institutions. As a result Alliance members came to depend more on their local organizations to sustain them in different aspects of their daily lives, and in doing so they enhanced the strength and pervasiveness of group constraints on their social relations.

The Grid Dimension

A recurring theme in Alliance writings was antipathy toward authority. "A man gets up in the pulpit, or sits on the bench," observed a writer quoted approvingly in an *Alliance* column, "and we allow ourselves to be bullied by ... [him], when, if he stood side by side with us ..., as a simple individual, his ideas would not have disturbed our clear thoughts an hour. Stand upon the pedestal of your own individual independence," the author continued, "summon these institutions about you, and judge them." As the publication of these hortatory comments reveals, Populists were receptive to challenges to what they conceived as hegemonic social structures. For them, an important constituting ideal of the American polity was that "men do not need any guardian. We need no safeguard. ... The best power this side of the ocean is the unfettered average common sense of the masses."[34] It was out of such a conviction that they had, as one member put it, "transferred ... [their] homage from hereditary kings and moneyed princes."[35]

Populists translated their enmity for authority into practice within their own alliances by keeping authoritative relations and role definition to a minimum. As Goodwyn observed, in their "self-generated" communities Populists transcended hierarchical relationships by "acting in democratic ways in their daily lives."[36] "We have no leaders," declared one group of Populists. "We formulate our demands in our own way. ... We never have and never will permit dictation inside, nor will we from outside the order."[37] Populist editor, writer, and senator, William A. Pfeffer, echoed that view, observing that in their "neighborhood assemblies ... out where the pure air of heaven sweeps over the fields," members of alliances "meet together upon a plane of perfect equality."[38]

Out of concern for their autonomy, Populists at their 1892 Omaha convention endorsed measures to prevent the stratification an emerging class of professional politicians threatened to reproduce in their organizations. So that the political amateur would not be supplanted by the more-sophisticated and wily party pol, they adopted an "ordinance for the purification of politics." Designed to keep power in the hands of "the people," this "fundamental law" prohibited persons "holding any office or position of profit, trust, or emolument under the federal or any state or municipal government" from sitting or voting in their conventions.[39]

To be sure, the Alliance system embodied some specialization of function and division of labor. Lecturers, for example, were appointed to bring information to local alliances. Yet even here the order muted the effects of social roles. Following Goodwyn's analysis, Gianna Pomota suggests that Populists' organizational practices allowed them to avoid institutionalizing distinctions between lecturers and the rank and file. The "social interaction" that characterized the "grassroots network" of their lecturing system, reasons Pomota, entailed a "sharing" of experiences. This, he conjectures, resulted in the transmission of "knowledge from the bottom up."[40]

The Alliance system further mitigated the impact of prescribed roles through its educational activities. Alliances used newspapers, local meetings, study groups, and common readings to ensure a broad distribution of information among members.[41] Thus when it came to the ability to understand and discuss salient political and economic issues, the distinction between lecturers and organizers and the rest of those in the movement was obscured. As Elizabeth Barr wrote,

> The upheaval that took place ... [was] a pentecost of politics in which a tongue of flame sat upon every man and each spake as the spirit gave him utterance. ... [Those] who lectured up and down the land were not the only people who could talk on the issues of the day. The farmers, the country merchants, the cattle-herders, they of long chin-whiskers, and they of broad-brimmed hats and heavy boots ... could preach the gospel of Populism. The dragon's teeth were sprouting in every nook and corner. ... Women with skins tanned to parchment by the hot winds, with bony hands of toil and clad, in faded calico, could talk in meeting and could talk right straight to the point.[42]

A final indication of the low-grid character of alliances can be discerned by measuring women's participation in the movement. Though not all members of alliances rejected social ascription based on gender, the Populist stance, when viewed against the backdrop of the social status accorded women at this juncture in U.S. history, can be considered quite progressive.[43] Women were usually allowed to join the movement on the "same equality with men." They attended local Alliance meetings prepared "to discuss, consult and deliberate on all subjects that are of common interest to mankind." Many also read papers at weekly gatherings, worked for political candidates sympathetic to the plight of farmers, attended and participated in state and national conventions, and addressed large rallies. Some, such as Mary Elizabeth Lease and Annie Diggs, gained national recognition for the quality of their perorations on the lecture circuit. For many, then, the "duties" of "sisters" did not "differ very materially" from those of the "brothers." Both men and women were instead "bound by the same obligation."[44] In a speech before the Woman's Council in Washington, D.C., Lease articulated the normative assumptions of populism regarding formally prescribed, gender-related modes of Alliance activity. "We are," she explained, "living in a day when old ideas tremble and are crumbling away. There is no difference between the intelligent woman and the intelligent man."[45]

Overall, within the constraints imposed on Alliance members' interactions with the outside world, Populists supported a life of voluntarism. Openly expressing their contempt for relations of authority, they avoided proliferating structuring principles within their own associations. At the same time, through their organizational dynamics and practices, they minimized the effects of the roles they introduced. Finally, by rejecting many social classifications adhered to by other organizations of this era, including several restrictions traditionally imposed on women, they avoided making access to roles contingent on ascriptive criteria.

The Egalitarian Bias of Populism

Recall that cultural theory postulates that those situated in a low-grid, strong-group social context dedicate themselves to eradicating social differences. Their goal is to bring about a greater equality of results. In populism, this ideal was reflected in the movement's political agenda, and it was advanced by Alliance members elected to state and national offices.

Populists contended that the egregious social inequalities of late-nineteenth-century America, a society of "tramps and millionaires," constituted a gross injustice.[46] These inequities, they contended, were "inimical" to American ideals and "repugnant to every fair-minded citizen."[47] As one Alliance member explained, "What one individual or class ... secures by virtue of superior capacity and opportunities above the general average of the comforts of life belongs of right to other individuals or class of individuals failing by lack of capacity and opportunity to secure an average."[48]

In response to existing class inequalities, Populists called for a system that "leveled up" the "great gulf" that divided "rich" from "poor,"[49] a world in which, as Lease put it, there would be "neither millionaires nor paupers."[50] Their ideal social order was one in which "each member" would be "equally nourished, equally exercised, and receive equal honor for equal exertion."[51] For them, this required scrupulous adherence to a redistributive ethic. "Some," declared one Populist writer, "are stronger than others; therefore their burdens should be heavier. Some are wiser than others; but their wisdom should be used for all. Service must not be bought and sold."[52]

Representative of Populists' commitment to equalizing results were reforms they advanced regarding the three issues that predominated their platforms: property, transportation and public utilities, and the monetary system.[53] Populists contended that all individuals were entitled to a "portion of the earth and its forces" so that they could "sustain life and gratify legitimate desires." To that end, they supported actions to bring about equal shares in the "provisions of nature" and the "means of production."[54] They also advocated public ownership of railroads, telegraphs, and telephones so that all would be served in the same way.[55] Finally, to equalize disparities between "money capital" and laborers, they demanded a return to the bimetallic standard; the issuance of paper notes as legal tender; and the institution of a subtreasury program that would require the government to provide low-interest loans to farmers who placed their nonperishable commodities in storage facilities constructed by the state. Though they were not avowed inflationists, Populists realized that extensive reform of the monetary system would afford debtors financial relief at the expense of the wealthier creditors and speculators.[56]

Populism's egalitarian sympathies also animated the movement's calls for reform of the political process. Of special importance were the 1892 Omaha Platform[57] demands calling for term limits for the president and vice president, popular election of senators, and the "legislative system" of initiative and referendum. All these resolutions, to use Giovanni Sartori's terms, were challenges to the governing relations of "superordination" and "subordination" that constitute the "vertical dimension" of politics.[58] As efforts to assert the popular will at the expense of institutions of indirect democracy, these proposals were explicit assaults on authority, power, privilege, and status.[59]

The egalitarian propensities of populism were also manifested in the behavior of officials elected under its label. In the Kansas state assembly, Populists initiated or endorsed bills that regulated business activities, protected laborers, equalized disparities in education, established public defenders' offices to provide defense for the indigent and insane, and protected women from "improper advances" by their employers. Analyses of voting patterns in the Kansas legislature also reveal that support for such reform legislation was widespread among Populist representatives.[60] Similarly, studies of the Fifty-second and Fifty-third Congresses that convened from December 1892 until March 1895 show that Populist representatives endorsed old-age-assistance policies, public works programs for the unemployed and impoverished, regulations to protect the rights of workers, public housing programs for the poor, and a host of other equalizing social and welfare policies, including public ownership of certain basic industries and utilities.[61]

To summarize, cultural theory posits that individuals who adopt low-grid–strong-group social relations commit themselves to the principle of equality. This egalitarian bias can be found in populism on several fronts. The movement's concern for greater equality of results, for instance, underlay its excoriation of America as a society that created only "tramps and millionaires." And it was an egalitarian predilection that animated the public policies advocated by Populists.

THE AMERICAN REGIME

A culture exists in a social context, not a vacuum. Adherents of each culture respond to and interact with others who espouse different ways of life. Their strategies and options are affected by the relative strengths of the alternative cultures with which they must compete.[62] Thus, to gain a better understanding of what it means to treat populism as an egalitarian culture, it is necessary to outline the mixture of cultures that defined late-nineteenth-century America.

The American social context during these years was primarily a combination of individualist and hierarchical cultures. And of the two, competitive individualism was dominant. This was, after all, the Gilded Age, the time of rugged individualism, social Darwinism, and Andrew Carnegie's gospel of wealth. Most historians concur that from the end of the Civil War until the turn of the century the laissez-faire ideal of classical political economy was "championed in America as it never was before and has never been since."[63] William Graham Sumner captured the prevailing sentiment when he argued that "the only help which is generally expedient is that which consists in helping a man to help himself." The legitimate "aim" of society, he explained, "should be to increase, multiply, and extend the chances. ... Such expansion is no guarantee of equality. On the contrary, if there be liberty, some will profit by the chances eagerly and some will neglect them altogether. Therefore, the greater the chances the more unequal will be the fortune of these two sets of men. So, it ought to be, in all justice and right reason."[64]

Though dominant, individualism did not by itself constitute the established order. It accommodated authoritative controls required to provide rationality and stability. Thus hierarchy appeared as an attendant of late-nineteenth-century capitalism in the form of large-scale aggregations of administrative power, that is, corporations.[65] This centralization, formalization, and differentiation of businesses in turn impacted beliefs, perceptions, and behaviors, setting in motion a process that Alan Trachtenberg has characterized as the "incorporation of America."[66]

In the public sector, hierarchy was constituted by a modest expansion in state power. This was brought about as both state and national governments set out to promote certain economic interests. But apart from an emergent "bureaucratic clientelism," there was a delimited role for hierarchical principles.[67] Changes in national institutions of government designed to meet the exigencies of industrial capitalism prior to the turn of the century were, as Stephen Skowronek noted, re-

ally more like exercises in "patchwork" than "reconstitution."[68] The prevalent
attitude dictated the subordination of the federal government to state governments, with both levels of government circumscribed by the laissez-faire ideal.[69]

Recognizing that populism was situated in a context in which the principal
threat to its preferred form of social relations was a way of life committed to self-
regulation clarifies the fundamental cultural challenge the movement confronted.
Populism's task, in effect, was to build up support for its preferred form of social
relations at the expense of the ideals and social relations of competitive individualism. At the same time, having individualism as its primary cultural competitor
limited the policy options that could be entertained by the movement. For populism, the only culturally rational course of action was to find a way to join forces
with hierarchy.

POPULISM CONFRONTS THE ESTABLISHMENT

Any interpretation of populism must be able to account for its Manichaean tendencies and the conspiratorial theories of politics, which even many critics of
Hofstadter's position have ascribed to the movement.[70] In the past, scholars working within the progressive and New Left paradigms addressed Populists' conspiratorial bent of mind by explaining it away. Progressive interpretations have generally viewed populism's scathing indictment of the system as an objective response
to farmers' problems. As Nugent concluded, "Populists have been accused of
'conspiracy mindedness'; for them, however, tangible fact quite eclipsed neurotic
fiction."[71] Similarly, New Left scholars like Goodwyn implied that populism's affinity for conspiracy theories was a product of what Alliance members discovered
about economic elites and the workings of corporate power in the day-to-day experiences in their cooperatives.[72]

The way these scholars addressed populism's Manichaean tendencies and conspiracy-mindedness, however, is not without its difficulties. Critics of this line of
reasoning, for instance, have noted that the "villainies" Populists alluded to in
their "sensational revelations of conspiracies which threatened the safety of the
republic" were in fact more often the product of inference than "research or investigation."[73] At times, even scholars associated with the progressive view admitted that Populists "were a provincial lot," that they "oversimplified" their
problems, and that "many of them were fascinated with the notion of conspiracy
and advanced conspiratorial theories of history, and some of them were given to
apocalyptic premonitions of direful portent."[74] Nugent himself conceded that
Populists were not the most "worldly-wise" when it came to understanding the
"hallmarks of urban industrial life in the nineteenth century." The movement, he
concluded, was "shot through with naivete and oversimplification."[75]

In contrast, some scholars working within the liberal exceptionalist paradigm
have explained populism's Manichaean cosmology and its predilection for conspiracy theories by stressing what they considered the movement's irrational side.

To them, adherence to this worldview was a psychological defense mechanism that enabled Populists to cope with their declining social status.[76] Though suggestive, this hypothesis is problematic. First, it assumes an untenable view regarding Populists' position in society. As Vann Woodward explained, years before the Populist uprising emerged, most of these farmers had already been eclipsed by others on the American social hierarchy.[77] Second, it begs the question that if Populists were so concerned about status, why were they so willing to accommodate groups who stood outside the mainstream of society? Indeed, most evidence collected on populism since the 1960s suggests that Alliance members were much more sensitive to the needs of diverse racial, ethnic, and religious groups than were others in society.[78]

A synthesis derived from cultural theory provides an alternative account of populism's Manichaean tendencies. As Douglas hypothesizes, Manichaean beliefs are cosmological correlates of egalitarian environments. Because the absence of internal structuring principles increases the likelihood of internecine conflict and schisms, affiliates of this mode of organizing sustain cohesion and shore up their group boundaries by portraying themselves as representatives of righteousness engaged in an apocalyptic struggle with the outside forces of evil. This is functional for their pattern of social relations,[79] for it increases the cost of group members' "exit option."[80] It is, egalitarians remind one another, "wicked to leave the good and join the bad."[81]

As seen from the perspective of cultural theory, Populists' objectives were twofold: first, to diminish the attractiveness of competing ways of organizing; and second, to accentuate the desirability of low-grid–strong-group social relations. They accomplished this by pointing to the innumerable evils perpetrated by the established cultures while they simultaneously emphasized the inherent goodness and superiority of their own way of life. As they envisaged it, they were the standardbearers of the "cause of justice," locked in a premillennial "struggle with all evil."[82]

Populists attacked the alternative ways of life while they stabilized their own social organization by mounting an assault on the predominant structuring principle of, to use their epithet, "competing individualism." For them, this social design of "active irreconcilable war on every side and in all things," which required workers to sacrifice "virtue for bread," had debauched an otherwise scrupulous citizenry. The myriad "evils" pervading society could not simply be ascribed to the frailties of human nature. They were instead consequences of a "false and vicious system."[83] Pitting individual against individual, "competing individualism" dissociated and degraded people. According to the Populist jeremiad, "We endeavor to fence off a little fold for the family, but make, after all, only wolf dens, the places where the selfish retire to enjoy the prey and live." Thus it was this "grabbing, grinding, and groveling in mammon worship" that was responsible for the erosion of "brotherly love," the decline of "patriotism," and the alienation of the "producer of wealth."[84] In short, "competing individualism" had transformed citizens into fatalists. "The materialism of to-day," Populists lamented, "does all the time segregate human lives. Take a man for instance who labors hard from fourteen to sixteen hours a day to obtain the bare necessities of life. ... He is brutalized both morally and physically. He has no ideas, only propensities. He has no beliefs, only instincts. He does not, often cannot, read. His contact with other people is only the relation of servant to master, of a machine to its director. ... This man's name is million. He is all about us."[85]

To Populists, the primary problem with "competing individualism" was that it proliferated flagrant inequalities. "The plutocracy of to day," they charged, "is the logical result of the individual freedom which we have always considered the pride of our system."[86] They furthermore contended that this evolution into plutocracy had untoward consequences, for it made it possible for the winners in this "selfish, struggling individualism" to forge a symbiotic relationship with the state.

Collusion between hierarchy and individualism, Populists maintained, created a "system of paternalism" not unlike the invidious "paternalism" of "rank" typified by feudalistic orders. As a result of insidious influence gained through wealth, the "plutocracy" corrupted political institutions, thus perverting the exercise of public power to buttress its position of privilege.[87] "The tyrants of modern civilization," explained a writer in the *Advocate*, "do not bind their subjects with bonds of blood and iron as did the conquerors of the past—their weapon is corruption forged by duplicity, and riveted by ignorance."[88]

In the Populist worldview, legislation was attributed to the machinations of railroad and oil magnates, corporate leaders and "unscrupulous pirates of Wall Street." This "overbearing, despotic, insulting monied aristocracy" used its wealth to select public officials and enact discriminatory "class laws." The result was "one law for the rich" and "another for the poor," with "Mr. Laws" having as his purpose the sanctioning of usury, extortion, and the monopolization of the gifts of "Providence" so that the wealthy might keep the "masses in subordination to the classes."[89] To Populists, this meant that government, and by implication, hierarchical authority, had ceded claims to legitimacy.

The emergent entrepreneurial class, Populists also charged, corrupted and manipulated other prominent institutions to disseminate an ideology that legitimated the existing order. It was this contention, for instance, that animated the Populist response to organized religion. "Defiled and flattered" by the "wealthy," religious leaders extolled the virtues of "obedience," "submissiveness," and "poverty" to keep the "mass of people" subservient to "high officials and money shoddied aristocracy."[90] In this indictment Populists not only explicitly attacked individualism by pointing to its corrupting influence but also undermined hierarchy by exposing the values on which it depends—obedience, sacrifice, and so forth—as nothing more than principles tainted by self-interest and invoked for the purpose of social control.

Alliance members reinforced their group boundaries by juxtaposing the inherent goodness and justness of their cause with the evil endemic to their cultural rivals. They envisaged themselves as "missionaries" engaged in battle with the "worshippers of the golden calf," representatives of the "voice of God preparing the people for the coming of Christ's kingdom."[91] Their task, as they understood it, was to discover a way to "kindle" that "divine spark which is torpid" in the worker's "soul." As is generally the case with egalitarians, Populists anticipated that human beings could be transformed and saved by replacing corrupt, coercive structural forms with social institutions based on cooperative principles. Once enacted, their programs would "inaugurate a reign of justice, thus leading to an equality of power if not condition." "Cruelty and oppression" would be eradicated. "Misery and want would disappear, and human brotherhood would be established on the earth."[92] The result would be "a return to the Christian impulses of our fathers, a repudiation of the alliance with Satan, an end to the daily confession at the shrine of the Golden Calf, and the restoration of, and a new lease of life for the American Republic."[93]

By portraying themselves as saintly missionaries engaged in an apocalyptic battle with diabolical outsiders, Populists were behaving in a culturally rational way. This dichotomization of the world and the conspiracy theories of politics that it engendered functioned to minimize defections from their life of voluntary collectivism. That is, adherence to a Manichaean outlook promoted the viability of their strong-group–low-grid social relations. By making it possible to confront and explain Populism's dualistic worldview, cultural theory is therefore able to provide an account that goes beyond existing interpretations. Moreover, it does so in a way that takes New Left interpretations of Populists one step further. By emphasizing the linkages between beliefs and preferences and patterns of social relations, cultural theory shows that populism's Manichaean cosmology can be derived from the antihierarchical, strong-group social forms that New Left analyses attributed to the movement.

POPULISM AND THE STATE

Much of the controversy surrounding who the Populists were and what they really wanted centers on the movement's conceptualization of state power. From a liberal exceptionalist perspective, Populists were self-interested, antistatist individuals who identified more with the "entrepreneurial radicalism" of their Jacksonian predecessors than they did with the philosophical assumptions of twentieth-century democratic liberalism.[94] Those working within the progressive paradigm underscore populism's support for an activist state that could correct the excesses of industrial capitalism. Finally, New Left scholars stress that populism's quintessential contribution to American political development was the effort it made to institute democratic forms. The essence of populism, as Goodwyn explained, was not the Omaha Platform but rather "its cultural assertion as a people's movement of mass democratic aspiration."[95]

Cultural theory emphasizes that those who prefer egalitarian relations oppose authority. Yet many measures favored by egalitarians are predicated on an interventionist government. The result is that egalitarians often have a highly ambivalent view of state power—at once critical and demanding. This paradoxical view of state power is evident in Populist political thought.

Populists believed that a competitive individualist culture had co-opted the state for the sake of providing a legal foundation for its position of preeminence. Still, according to their view, government was not the principal villain, for it had only abetted, not created, monopoly power and resulting social inequalities. Populists recognized, as Jacksonians had not, that since private monopolies were not direct creatures of the state, there was no guarantee that removing governmental support for hegemonic monopolism would bring about its demise.[96] "We have violated the social law [that each shall find his happiness only in the happiness of all] so long," one Alliance member reminded others, "that our whole social system has become diseased and we cannot reform so as to recover social health."[97]

To restore the body politic to health, many Populists thus turned to the state, which they believed could serve as a "leveling distributive mechanism."[98] In their hands, government was to be a policy "instrument, not of the rich, but of the people; its object not the perpetuation of monopoly, but the happiness of society." The state's ultimate goal was to ensure that "the products of labor must be for all; services must be rendered for all; the fruits of genius must be shared by all."[99] Populists believed that government could be used to secure for each citizen his "equal share" of providential benefits and "defend that citizen in the use of it" by taking "away the power of men to keep what they do not need and do not use themselves from people who do need and wish to use what heaven designed should be used."[100] To some, this meant using government to impose a graduated tax, "the most just and equitable method of taxation that could be devised," on those who amassed prodigious amounts of wealth. For others, this entailed using government's powers to expropriate and redistribute land held by those who had more than their fair share; to set ceilings on the amount of land that could be owned by any one person; and to regulate access to natural resources.[101] Then, too, Populists contended that government should "by enactments procure and secure to the workers ... [their] equal, rightful share of the labor-saving, wealth-making power of steam electricity and machinery" and thus diminish differences between laborers and capitalists.[102] A vocal minority even argued that the "best features" of the government were those that were "purely socialistic" and advocated extending these incipient socialist practices. In their eyes, governmental agencies that had conducted themselves most admirably in the past were quasi-socialist institutions like the post office and public school system, for they had performed a leveling function by ensuring that everyone received the same services and benefits.[103]

Although Populists were willing to use government as an egalitarian policy instrument, they were cognizant that collaboration with hierarchical institutions had to be based on ideals that buttressed their preferred form of social relations. "The problem of to-day," declared Lorenzo Lewelling, the Populist governor of Kansas, "is how to make the State subservient to the individual, rather than to become his master. Government is a voluntary union for the common good." With the problem so formulated, the aim of populism was to usher in a "new era in which the people shall reign, and if found necessary they will 'expand the powers of government to solve the enigmas of the times.'"[104] As Lewelling implied, state intervention was not something Populists regarded without apprehension. It had to be "found necessary," and it had to be restricted to solving the "enigma of the times." While supporting measures that expanded federal regulation and increased assistance for the "producers of wealth" and the indigent, Populist legislators attacked the proliferation of bureaucratic structures and procedures and challenged growth in governmental expenditures.[105] To Populists, government was, to use Norman Pollack's words, "a mere instrument, a structural convenience to ensure equitableness."[106] State intervention was justifiable only to the extent that it advanced egalitarian objectives. Frank Doster, a noted Populist and chief justice of the Kansas Supreme Court, explained. "All government and all necessity for government," he averred, "grows out of the fact of inequalities and that government which does not provide for the leveling and equalizing of the conditions which grow out of the unrestricted exercise of the natural powers of its citizens has failed in the purpose of its creation."[107]

In sum, Populists were not unambiguous supporters of expanded governmental authority. Unless it promoted equality, an activist state was suspect. This formulation enables us to see the deficiencies of existing interpretations of populism as well as to build upon the strengths of each approach.

Liberal exceptionalist syntheses have correctly identified populism's concerns about state power and what Christopher Lasch has labeled as its "anti-bureaucratic" ethos,[108] but they have been hard-pressed to account for Populist proposals for reform that entailed increased state intervention. Unlike their Jacksonian forebears, Populists were not uniformly hostile to the use of state authority and the expansion of governmental powers. Most Populists had abandoned their faith in the workings and beneficence of an unregulated market. To them, state intervention was necessary to bring about an equality of conditions that a laissez-faire economy could no longer provide. At the same time, a cultural interpretation recognizes that Populists were not unabashed supporters of state power. They advocated increased governmental controls and involvement but did so *only* under the condition that an expansion in authority served egalitarian ends.

Progressive accounts have accentuated populism's demands for increased governmental action to help the disadvantaged and have cast Populists in the role of state builders but have been hard-pressed to account for the movement's fear of public authority and administrative power. Cultural theory, however, provides an explanation for populism's ambivalence regarding an activist state. Cultural theory accounts both for the Populists' willingness to align themselves with the state and for their concerns about expanding state power. At the same time, cultural theory also refines progressive accounts by directing attention to the fact that the Populist insurgency represented more fundamental change than is commonly assumed by scholars working within the progressive framework. A cultural perspective suggests that the Alliance movement demanded more than a correction of economic and political abuses by showing that it represented a commitment to defend and advance a specific form of social relations

Finally, although a cultural analysis confirms the New Left view that Populists desired to create nonhierarchical, democratic institutions, it modifies that view by directing attention back to the movement's conceptualization of government. The problem with the New Left version of populism is that it focuses on the movement's democratizing processes at the expense of considering the importance of the role Populists assigned to the state. As Goodwyn argues, a principal Populist insight that would be useful for today's activists is not to "worry whether [your political] agenda has immediate prospects for instant acceptance: just be sure it is real—that is, that it reflects what people really want."[109] Such a view, however, is problematic because it not only ignores the Populist calls for programmatic reforms but also misses the linkage between the Populist program and the social relations the movement was attempting to sustain. In contrast, a cultural perspective stresses that Populists recognized that active governmental intervention could neither be divorced from nor subordinated to their social practices. For them, the state had a specific role to play in helping them realize their way of life. As one Populist put it, government was to be an "agency through which the associated people of the nation would carry on universal co-operation. It would not be paternalism; that would be dead; but fraternalism—an association of brothers for the common good."[110] A cultural analysis thus treats the Populists' reform agenda and their support for state activism as central to the Populists' strategy of bringing about the equality of conditions required for the realization of their nonhierarchical and democratic communal relations.

CULTURAL THEORY AND POPULISM

Though the interpretation advanced in this work is limited to the cases examined, the evidence suggests that populism can be usefully conceptualized as a distinctive cultural type within a social context characterized by the interaction of competing cultures. Using indicators of the social dimensions of grid and group to classify Populists in Kansas and Nebraska suggests that it is possible to locate this agrarian uprising in the egalitarian quadrant of the grid-group typology. The preceding discussion has also shown that many of those associated with this insurgency supported actions and policies designed to bring about a greater equality in results, as is expected for individuals who espouse strong-group–low-grid social relations.

Cultural theory makes it possible to provide an account that transcends existing explanations by incorporating and explaining the disparate traits ascribed to populism by studies conducted from within the progressive, liberal exceptionalist, and New Left interpretive frameworks. First, after showing that existing approaches have so far been unable to provide a compelling explanation of populism's Manichaean cosmology and conspiracy-mindedness, cultural theory was enlisted to offer an alternative thesis regarding these phenomena. From the perspective of cultural theory, populism's bipolar worldview and its affinity for conspiracy theories can be understood as culturally rational responses designed to maintain egalitarian social relations.

Conceiving of populism as an egalitarian movement also sharpens our insight into Populist thinking and behavior regarding an interventionist government. A comparison of the egalitarian thesis with contending interpretations revealed that cultural theory shows that Populist thinking regarding state power was far more complex and ambiguous than has been assumed. On the one hand, like liberal exceptionalist and New Left views, cultural theory underscores populism's distrust of state institutions and hierarchical controls. Indeed, cultural theory views such beliefs as concomitants of the movement's egalitarian social relations. Yet it does so in a way that provides an explanation of what progressive accounts have correctly discerned as Populist support of an interventionist state. What cultural theory shows is that for populism an activist government was legitimate only insofar as it produced a greater equality of results, an equality that "competing individualism" was seen as being unable to provide. Thus, by specifying the precise conditions on which Populist support for an interventionist state was contingent, cultural theory corrects the excesses of those who accentuated one side of the movement's attitudes toward the state at the expense of others.

NOTES

I am especially indebted to Aaron Wildavsky and Richard Ellis for comments and suggestions on earlier drafts of this chapter.

1. James Turner, "Understanding the Populists," *The Journal of American History* 67(September 1980), 354.

2. See Richard Hofstadter, *The Progressive Historians: Turner, Beard, Parrington* (New York: Knopf, 1968).

3. Samuel P. Huntington, *American Politics: The Promise of Disharmony* (Cambridge, Mass.: Harvard University Press, 1981), 6.

4. John Hicks, *The Populist Revolt* (Minneapolis: University of Minnesota Press, 1931), 2, 54–95, 237, 405–406, 422–423.

5. C. Vann Woodward, *The Burden of Southern History* (New York: Vintage Books, 1960), chap. 7. Walter T.K. Nugent, *The Tolerant Populists: Kansas, Populism, and Nativ-

ism (Chicago: University of Chicago Press, 1963). Gene Clanton, "Populism, Progressivism and Equality," *Agricultural History* 51(July 1977), 559–581; Clanton, "'Hayseed Socialism' on the Hill: Congressional Populism, 1891–1895," *Western Historical Quarterly* 15(April 1984), 139–162; and Clanton, *Kansas Populism: Ideas and Men* (Lawrence: University of Kansas Press, 1969).

6. Gene Clanton, *Populism: The Humane Preference in America, 1890–1900* (Boston: Twayne, 1991),

7. Norman Pollack, *The Populist Response to Industrial America* (New York: W. W. Norton, 1962), 4, 6–7, 9, 11–12.

8. Norman Pollack, *The Just Polity: Populism, Law, and Human Welfare* (Urbana: University of Illinois Press, 1987), 1–16, 18, 35–36, 343–345. See also Pollack, *The Humane Economy: Populism, Capitalism, and Democracy* (New Brunswick, N.J.: Rutgers University Press, 1990).

9. Alexis de Tocqueville, *Democracy in America,* 2 vols. (New York: Vintage Books, 1945), vol. 1, chap. 2. Louis Hartz, *The Liberal Tradition in America* (New York: Harcourt, Brace & World, 1955).

10. Huntington, *American Politics,* 6.

11. H. Mark Roelofs, *The Poverty of American Politics: A Theoretical Interpretation* (Philadelphia: Temple University Press, 1992), 29–33.

12. Richard Hofstadter, *The Age of Reform: From Bryan to F.D.R.* (New York: Vintage Books, 1955), 61–62, 70–71, 73, 77–80.

13. For an overview and criticism of revisionism and the responses to it, see Michael Paul Rogin, *The Intellectuals and McCarthy: The Radical Specter* (Cambridge, Mass: MIT Press, 1967), chap. 6; Vann Woodward, *Burden of Southern History,* chap. 7; and Nugent, *Tolerant Populists,* chap. 2.

14. Victor Ferkiss, "Populist Influences on American Fascism," in Theodore Saloutos, ed., *Populism: Reaction or Reform?* (New York: Holt, Rinehart and Winston, 1966), 69–77.

15. Peter Viereck, "The Revolt Against the Elite," in Daniel Bell, ed., *The Radical Right* (Garden City, N.Y.: Doubleday, 1963), 136–137. In that same volume see Talcott Parsons, "Social Strain in America," 189; David Riesman and Nathan Glazer, "The Intellectuals and the Discontented Classes," 87–113; and Seymour Martin Lipset, "The Sources of the 'Radical Right,'" 259–312.

16. K. D. Bicha, "The Conservative Populists: A Hypothesis," *Agricultural History* 47(January 1973), 10, 11, 14–15, 17; and *Western Populism: Studies in Ambivalent Conservatism* (Lawrence, Kans.: Coronado Press, 1976), chaps. 1, 6–7.

17. Gerald N. Grob and George Athen Billigs, *Interpretations of American History,* 5th ed. vol. 2 (New York: Free Press, 1987), 18–19; and Worth Robert Miller, *Oklahoma Populism: A History of the People's Party in the Oklahoma Territory* (Norman: University of Oklahoma Press, 1987), 261.

18. Lawrence Goodwyn, *Democratic Promise: The Populist Revolt in America* (New York: Oxford University Press, 1976), xviii, 88, 208, 195–196, 540–543.

19. Margaret Canovan, *Populism* (New York: Harcourt, Brace, and Jovanovich, 1981), 11.

20. Mary Douglas, "Cultural Bias," in *In the Active Voice* (London: Routledge & Kegan Paul, 1982), 202. James Hampton, "Giving the Grid/Group Dimensions an

Operational Definition," in Mary Douglas, ed., *Essays in the Sociology of Perception* (London: Routledge & Kegan Paul, 1982), 66–67.

21. *Farmers' Alliance* (Lincoln, Neb.), February 8, 1890; *Advocate* (Topeka, Kans.), February 18, 1891; December 28, 1892; January 6, 1892; *Farmers' Alliance,* February 20, 1891; *Alliance-Independent* (Lincoln, Neb.), January 4, 1894; *Farmers' Advocate* (Topeka, Kans.), June 19, 1891; and *Platte County Argus* September 3, 1896, reprinted in Norman Pollack, ed., *The Populist Mind* (Indianapolis, Ind.: Bobbs-Merrill, 1967), 42. See also Canovan, *Populism,* 51–53.

22. See Stanley B. Parsons, *Populist Context: Rural Versus Urban Power on a Great Plains Frontier* (Westport, Conn.: Greenwood Press, 1973), chap. 5; and Scott G. McNall, *The Road to Rebellion: Class Formation and Kansas Populism, 1865–1900* (Chicago: University of Chicago Press, 1988), chap. 6.

23. See McNall, *Road to Rebellion,* 186.

24. See Ibid., 197; and Nugent, *Tolerant Populists,* 60.

25. *Farmers' Advocate,* August 14, 1891.

26. *Farmers' Alliance* August 9, 1890. *Advocate,* November 23, 1892.

27. *Farmers' Alliance,* December 20, 1890; February 21, 1891. *Farmers' Advocate,* August 14, 1891. *Advocate,* May 13, 1891; and November 23, 1892.

28. McNall, *Road to Rebellion,* 188, 192, 193, 195, 234. Clanton, *Populism,* 166–167.

29. Goodwyn, *Democratic Promise,* 185, 311.

30. Peter H. Argersinger, "Pentecostal Politics in Kansas: Religion, the Farmers' Alliance and the Gospel of Populism," *Kansas Quarterly* 1(Fall 1969), 24–59.

31. Parsons, *Populist Context,* 68–73.

32. *Advocate,* November 26, 1890.

33. *Farmers' Advocate,* February 20, 1891. *Farmers' Alliance,* September 3, 1891; May 4, 1893.

34. *The Alliance* (Lincoln, Neb.), July 17, 1889.

35. *Alliance-Independent,* January 4, 1894; November 3, 1892.

36. Lawrence Goodwyn, *The Populist Moment: A Short History of the Agrarian Revolt in America* (New York: Oxford University Press, 1978).

37. *Advocate,* February 8, 1893.

38. Argersinger, "Pentecostal Politics," 28.

39. *Advocate,* March 28, 1894.

40. Gianna Pomota, "A Common Heritage: The Historical Memory of Populism in Europe and the United States," in Harry Boyte and Frank Riessman, eds., *The New Populism: The Politics of Empowerment* (Philadelphia: Temple University Press, 1986), 42–43. Also see Lawrence Goodwyn, "Populism and Powerlessness," in *New Populism,* 26, 28; and Goodwyn, *Democratic Promise,* 74, 126, 542, 543.

41. See Hicks, *Populist Revolt,* 130; and McNall, *Road to Rebellion,* 207–208.

42. Hicks, *Populist Revolt,* 159.

43. See Marilyn Dell Brady, "Populism and Feminism in a Newspaper by and for Women of the Kansas Farmers' Alliance," *Kansas History* 7(Winter 1984-1985), 280–290.

44. *Advocate,* July 22, 1891; November 26, 1890; March 29, 1893.

45. *Farmers' Advocate,* March 13, 1891.

46. *Alliance,* June 12, 1889. Also see *Farmers' Alliance,* February 8, 1890; April 26, 1890; November 19, 1891. *Alliance-Independent,* November 10, 1892; June 15, 1893.

Wealth Makers (Lincoln, Neb.), April 5, 1894. *Advocate,* July 22, 1891; January 13, 1892; July 6, 1892; June 14, 1894.

47. *Advocate,* January 20, 1892.

48. Ibid., July 22, 1891.

49. Ibid., January 20, 1892.

50. *Alliance-Independent,* July 14, 1892.

51. *Advocate,* January 20, 1892. Also see *Alliance-Independent,* October 15, 1891; November 16, 1893; and *Wealth Makers,* June 14, 1894.

52. *Wealth Makers,* July 19, 1894.

53. As one Populist letter writer explained, the movement's platforms indicated that one of its principal objectives was to "establish the economic equality of man" (*Advocate,* January 6, 1892).

54. *Advocate,* January 20, 1892. *Alliance-Independent,* October 15, 1891; November 16, 1893. *Wealth Makers,* June 14, 1894.

55. *Advocate,* August 15, 1894, in Pollack, ed., *Populist Mind,* 58. *Advocate,* July 6, 1892; September 19, 1894. *Alliance-Independent,* March 2, 1893.

56. See Clanton, *Populism,* chap. 5; Nugent, *Tolerant Populists,* 102–109; and *Alliance-Independent,* March 1, 1894.

57. See *Advocate,* July 6, 1892.

58. Giovanni Sartori, *The Theory of Democracy Revisited,* 2 vols. (Chatham, N.J.: Chatham House, 1987), vol. 1, 131.

59. *Advocate,* August 15, 1894, in Pollack, *Populist Mind,* 58.

60. See Argersinger, "Ideology and Behavior"; and Clanton, *Populism,* chap. 5.

61. Clanton, *Populism,* 125–137.

62. See, for example, Richard Ellis and Aaron Wildavsky, *Dilemmas of Presidential Leadership: From Washington Through Lincoln* (New Brunswick, N.J.: Transaction, 1989).

63. Sidney Fine, *Laissez Faire and the General Welfare State: A Study of Conflict in American Thought, 1865–1901* (Ann Arbor: University of Michigan Press, 1964), 29.

64. William Graham Sumner, "Sociology," in Perry Miller, ed., *American Thought: Civil War to World War I* (New York: Holt, Rinehart and Winston, 1968), 72–92. Sumner, *What Social Classes Owe to Each Other* (Caldwell, Ida.: Caxton Printers, 1986), 141–145.

65. See Peter George, *The Emergence of Industrial America: Strategic Factors in American Economic Growth Since 1870* (Albany: State University of New York Press, 1982), chap. 5; and Alfred D. Chandler, "The Rise of Big Business: 'The Coming of Big Business,'" in Alfred D. Chandler, Stuart Bruchey, and Louis Galambos, eds., *The Changing Economic Order: Readings in American Business and Economic History* (New York: Harcourt, Brace and World, 1968), 268–279.

66. Alan Trachtenberg, *The Incorporation of America: Culture and Society in the Gilded Age* (New York: Hill and Wang, 1982).

67. James Q. Wilson, "The Rise of the Bureaucratic State," in Francis E. Rourke, ed., *Bureaucratic Power in National Policy Making* (Boston: Little, Brown, 1986), 125–148.

68. Stephen Skowronek, *Building a New American State: The Expansion of National Administrative Capacities, 1877–1920* (New York: Cambridge University Press, 1982), 16.

69. See Leonard White, *The Republican Era, 1869–1901* (New York: Macmillan, 1958).

70. See Rogin, *Intellectuals and McCarthy,* chap. 6; and Christopher Lasch, *Agony of the American Left* (New York: Alfred A. Knopf, 1969), chap. 1.

71. Nugent, *Tolerant Populists,* 231.

72. On this point see Canovan, *Populism,* 50.

73. Oscar Handlin, "Reconsidering the Populists," *Agricultural History* 39(April 1965), 72.

74. Vann Woodward, *Burden of Southern History,* 159.

75. Nugent, *Tolerant Populists,* 104, 105.

76. For a discussion of the "status-anxiety" hypothesis, see Hofstadter, *Age of Reform.* Although Hofstadter himself was not always clear as to whether this hypothesis actually applied to Populists, those who have followed his lead have used concern for status to explain Populists' attraction to conspiratorial theories of history. On this point, see Robert M. Collins, "The Originality Trap: Richard Hofstadter on Populism," *Journal of American History* 76(June 1989), 150–167.

77. Vann Woodward, *Burden of Southern History,* 153.

78. Ibid.; also see Nugent, *Tolerant Populists.*

79. See Mary Douglas, *Natural Symbols* (New York: Pantheon, 1992), 107–124.

80. Albert O. Hirschman, *Exit, Voice, and Loyalty* (Cambridge, Mass.: Harvard University Press, 1970).

81. Mary Douglas, *Risk and Blame: Essays in Cultural Theory* (London: Routledge, 1992), 140.

82. *Alliance-Independent,* January 4, 1894. Also see *Alliance-Independent,* August 11, 1892, in Pollack, *Populist Mind,* 40; and *Farmers' Alliance,* November 19, 1891.

83. *Advocate,* January 6, 1892; April 11, 1894. *Farmers' Alliance,* December 6, 1890. *Farmers' Alliance,* May 7, 1891, in Pollack, *Populist Mind,* 3, 4.

84. *Wealth Makers,* July 19, 1894; June 7, 1894. *Farmers' Alliance,* May 7, 1891, in Pollack, *Populist Mind,* 4. *Alliance-Independent,* February 15, 1894; December 28, 1893.

85. *Farmers' Alliance,* May 7, 1891, in Pollack, *Populist Mind,* 3–4.

86. *Farmers' Alliance,* February 28, 1891. *Alliance-Independent,* December 28, 1893.

87. *Platte County Argus,* February 28, 1891, in Pollack, *Populist Mind,* 447.

88. *Advocate,* July 29, 1891.

89. *Alliance-Independent,* December 15, 1892; February 15, 1894. *Alliance,* October 19, 1889. *Farmers' Alliance,* September 3, 1891; October 15, 1891. *Wealth Makers,* May 31, 1894. *Advocate,* November 4, 1891; August 23, 1893. *Platte County Argus,* September 3, 1896, in Pollack, *Populist Mind,* 41–44.

90. *Advocate,* January 20, 1892; March 30, 1892.

91. Argersinger, "Pentecostal Politics," 31. *Advocate,* July 20, 1892.

92. *Advocate,* February 28, 1894; April 11, 1894. For the egalitarian conception of human nature, see Michael Thompson, Richard Ellis, and Aaron Wildavsky, *Cultural Theory* (Boulder: Westview Press, 1990), 33–36.

93. Argersinger, "Pentecostal Politics," 31.

94. See especially Hofstadter, *Age of Reform;* and Bicha, "Conservative Populists."

95. Goodwyn, *Populist Moment,* 294; and Goodwyn, "Populism and Powerlessness," 26.

96. Russell L. Hanson, *The Democratic Imagination in America: Conversations with Our Past* (Princeton: Princeton University Press, 1985), 198–199.

97. *Advocate,* September 19, 1894. *Farmers' Alliance,* March 21, 1891. *Wealth Makers,* October 4, 1894.

98. Douglas, "Cultural Bias," 225. Mary Douglas and Baron Isherwood, *World of Goods: Towards an Anthropology of Consumption* (London: Allen Lane, 1979), 37.

99. *Advocate,* September 19, 1894. *Farmers' Alliance,* March 21, 1891. *Wealth Makers,* October 4, 1894.

100. *Advocate,* April 8, 1891; April 15, 1891; September 19, 1894. *Farmers' Alliance,* March 21, 1891.

101. *Advocate,* January 13, 1892; February 15, 1893; August 23, 1893. *Farmers' Alliance,* March 21, 1891.

102. *Advocate,* January 11, 1893; April 11, 1894; September 19, 1894. *Farmers' Alliance,* October 22, 1891, in Pollack, *Populist Mind,* 20. *Wealth Makers,* October 4, 1891.

103. Clanton, *Kansas Populism,* 147. *Farmers' Alliance,* February 28, 1891.

104. *People's Party Paper* (Atlanta), January 20, 1893, in Pollack, *Populist Mind,* 52–53.

105. Bicha, "Conservative Populists," 14–15; and Clanton, "Hayseed Socialism," 157.

106. Pollack, *Just Polity,* 164.

107. Ibid., 137.

108. Lasch, *Agony of the American Left.*

109. Goodwyn, "Populism and Powerlessness," 26.

110. *Advocate,* September 19, 1894.

CHAPTER 6

The Social Construction
of Slavery

Richard J. Ellis

Cultural theory begins from the premise that the world is socially constructed. To claim that the world is socially constructed is to say more than just that the world is filtered through categories rather than directly experienced. It is to say as well that the constructions we place on the world (human nature is self-interested, the environment is fragile, global warming is making the world uninhabitable, poverty is the fault of the individual, natural resources are plentiful) are derived from our social relations. How we construct the world is shaped by the social relations we inhabit or wish to inhabit.

In this chapter I explore the social construction thesis by examining the understanding of slave culture in the United States that emerged in the wake of the civil rights movement of the 1960s.[1] That an observer's cultural bias shapes what she looks for and what she finds is no great surprise. Indeed, such a proposition is a truism in the social sciences—though some insist on claiming this as a revolutionary discovery of postmodernism. Mary Douglas's contribution is to provide a theory that specifies types of biases and predicts how each bias will shape perceptions.

To focus on the way in which observers have constructed slave life so as to fit a particular cultural bias is not to say that these constructions are without validity or that all such constructions are equally valid. To allow that knowledge is socially constructed is not to suggest that empirical claims cannot be tested. Indeed, my aim in this chapter is not only to show how slavery has been socially constructed by recent scholarship but also to show how these constructions ignore or underestimate the fatalistic nature of so much of slave culture. Cultural theory can thus make sense not only of how others have interpreted slavery but also of the social relations and accompanying cultural biases of slavery itself.

Because slaves left relatively little in the way of conventional historical records—diaries, letters, memoirs—there is probably greater scope to interpret slave culture in accord with one's own cultural bias than there would be with, say, the culture of slaveowners or abolitionists or industrial capitalists. The more ambiguous or incomplete the evidence, the greater the freedom of interpretation. But it is far more than availability of data that explains why slaves are such a rich source of social constructions. All marginal groups, whether the poor, the underclass, the homeless, or the proletariat, are vitally important in the contest between rival cultures. If the poor lack the talent, industriousness, or character possessed by the more successful members of society, the successful entrepreneur can justify his own position and the system that placed him at its apex. If these groups are systematically oppressed by the dominant groups, they stand as a permanent indictment of the injustice of the current regime. The meaning of the downtrodden's experience is thus contested and constructed by others in order to advance their preferred ways of life.

ROMANCING THE OPPRESSED

Particularly revealing is the social construction of slave culture that emerged during the 1970s in the work of George P. Rawick, John Blassingame, Eugene Genovese, Herbert G. Gutman, Lawrence W. Levine, and Thomas L. Webber.[2] There is much that is valuable in this rich literature, and much that sheds new light on the character of the slave experience. But this scholarship also tells us as much about the cultural biases of contemporary scholars as it does about life as a slave in the Old South. In large part it can be understood as an effort to construct the slave experience in such a way as to fit a contemporary egalitarian or communitarian bias.

Although the analyses differ in important respects, the authors share a concern with highlighting slave community and resistance rather than psychological damage and resignation. Their interpretations of slave culture evidence the classic egalitarian tendency to romanticize the oppressed, to find virtue and authenticity in the noble suffering of the downtrodden. Just as Russian populists looked upon serfs not only as damning evidence of the brutality of the system but "as embodiments of simple uncorrupted virtue, whose social organization ... was the natural foundation on which the future of Russian society must be rebuilt,"[3] so these authors look into the lives of the slaves for an indictment of the established powers as well as for a reaffirmation of their own preferences for noncoercive, egalitarian community. This egalitarian bias leads these researchers to underestimate the fatalism of slave life and to exaggerate the communitarian and egalitarian aspects of slave culture.

The paradox of a cohesive and resourceful community existing in the midst of a brutally exploitive labor system is resolved in this literature by distinguishing between the work environment and life in the slave quarters. Whatever the oppression slaves experienced in the fields, in the living quarters slaves found themselves amidst a noncoercive and supportive community. "While from sunup to sundown, the American slave worked for another and was harshly exploited,"

Rawick explains, "from sundown to sunup he lived for himself and created the behavioral and institutional basis which prevented him from becoming the absolute victim."[4] Blassingame goes still further, arguing that "the social organization of the quarters was the slave's primary environment which gave him his ethical rules and fostered cooperation, mutual assistance, and black solidarity." Within the slave quarters, "recreational activities led to cooperation, social cohesion, tighter communal bonds, and brought all classes of slaves together in common pursuits."[5] In the face of tremendous adversity, slaves thus created an autonomous life of community, solidarity, cooperation, and equality.

The thesis that the slave quarters represented an autonomous, noncoercive community of equals is most fully elaborated in Webber's *Deep Like the Rivers*. Within these quarters, Webber argues, slaves carved out "a society within a society," which gave slave culture "a community structure [that] set blacks apart from whites and enabled them to form and control a world of their own values and definitions." A slave's identification with the slave community was furthered in a number of ways: clandestine religious meetings gave blacks a feeling of cohesive fellowship and allowed slaves to "experience moments of peace, ecstasy, fellowship, and Freedom"; and storytelling "frequently took the form of a community happening" that gave slaves "a sense of communal spirit and camaraderie with their fellows" as well as "a feeling of identification with the larger community of American slaves." No matter how far slaves might travel "from their quarter home, these feelings of communality and kinship would always be rekindled with the soulful singing of a quarter song or the ... performance of a quarter story." Webber is particularly impressed by the egalitarian spirit within the slave quarters. "There is little in the slave narratives," Webber finds, "to suggest that the quarter community made a strong delineation among people, either with respect to innate ability or role, according to their sex. One is struck by the absence of the familiar theme of male superiority and by the lack of evidence to support the view that the quarters was a female-dominated society. The black source material suggests, rather, a general equality between females and males."[6]

The idea that the lives of the oppressed were more egalitarian than the lives of the oppressors surfaces repeatedly in a number of these works. Angela Davis, for instance, agrees that domestic life in the slave quarters was characterized by sexual equality. Slaves, Davis writes, "transformed that negative equality which emanated from the equal oppression they suffered as slaves into a positive equality: the egalitarianism characterizing their social relations."[7] Genovese agrees that "what has usually been viewed as a debilitating female supremacy was in fact a closer approximation to a healthy social equality than was possible for whites."[8] And Rawick portrays the slave community as approximating a utopian socialist cooperative "in which all adults looked after all children and there was little division between 'my children for whom I'm responsible' and 'your children for whom you're responsible.'"[9]

The tendency to romanticize the oppressed is evident even in such a masterful and nuanced work as Eugene Genovese's *Roll, Jordan, Roll.* Genovese marvels at the way slaves "transformed the ghastly conditions under which they labored into living space within which they could love each other." Much like the abolitionists who, as Kenneth Stampp notes, frequently portrayed blacks as "innately gentle and Christian people," Genovese suggests that slave family members treated one another with "tenderness, gentleness, charm, and modesty." Slaves were "compassionate people," with a "vibrant love of life and of each other," "a people ... who never lost faith in a future built on human brotherhood." Their distinctive religion not only possessed a "humanism that affirmed joy in life in the face of every trial" but constituted "a critical world-view in the process of becoming." And in "the call-and-response pattern" of the black congregations, Genovese saw a model of egalitarian life in which slaves affirmed "community solidarity and yet demanded the fullest expression of the individual."[10]

Lawrence Levine's great work, *Black Culture and Black Consciousness,* similarly accents the way that slaves through their religion as well as their music and folk beliefs "created and maintained a world apart which they shared with each other and which remained their own domain, free of control of those who ruled the earth." Slave spirituals, according to Levine, were the product of "an improvisational communal consciousness" and allowed the slave "the comfort of basking in the warmth of the shared assumptions around him." Christianity solidified the "slaves' sense of communality" and reinforced "their feelings of self-worth and dignity," and magical folk beliefs not only "provided hope, assurance, and a sense of group identification" but even offered the slaves "sources of power and knowledge alternative to those existing within the world of the power class."[11]

The primary intellectual foil for the communitarian interpretation of slave life is Stanley Elkins's seminal *Slavery* (1958), which likened slavery to life in a Nazi concentration camp. It is Elkins that Rawick has primarily in mind when he complains that historians "have presented the black slave as dehumanized victims, without culture, history, [or] community." And it is at Elkins that Levine takes aim when he criticizes historians for treating black history "not as cultural forms but as disorganization and pathology."[12] This dichotomy between culture and pathology, however, is false and misleading. *Every* cultural form has its pathologies. The question should not be Did slavery produce pathology or culture? but rather What cultural forms with what associated pathologies did slavery engender?

THE SOCIAL RELATIONS OF SLAVERY

To draw attention to the ways in which contemporary research on slave culture has been fueled by an egalitarian cultural bias is not to suggest that egalitarians' descriptions of slave culture are without validity. The slave quarters, at least on large plantations where the slave quarters were clearly set off from the master's residence,[13] did enable slaves to carve out pockets of autonomy separate from the influence of their masters. The communitarian emphasis is a useful corrective to Stanley Elkins's concentration-camp analogy, which greatly underrepresented the extent of psychological and cultural breathing space allowed slaves. But if the concentration-camp analogy is off the mark, so too is the vision of the slave quarters as an egalitarian cooperative.

The excesses of the egalitarian interpretation of slave culture are nicely brought out by Peter Kolchin's comparative study of Russian serfdom and American slavery, *Unfree Labor.* By comparing the experience of American slaves with that of Russian serfs, Kolchin shows how relatively circumscribed was the autonomy of slaves and how relatively undeveloped was slave community. Compared with Russian serfs, American slaves "found it more difficult to create their own collective forms and norms, and their communal life was more attenuated." Although conceding that the slave quarters often functioned as "a refuge from white control," Kolchin also points out that compared to the peasant commune, "institutionally the slave community remained undeveloped, never assuming the concrete forms and functions that would enable it to serve as a basis around which the slaves could fully organize their lives." When serfs wished to redress a grievance, "they turned instinctively to the commune, collectively petitioning their owners, local government officials, or the tsar." Slaves, in contrast, sought redress primarily as isolated individuals. "Seen in the light of the peasant obshchina," Kolchin continues, "the absence of any communal organization among American slaves is striking." Slave drivers, for instance, were chosen not by other slaves but by the master. In sum, the slave community "lacked the formal institutional basis of the peasant obshchina." This absence, Kolchin explains, did not "preclude the existence of communal sentiment and behavior among the slaves." But it did "severely restrict the ability of slaves to express their communal feelings, in the process limiting the collective nature of their life and culture."[14]

Not only was group life less cohesive and less-developed among American slaves than among Russian serfs, the slave community was also far less autonomous vis-à-vis dominant groups in society. The slave community was always precarious and often ill-equipped to resist interference by slaveholders. It is true that absolute regulation of the slaves' lives was impossible and that pockets of autonomy inevitably opened up. But, as Kolchin reminds us, slaves were significantly worse off on this score than Russian serfs, who "were usually subject to less regulation and were therefore freer to lead their lives as they wished."[15]

The slave experience was, to be sure, extremely varied; there certainly was no single slave culture. Slaves on small agricultural units sometimes worked side by side in the field with their masters; those on larger estates might only infrequently get a glimpse of their master. Some slaves worked under the close supervision of watchful overseers; others were allowed to hire out their own time. Some owners intervened extensively in the personal lives of their slaves; others preferred to let the slaves manage their own domestic affairs. Some lived under the master's roof; others lived in separate slave quarters at a considerable distance from the Great

House. Some slaves lived out their entire lives on a single estate in relatively stable families; others were repeatedly torn from family and friends. Some were brutally whipped into submission; others avoided punishment altogether. Some labored in the city, where opportunities for contact with outsiders were relatively plentiful; others lived on isolated, self-contained plantations cut off from the outside world. The degree of individual autonomy and group life that a slave experienced thus varied immensely.

So great is the variety of slave experience that some historians have suggested that any attempt to isolate a dominant behavioral or personality pattern is bound to fail.[16] It is no doubt true that no model can capture all of the complex reality of slavery. "Neither slavery nor slaves," Genovese wisely cautions, "can be treated as pure categories, free of the contradictions, tensions, and potentialities that characterize all human experience."[17] But this does not mean that we must accept Blassingame's conclusions that "the slave was no different in most ways from most men" and that "the same range of personality types existed in the quarters as in the mansion."[18] Can it be that slavery matters so little? How can there be so little connection between the way people live and the way people think? The diversity of the slave experience should make us wary of sweeping generalizations about slave culture, but we ought not to shrink from the important task of specifying the effects that slavery as a system of social relations has on values and beliefs, and how these values and beliefs in turn sustain slavery as a mode of social organization.

The life of a southern slave tended to be tightly prescribed. A slave generally could not leave the estate without a pass stating the destination and time of return. No slave was to be out of his cabin after "hornblow," and it was considered prudent for the overseer or master to inspect cabins at night to see that no slaves were missing. Overseers were required to stay in the fields as long as the hands were at work. A slave was not to sell or trade anything without a permit. Gambling with whites or other slaves was illegal. Some slave codes made it illegal for slaves to raise cotton, swine, horses, mules, or cattle. Many masters forbade slaves to have whiskey in the cabin, quarrel or fight, or use abusive language.[19]

Slaves' interactions with those of a different status were closely regulated by slaveowners. Free blacks and whites were often forbidden to work or even talk with slaves. One planter, for instance, fired a white mechanic for "talking with the negroes." To insulate slaves, some planters bought up the lands of lower-class whites living on the outskirts of the plantation. Masters rarely allowed slaves to marry free blacks; most were reluctant even to allow slaves to marry other slaves living on nearby plantations.[20]

To be sure, these laws and rules were not always adhered to in practice. For instance, although slave codes made it illegal for any person, even the master, to teach a slave to read or write, some masters did so anyway. Other slaves learned to read at the risk of being severely punished. Slaves in urban environments tended to find their opportunities for interaction with others of different circumstance and station to be much more plentiful than did slaves living on large, isolated plantations in the Deep South. There were more areas for initiative and autonomy than is suggested by looking only at formal legal codes and instructional manuals.

Nevertheless, if these ideal prescriptions and formal codes were not always followed to the letter, it remains true that the lives of most slaves were closely regulated. "It was the lot of the ordinary bondsman," concludes Kenneth Stampp, "to work under the close supervision of his master or of some employer who hired his services." Kolchin finds that compared with Russian serfs or even Jamaican slaves, who often supported themselves on private plots of land, American slaves "had little occasion to engage in their own economic activity and found it correspondingly difficult to accumulate property." Instead, "most slaves had resident masters who constantly meddled in their lives and strove to keep them in total dependence."[21]

Not only were slaves' lives closely regulated and tightly circumscribed (high grid), but slaves were excluded from the group making the rules that bound them (low group). The slaves' exclusion from the decisionmaking group belies slaveholder claims to an inclusive hierarchy in which there was a place for everyone and everyone in his place. In contrast to in Russia, where the serf's "commune represented the lowest level of authority in a chain of command that linked the peasant to the tsar,"[22] in America slaves faced a rigid wall of exclusion. Rather than making finely graded distinctions among people according to station, characteristic of hierarchy, southern law tended to define slaves as chattel rather than people.

There is merit in recent research that has shown how slaves carved out something of a communal life in the slave quarters or gained a sense of community in their spirituals. As we have already seen, however, a comparative perspective reveals the relative weakness of these slave communities compared with the high-group solidarity (as well as local chauvinism and hostility to outsiders) common among peasants.[23] That slave life in America was distinguished more by individual atomization than by group solidarity can be seen even in the patterns of resistance among slaves, which were overwhelmingly individualistic. Collective action against slavery was extremely rare.

A common experience of oppression is often assumed to mold an oppressed group into a cohesive unit. But the evidence collected by scholars examining social interaction in such institutions as prisons and mental hospitals strongly suggests that atomization is the more likely outcome. Erving Goffman, for instance, found that "although there are solidarizing tendencies" in total institutions, they tend to be limited. "Constraints which place inmates in a position to sympathize and communicate with each other do not necessarily lead to high group morale and solidarity. [Often] the inmate cannot rely on his fellows, who may steal from him, assault him, and squeal on him. ... In mental hospitals, dyads and triads may keep secrets from the authorities, but anything known to a whole ward of patients is likely to get to the ear of the attendant."[24] Much the same obstacles to group solidarity are evident in the lives of southern slaves.

Individual flight was by far the most common form of slave resistance. The decision to flee was usually reached individually rather than collectively for the very good reason that cooperation involved the risk of betrayal. Frederick Douglass was one of many slaves to discover the perils of joint action when one of his "band of brothers" informed the authorities of their plan of escape. Douglass learned his lesson: Next time he kept the plan to himself and escaped on his own.[25] "The difficulty of movement for southern blacks," Kolchin observes, only "served to reinforce their noncollective ethos." Closely controlled and insulated from free social intercourse, "most fugitives escaped on foot, traveled by night and slept in the woods by day, and were properly leery of both whites and blacks."[26] This individualistic pattern of resistance differs markedly not only from the Russian experience—it was not uncommon for all the serfs on an estate to flee together—but also from the experience of American slaves born in Africa who not infrequently "ran off in groups or attempted to establish villages of runaways on the frontier."[27] The distinctive pattern of resistance offered by American-born slaves, Kolchin concludes, indicates both "the difficult conditions faced by slaves seeking to engage in communal endeavors and the generally noncollective nature in which they responded to their bondage."[28]

Brer Rabbit and Amoral Individualism[29]

Nowhere is the atomized aspect of slave culture more clearly revealed than in the Brer Rabbit stories. Those who have given an egalitarian or communitarian construction to slave culture have often interpreted these as tales of resistance, a form of wish fulfillment in which weakness overcomes strength, slave defeats master.[30] That this explains something of the slaves' fascination with the Brer Rabbit stories seems plausible. But to leave the analysis at this point is woefully inadequate, for it misses the amoral, atomized world depicted in these folktales.

The recurring motif in these stories, as Michael Flusche documents, is less that the weak triumph over the strong than that survival in this world necessitates distrust and deceit. Cunning and deception triumph not over strength and oppression but over gullibility and trust. It is not "the theme of the ultimate victory, of the Lord delivering Daniel" that one finds in these tales. Rather the tales are "a humorous statement of the treacherous ways of society. They point to the fate of the man who trusts his neighbor exceedingly." "Most of the stories," Flusche explains, "took for granted that deep hostility existed between the characters, however they might disguise it." The relationship between the animals in the stories is invariably portrayed as adversarial. There is no friendship, no cooperation, no pooling of resources, and no collective action. "The perpetual struggle constantly prevented the animals from working together, in spite of the supposed geniality. Attempts at co-operation for parties, for farming, or for storing food, constantly fell apart because someone sabotaged the efforts for his own advantage—typically to eat the butter." Brer Rabbit's world was one in which "alliances were illusory and each man had to fight his battles alone; every other man was a potential enemy or rival in spite of his smiles and grins, and only the fool was unwary."[31]

Those animals who place their trust in the word of another animal invariably end up meeting a sticky end. Brer Rabbit usually comes out ahead because he discerns and exploits the other animals' weaknesses and presumes that no one means him any good. "His completely cynical view of manners and social relations," Flusche explains, "enabled him always to get the better of his opponents; repeatedly they presumed good will on his part when he provided a facade of consideration and altruism." When, for instance, Brer Wolf begs Brer Rabbit to shelter him from pursuing dogs, Brer Rabbit offers the wolf a chest in which to hide. Locking the wolf in the chest, Brer Rabbit then scalds his victim to death by pouring boiling water through a hole in the top, all the while assuring Brer Wolf that the pain is only fleas biting him.[32]

When Brer Rabbit temporarily drops his guard and trusts another to play by the rules he, too, ends up a loser. Brer Tarrypin bests Brer Rabbit in a race by positioning members of his family at regular intervals along the course to be there when the rabbit passes. Remaining near the finish line throughout the race, Brer Tarrypin steps over just as Brer Rabbit comes into sight.[33] Unlike the Aesop tortoise-and-the-hare fable, which teaches the virtue of perseverance ("slow but sure"), the Brer Rabbit variant lauds treachery. Those gullible few who try to run a fair race invite defeat and humiliation. Competition, like cooperation, is a fraud in which victory goes not to the swift or the strong or the persevering but to the deceitful.

The social environment depicted in these tales is violent, cruel, and remorseless. By Flusche's count, "in about half the tales, by sudden inspiration or deliberate forethought, one animal burned, scalded, or hacked another."[34] Violent acts are not justified as the just comeuppance due to an oppressor or bully, or as the righteous wreaking vengeance on the wicked. Instead the violence is spiteful, vindictive, even gratuitous and purposeless. Brer Rabbit not only persuades other animals to help him out of traps but tricks them into taking his place. A lady who resists his wooing he kills, skins, and smokes over hickory chips. After persuading his neighbors to help him build a springhouse, Brer Rabbit has them all drowned. And on and on.[35]

Trickery may enable a slower or weaker creature to outsmart a faster or stronger one, but the cunning is corrosive of social relationships. There is nothing Brer Rabbit will not do to his fellow animals in order to survive. Loyalty and self-sacrifice, even pity and regret, are emotions foreign to Brer Rabbit's amoral world. Even his own family is not exempt from his self-interested scheming. In one story, Brer Wolf seeks revenge upon Brer Rabbit for having boiled Wolf's grandmother and tricking Wolf into eating her. To save himself, Brer Rabbit sacrifices his own wife and children.[36]

Why did slaves find these stories so appealing? Why did they relish telling their young tales with such overtly amoral, even antisocial, messages? Interviews with former slaves suggest that many believed the stories accurately portrayed a hostile, compassionless world in which cooperation was futile and trust dangerous. Brer Rabbit was admired for his ability to survive and even advance his material fortunes in the face of a harsh environment in which one animal's gain was invariably another's loss. Asked to explain what the Brer Rabbit stories meant to him, one ex-slave explained: "I is small man myself; but I ain't nevver 'low no one for to git 'head of me. I allers use my sense for help me 'long, just like Brer Rabbit." That his master had made him a driver on the plantation so he did not have to work as hard and got more rations of food and clothes than other slaves, he attributed to "usin' my sense." Another former slave believed that the moral of these stories was "Learn not to trust ... people whom you do not know." And another reported the moral as "When two fellows are in your way, you must make them fight, then you will always save your skin."[37] This testimony suggests that many slaves understood the Brer Rabbit stories as an allegory for all social relationships, not just for the relationship between master and slave.

A passage from the slave narrative of William Wells Brown shows how the amoral individualism of Brer Rabbit was sometimes acted out in real life by slaves. Brown was at the time hired out to a slavetrader by the name of Walker. On this occasion, Brown was called upon to serve wine to several men negotiating with Walker about the purchase of some slaves. Brown filled the glasses perilously high, and the visitors spilled wine on their clothes. Walker deemed it necessary to punish the slave for his act of carelessness and so the next morning sent Brown to deliver a note and a dollar to the jailer. Suspecting "that all was not right," Brown showed the message to a sailor who informed the slave that the note instructed the jailor to whip him. The slave's response to this predicament was straight out of the pages of Brer Rabbit:

> While I was meditating on the subject I saw a colored man about my size walk up, and the thought struck me in a moment to send him with my note. I walked up to him, and asked him who he belonged to. He said he was a free man, and had been in the city but a short time. I told him I had a note to go into the jail, and get a trunk to carry to one of the steamboats; but was so busily engaged that I could not do it, although I had a dollar to pay for it. He asked me if I would not give him the job. I handed him the note and the dollar, and off he started for the jail.

The result was that the unsuspecting black man got a severe flogging and the cunning Brown escaped without physical harm. Unlike Brer Rabbit, however, Brown later felt deep remorse at the deception he had practiced on his fellow man, citing this incident as an example of how "slavery makes its victims lying and mean."[38]

Even those slave stories that unambiguously referred to the master-slave relation share the atomized structure of the Brer Rabbit stories. In the Old Master and

John tales, for instance, John the slave tries to trick his master for his own advantage, not for the benefit of the slave community as a whole.[39] Notably absent from slave folklore, observes Kolchin, were "mythological stories ... [that] emphasized classical elements of heroism, self-sacrifice, and group solidarity. ... Slave tales contain few depictions of courageous or noble behavior; there are no dragon slayers, giant killers, or defenders of the people." Even the animal trickster tales told by Russian serfs "often expressed a communal solidarity lacking in the slave stories. Animal tales that reflected a devil-take-the-hindmost amorality constituted a much smaller fraction in Russia ... than in America." In sum, Kolchin concludes, "Peasant folklore, unlike that of American blacks, contained substantial elements of social consciousness expressing lofty ideals of heroism, generosity, and struggle for the common good."[40]

The folklore of American slaves is not about affirming collective identity or about arousing collective resistance to slavery. Rather it speaks to individual survival in a hostile environment of atomized subordination. The recurring themes of these stories, as Flusche argues, "suggest that slavery tended to engender an atomistic, individualistic world view among the slaves."[41] But this is not the individualism of the aspiring entrepreneur, who sees the world as his oyster; it is instead the individualism of the ineffectual who finds himself prevented from joining with others by virtue of a tightly regulated environment. Neither the entrepreneur nor the ineffectual puts much store in group solidarity. But the entrepreneur has the social freedom to negotiate for himself, to join with others to advance his fortunes, to build networks, or even to drop out. The ineffectual has no such freedom, for his life is prescribed by others.

FATALISM AS A RATIONAL RESPONSE TO A CAPRICIOUS ENVIRONMENT

Contemporary observers of slavery often described American slaves as fatalistic, apathetic, indifferent, resigned. Some analysts have dismissed this testimony as nothing more than slaveholder propaganda designed to justify the enslavement of blacks. It is true that efforts by members of the southern medical profession to explain slave passivity in terms of innate racial makeup were unambiguously racist. But it is also true, as Genovese points out, that "too many contemporaries, black and white, described this fatalism to permit its dismissal as a figment of white racist imagination."[42] It was Frederick Douglass, not a pro-slavery apologist, who recalled living "among slaves, who seemed to ask, 'Oh, what's the use?' every time they lifted a hoe."[43]

Fatalism is a learned response to a social environment in which there is only a tenuous connection between preferences and outcomes. If slaves felt that there was little they could do to significantly alter their circumstances, it was because for most of them this was the hard reality. They felt that life was like a lottery because it often was. Living in a capricious world in which one could be punished on a whim or separated from family members without consent made it difficult for slaves to develop a self-reliant cosmology. Some unusual individuals in unusual circumstances did; most did not.

Fatalism is not, of course, an attitude limited to slaves. Misfortune, disaster, sickness, and death strike all human lives. Our control over the physical environment is often precarious, a truth that earthquakes, floods, and other natural disasters periodically bring home to even the most self-reliant individualists. Lack of control over nature's course is part of the human condition and thus creates a degree of fatalism in all of us. Indeed, an understanding that there are things beyond an individual's control is perhaps the beginning of wisdom. But if no individual has total control over his physical environment, some individuals have greater control than others. Poor people usually live with much greater uncertainty, many fewer resources to resist nature's vagaries, and a much higher incidence of death and sickness. As one moves in the direction of these more vulnerable social worlds, a fatalistic orientation becomes increasingly rational.

The death of a master was one of many events in a slave's life that revealed the capriciousness and vulnerability of a slave's existence. In his autobiography, Frederick Douglass vividly recalls the terrifying sense of uncertainty and lack of control that he felt upon his master's death. The master's estate was to be divided among two children, Andrew and Lucretia. The slaves knew Master Andrew to be a cruel and profligate drunkard; Mrs. Lucretia, however, was widely acknowledged to be kind and considerate. To fall into the hands of Master Andrew meant not only brutal treatment but also the strong possibility of being sold away to the Far South if he fell in debt. The prospects for those slaves who went to Mrs. Lucretia were inestimably brighter. But the slaves' preferences counted for nothing. The master's property—slaves together with cattle, pigs, and horses—was valued and divided without consulting the slaves in any way. "We had no more voice in the decision of the question," Douglass remembers, "than the oxen and cows that stood chewing at the haymow. One word from the appraisers, against all preferences or prayers, was enough to sunder all the ties of friendship and affection. ... Thus early, I got a foretaste of that painful uncertainty which slavery brings."[44]

It is not that slaves lack preferences. Rather it is, as Douglass saw, that "neither their aversions nor their preferences avail them anything." Being "only a slave," Douglass lamented, "my wishes were nothing."[45] It is difficult to sustain preferences where they have little or no effect upon outcomes. Over a lifetime, many will learn that to formulate a preference serves no positive purpose. Resignation to one's lot becomes a rational adaptation, reducing cognitive dissonance by teaching the slave not to want what he can't have.[46]

Chance figured prominently in the lives of most slaves. It was a world, Kenneth Stampp observes, "full of forces which [they] could not control."[47] This capricious environment generated a cosmology that attributed success less to individual effort than to good luck. Douglass recalls, for instance, how his grandmother's success in preserving seedling sweet potatoes was widely attributed by her neighbors to good fortune: "It happened to her—as it will happen to any careful and thrifty person residing in an ignorant and improvident community—to enjoy the reputation of having been born to 'good luck.' "[48] The slaves' arbitrary social world gave scant encouragement to the belief that there was a just or predictable relation between individual effort and success.

Although it is true, as Robert Fogel and Stanley Engerman have stressed, that slaves who were especially diligent were sometimes promoted from fieldwork to managerial or artisan positions, many other hardworking slaves were abruptly and arbitrarily shifted or sold with little or no relation to their work performance. Slave autobiographies are filled with such stories. One slave, who was the son of a groom's assistant, started out his youth taking care of horses. Upon the owner's death, however, the widow abruptly sold the horses and assigned those responsible for tending them to field work. Another slave from Kentucky began life as the pet of his white father and owner only to be suddenly sold away to Alabama to work in the fields.[49] The narrative of William Wells Brown dramatically illustrates the random character of slave mobility. Born in Kentucky, Brown was hired out by his master at a young age as a house servant to a Major Freeland, a drunkard and a gambler who cruelly abused his slaves. After a short time, Major Freeland failed in business and Brown was then employed on a steamboat, where he spent what he described as "the most pleasant time ... I had ever experienced." At the end of the sailing season, he was hired out to a hotel keeper, who was perhaps the most "inveterate hater of the negro ... [who] ever walked on God's green earth." After a brief, unhappy time at the Missouri Hotel, Brown was hired out to Elijah P. Lovejoy, a well-known abolitionist publisher and editor. In Lovejoy's employment, Brown was well-treated and even obtained a little learning. After only a short time with Lovejoy, however, Brown was severely beaten in the street and forced to return to his master. After recovering from the beating, he was hired out as a steward to a steamboat captain, a situation Brown again found pleasant. But this, too, was short-lived. For the captain left his boat at the end of the summer, and Brown was returned home to work in the fields on his master's farm. Shortly thereafter, he was moved from the field to the house to work as a waiter. Sometime later, he was hired out to work for a slavetrader, a job Brown found odious in the extreme. After serving out the year with the slavetrader ("the longest year I ever lived"), Brown returned home and attempted to escape. The effort failed and he was ordered to work in the field but soon thereafter was sold as a house servant to a merchant tailor (from whom he soon escaped).[50] Of these many changes in employment, none are traceable to personal effort or skill. There is a clear progression neither of upward nor downward mobility. Working conditions seem to vary randomly: sometimes better, sometimes worse. Decisions about careers are imposed from without, and to the slave, at least, there seems no rhyme or reason behind them. In such an uncertain and random environment, an ideology of resignation and chance appears more rational than an ideology of self-improvement.

Slaveowners often complained of their slaves' passivity and indifference toward the future, but at the same time they promoted the very fatalistic characteristics they deplored. The editor of the *Southern Planter,* for instance, advised his readers that "no laborer should have his attention distracted or his time occupied in thinking about what he should do next: the process of thought and arrangement should devolve wholly upon the superintendent."[51] Another defended restricting slave movement on the grounds that such a policy ensured that "they do not know what is going on beyond the limits of the plantation, and [thus] feel satisfied that they could not ... accomplish anything that would change their condition."[52] Initiative and foresight were double-edged swords: They were qualities that could make for a more responsible and productive work force as well as a more rebellious one.

Fatalism was not uniformly pervasive among southern slaves. Large plantations with absentee owners in new areas of the Southwest were particularly prone to produce a fatalistic bias. Slaves on these plantations were often ill-treated and "profoundly apathetic, full of depression and gloom, and seemingly less hostile than indifferent toward the white man who controlled him."[53] Where a modicum of social space opened up, as occurred when slaves were permitted to hire themselves out, nonfatalistic personalities were capable of developing.[54] The greater degree of social space afforded the skilled slaves (coopers, blacksmiths, bricklayers, and carpenters) explains their greater spirit of independence and initiative when compared with the closely supervised field hands.[55] Variation in cultural bias corresponded to variation in social experiences.

Frederick Douglass is a prominent example of a slave who was certainly no fatalist. But his social experiences were also exceptional. At the age of ten, Douglass was removed from a large Maryland plantation and sent to live with a Baltimore family. Here he found that "the crouching servility of a slave, usually so acceptable a quality to the haughty slaveowner, was not understood nor desired." His new mistress even began to teach Douglass to read before her husband put a stop to it. The relative freedom of Baltimore ("A city slave," Douglass wrote, "is almost a free citizen ... compared with a slave on [a] plantation") afforded him the opportunity to work and associate with free men and to read speeches "filled with the principles of liberty." Douglass himself acknowledged that "but for the mere circumstance of being thus removed before the rigors of slavery had fastened upon me; before my young spirit had been crushed under the iron control of the slave-driver, instead of being, today, a freeman, I might [still] have been wearing the galling chains of slavery." Douglass's autobiography, in short, is a fascinating and self-conscious case study in the social conditions and qualities of mind necessary to escape what Douglass described as the "spirit-devouring thralldom" of bondage.[56]

Slave uprisings or escapes were almost invariably led by the exceptional slave who, like Douglass, had experienced a substantial degree of social autonomy. Douglass testified that "perhaps not one of [my co-conspirators], left to himself, would have dreamed of escape as a possible thing. Not one of them was self-moved in the matter. They all wanted to be free; but the serious thought of running away, had not entered into their minds, until I won them to the undertaking."[57] The few slave revolts that did occur, Elkins points out,

> were in no instance planned by plantation laborers but rather by Negroes whose qualities of leadership were developed well outside the full coercions of the planta-tion-authority system. Gabriel, who led the revolt of 1800, was a blacksmith who lived a few miles outside Richmond. Demark Vesey, leading spirit of the 1822 plot at Charleston, was a freed Negro artisan who had been born in Africa and served several years aboard a slave trading vessel; and Nat Turner, the Virginia slave who fomented the massacre of 1831, was a literate preacher.[58]

Rebellions as well as runaways were concentrated among urban, skilled slaves who had greater social space and had experienced more lenient treatment.[59] From a cultural point of view, the social source of resistance is as significant as the rela-tive absence of slave rebellions. Both testify to the reciprocal relationship be-tween a fatalistic bias and the social relations of slavery.

FATALISM AND FREEDOM

That antebellum slaves were fatalistic does not mean they did not desire freedom. There is no reason to doubt the word of a former slave who told an interviewer that slaves used to "pray constantly for the 'day of their deliverance.'"[60] But if most slaves dreamed for freedom, few had much reason to think such an objective was attainable through their own efforts.[61] They could pray, wait patiently, and hope, but they could not act on this dream. Deliverance could come from without or above but not from within. The great mass of slaves, reported ex-slave Henry Bibb, "know that they are destined to die in that wretched condition, unless they are delivered by the arm of Omnipotence."[62] Raising one's own arm in resistance was insufficient without outside assistance and unnecessary with it.

Edward Banfield uncovered a parallel pattern of behavior among peasants of southern Italy. Although "getting ahead" is a recurring theme of peasant exis-tence, Banfield found that the peasant "sees that no matter how hard he works he can never get ahead. ... He knows ... that in the end he will be no better off than before." The peasants studied by Banfield wait for fortune to smile upon them. They wait, for instance, for the "call" that will enable them to take their family to the more prosperous regions of the North or, even better, for the "call" from a rel-ative in America that will enable them to migrate to the United States. They wait and they hope and they pray, but there is little they can do, or so they believe, to realize the desired outcome. "The idea that one's welfare depends crucially upon conditions beyond one's control—upon luck or the caprice of a saint" acts as a tremendous check upon individual initiative.[63] What distinguishes fatalists from adherents to other ways of life is not the desire for a better life but the feeling that fate and society conspire to prevent them from improving their condition.

Much the same is true of today's so-called underclass. No doubt the urban poor wish to be rich. No doubt they hope to get ahead and escape poverty. What is often missing, however, is the belief that getting ahead and escaping the coils of poverty is attainable through sustained individual or collective effort. The belief that individual initiative and collective action are inefficacious becomes self-fulfilling. Believing that there is little they can do to significantly alter their lives, their lives in fact remain unaltered.

This is not to suggest fatalism is all in the head. A fatalistic bias can flourish only where social institutions sustain that bias as an adaptive and rational posture. In a world in which there are no escapes and few rewards, passivity and resignation are more rational and adaptive than the individualist's incurable entrepreneurial optimism. As the young Indian boy living on the Bombay streets in the film *Salaam Bombay!* eventually discovers, certain social environments reward resignation and withdrawal over initiative and cooperation.

The fatalistic cultural bias of southern slaves was sustained by a hostile, random, and tightly prescribed social environment. Although slaves sometimes benefited from the pockets of social space that opened up in urban areas, in the slave quarters, or in the practice of hiring out, most slaves most of the time had little choice about the type of work to be done or how it was to be performed. Excluded from the group that made the key decisions affecting their lives—where to live, when to move, where to work—fatalistic resignation was an adaptive and rational cultural response for most slaves. That so many contemporary observers have played down or ignored this aspect of slave culture shows that it is not slaves alone who are in the grips of cultural bias.

NOTES

I would like to thank Reuben Deumling for his able research assistance.

1. Of course, social construction of the slave experience did not begin in the 1960s and 1970s. From the outset, understanding slavery has been inextricably entangled with contemporary cultural struggles. The social construction of slave life was hotly contested in the decades prior to the Civil War as pro-slavery ideologists insisted that slaves were content members of a caring hierarchy and abolitionists responded that slaves were an oppressed people with special virtues. And it is impossible to understand the hold that Ulrich Phillips's scholarship had on the academic community without understanding the racist worldview that his hierarchical social construction served. Phillips's construction of slavery as hierarchy as well as Elkins's construction of slaves as fatalists and Robert Fogel and Stanley Engerman's construction of slaves as individualists are analyzed at length in Rich-

ard J. Ellis, *American Political Cultures* (New York: Oxford University Press, 1993), 121–126.

2. George P. Rawick, *From Sundown to Sunup: The Making of the Black Community* (Westport, Conn.: Greenwood Press, 1972). John Blassingame, *The Slave Community: Plantation Life in the Antebellum South* (New York: Oxford University Press, 1972). Eugene Genovese, *Roll, Jordan, Roll: The World the Slaves Made* (New York: Pantheon, 1974). Herbert G. Gutman, *The Black Family in Slavery and Freedom, 1750–1925* (New York: Vintage, 1976). Lawrence W. Levine, *Black Culture and Black Consciousness: Afro-America Folk Thought from Slavery to Freedom* (New York: Oxford University Press, 1977). Thomas L. Webber, *Deep Like the Rivers: Education in the Slave Quarter Community* (New York: W. W. Norton, 1978).

3. Isaiah Berlin, "Russian Populism," reprinted in *Russian Thinkers* (Harmondsworth: Penguin, 1978), 211.

4. Rawick, *From Sundown to Sunup,* xix.

5. Blassingame, *The Slave Community,* 1979 rev. ed., 105–106.

6. Webber, *Deep Like the Rivers,* xii–xiii, 205–206, 215, 222, 223, 149.

7. Angela Davis, *Women, Race, and Class* (New York: Random House, 1981), 18.

8. Genovese, *Roll, Jordan, Roll,* 500.

9. Rawick, *From Sundown to Sunup,* 93.

10. Genovese, *Roll, Jordan, Roll,* 472, 204, 457, 283, 659, 271. Other quotations by Genovese are taken from David Herbert Donald's review of *Roll, Jordan, Roll,* "Writing About Slavery," in *Commentary* 59(January 1975), 87. The quotation by Stampp is from Kenneth M. Stampp, "A Humanistic Perspective," in Paul A. David, Herbert G. Gutman, Richard Sutch, Peter Temin, and Gavin Wright, eds., *Reckoning with Slavery: Critical Essays in the Quantitative History of American Negro Slavery* (New York: Oxford University Press, 1976), 15. Also see George M. Fredrickson, *The Black Image in the White Mind* (New York: Harper & Row, 1971), 101–102.

11. Lawrence Levine, *Black Culture and Black Consciousness,* 80, 29, 33, 63.

12. Rawick and Levine, quoted in Stanley M. Elkins, *Slavery: A Problem in American Institutional and Intellectual Life,* 3rd ed. (Chicago: University of Chicago Press, 1976), 280–281. If Elkins's concentration-camp analogy was flawed, the questions Elkins posed about the relationship between social structure and cosmology remain important. Elkins's enduring contribution was to focus attention on the way in which "the social system represented by American plantation slavery might have developed a sociology and social psychology of its own" (Elkins, *Slavery,* 23). Elkins tried to identify the structural elements of the plantation system "that could sustain infantilism as a normal feature of behavior" (Elkins, *Slavery,* 86). Recent research on slave culture has been so intent on affirming slave autonomy and community that it has sometimes slighted the important problem of specifying the effects that slavery actually had on slaves' beliefs and behavior.

13. The importance of the size of the plantation is nicely brought out in Robert William Fogel, *Without Consent or Contract: The Rise and Fall of American Slavery* (New York: W. W. Norton, 1989), esp. 182–185.

14. Peter Kolchin, *Unfree Labor: American Slavery and Russian Serfdom* (Cambridge, Mass.: Harvard University Press, 1987), 196, 200, 205–207.

15. Ibid., 233, 156; also see 357.

16. See Kenneth M. Stampp, "Rebels and Sambos: The Search for the Negro's Personality in Slavery," *Journal of Southern History* 37(August 1971), 367–392; Stampp, "A

Humanistic Perspective," 29; and Blassingame, *Slave Community.*

17. Eugene D. Genovese, "Rebelliousness and Docility in the Negro Slave: A Critique of the Elkins Thesis," reprinted in *In Red and Black: Marxian Explorations in Southern and Afro-American History* (New York: Vintage, 1972), 95. Elkins was not unaware of this. See Elkins, *Slavery,* 86–87, 103–104, 137–138.

18. Blassingame, *Slave Community,* 320. Also see Elkins, *Slavery,* 279.

19. Kenneth M. Stampp, *The Peculiar Institution: Slavery in the Ante-Bellum South* (New York: Knopf, 1956), 149–150, 209.

20. Ibid., 149–151.

21. Ibid., 73. Kolchin, *Unfree Labor,* 348–349.

22. Kolchin, *Unfree Labor,* 201.

23. Ibid., 331.

24. Erving Goffman, *Asylums: Essays on the Social Situation of Mental Patients and Other Inmates* (Garden City, N.Y.: Anchor, 1961), 60. In *The Prison Community* (New York: Holt, Rinehart and Winston, 1958), Donald Clemer found that "the prisoner's world is an atomized world. … Trickery and dishonesty overshadow sympathy and cooperation. … It is a world of 'I,' 'me,' and 'mine,' rather than 'ours,' 'theirs,' and 'his'" (297–298). Also see Michael Flusche, "Joel Chandler Harris and the Folklore of Slavery," *Journal of American Studies* 9(December 1975), 362; and George M. Fredrickson and Christopher Lasch, "Resistance to Slavery," *Civil War History* 13(December 1967), 315–329.

25. Kolchin, *Unfree Labor,* 278. Frederick Douglass, *My Bondage and My Freedom* (New York: Dover, 1969; first published 1855), 269. Gilbert Osofsky, ed., *Puttin' On Ole Massa* (New York: Harper & Row, 1969), 19.

26. Kolchin, *Unfree Labor,* 289, 286.

27. Ibid., 289. Gerald W. Mullin, *Flight and Rebellion: Slave Resistance in Eighteenth-Century Virginia* (New York: Oxford University Press, 1972), 34.

28. Kolchin, *Unfree Labor,* 291.

29. The term "amoral individualist" is from Edward Banfield, *The Moral Basis of a Backward Society* (New York: Free Press, 1958), 83.

30. Blassingame, *Slave Community,* 127–128.

31. Flusche, "Folklore of Slavery," 358–360.

32. Ibid., 359.

33. Ibid., 360.

34. Ibid., 358.

35. Elkins, *Slavery,* 283.

36. Ibid.

37. Flusche, "Folklore of Slavery," 360–361.

38. "Narrative of William Wells Brown, a Fugitive Slave," in Osofsky, *Puttin' On Ole Massa,* 198–200.

39. Flusche, "Folklore of Slavery," 361.

40. Kolchin, *Unfree Labor,* 230–232.

41. Flusche, "Folklore of Slavery," 361.

42. Genovese, *Roll, Jordan, Roll,* 638.

43. Douglass, *My Bondage,* 34.

44. Ibid., 175.

45. Ibid., 184, 183.

46. This thesis is developed in the work of Paul Veyne and discussed in Jon Elster, *Making Sense of Marx* (Cambridge: Cambridge University Press, 1985), 20–21, 505.

47. "And so," Stampp goes on to explain, a slave "tended to be a fatalist and futilitarian, for nothing else could reconcile him to his life" (*Peculiar Institution*, 361).

48. Douglass, *My Bondage*, 36.

49. Kolchin, *Unfree Labor*, 351.

50. "Narrative of William Wells Brown," in Osofsky, *Puttin' On Ole Massa*, 184, 202.

51. Genovese, *Roll, Jordan, Roll*, 638.

52. Stampp, *Peculiar Institution*, 149.

53. Stampp, "Rebels and Sambos," 386.

54. Many slaveholders who understood the reciprocal relation between slavery and fatalistic submission vehemently opposed hiring out. "No higher evidence can be furnished of [hiring out's] baneful effects," wrote a South Carolinian, "than the unwillingness it produces in the slave, to return to the regular life and domestic control of the master" (Stampp, *Peculiar Institution*, 147).

55. Elkins, *Slavery*, 137. Kolchin, *Unfree Labor*, 348. Stampp, *Peculiar Institution*, 147.

56. Douglass, *My Bondage*, 142, 145, 147, 157–159, 138–139, 272.

57. Ibid., 279.

58. Elkins, *Slavery*, 138.

59. See ibid.; Fredrickson and Lasch, "Resistance to Slavery," 225; and Kolchin, *Unfree Labor*, 318, 255.

60. Robert Smalls, in John W. Blassingame, ed., *Slave Testimony: Two Centuries of Letters, Speeches, Interviews, and Autobiographies* (Baton Rouge: Louisiana State University Press, 1977), 377.

61. See Kolchin, *Unfree Labor*, 320; and Stampp, *Peculiar Institution*, 97.

62. "Narrative of the Life and Adventures of Henry Bibb," in Osofsky, *Puttin' On Ole Massa*.

63. Banfield, *Moral Basis of a Backward Society*, 64, 58–59, 88, 109. Also see the analysis of Banfield in Michael Thompson, Richard Ellis, and Aaron Wildavsky, *Cultural Theory* (Boulder: Westview Press, 1990), 223–227.

CHAPTER 7

Cultural Theory and Historical Change: The Development of Town and Church in Puritan New England

Dean C. Hammer

That something happened to American Puritan social relations after the mid-1630s has been a consistent theme of Puritan scholarship; what that something was remains less clear. Richard Bushman, whose declension thesis reflects a prevalent theme of scholarship of the 1960s and 1970s, sees the Puritans as employing a "traditional image of society as an organism," emphasizing "order above all other social virtues." This order then disintegrated in the face of economic ambitions and, later, the religious enthusiasm of the Great Awakening.[1] So, too, Darrett Rutman and Kenneth Lockridge depict Puritanism as a utopian communal ideal that gave way to provincialism, commercialism, and selfishness.[2] Sacvan Bercovitch, departing from this declension thesis, sees early Puritan leaders like John Winthrop as "bespeak[ing] a moment of cultural transition" from a deferential to a modern, individualistic, capitalist ethic.[3] In reaction to the identification of Puritanism with modernity, Theodore Bozeman seeks to locate a dimension in Puritanism that expresses itself as a primitivist interest in the restoration of a biblical commonwealth.[4]

There is more than a faint echo in these writings of such categories as *Gemeinschaft* and *Gesellschaft,* organic and mechanical solidarity and traditional and modern forms of social organization, respectively. Yet, like trying to cover oneself with a blanket that is too short, scholars who use these categories are able to explain one aspect of Puritan social relations in the 1630s only as they make inexplicable another. Bushman's association of tradition with an emphasis on order, for example, seems unable to account for the fluid lines of political and religious authority that existed in the Puritan community prior to 1636.[5] In Bercovitch's equation of modernity with individualism, he strips Puritanism of its hierarchical

137

elements, which become more, rather than less, pronounced in the first decade of settlement. Bozeman's discussion remains ambiguous about the nature of Puritan social organization, though he points to a continuity in Puritan understandings of the nature of authority that belies the important changes in the actual practice of authority in the first decade of settlement.

Cultural theory offers the possibility of explaining these variations in Puritanism. It does this not by trying to fit Puritan social relations into a traditional-modern dichotomy but by providing a more variegated typology of ways of life that allows us to identify these different social relations within Puritanism. Using cultural theory, one can identify two distinct forms of Puritan organization: an egalitarian one that emphasized strong group cohesiveness and low, often ambiguous, internal differentiation; and a hierarchical organization that maintained strong group boundaries but exhibited increasingly centralized control and more rigid role differentiation. At any given time these two forms were always present in Puritan society. Although no one form of social organization decisively wins, the balance does tip in a large number of Puritan communities from egalitarianism to hierarchy. We can see the beginnings of this shift in Boston and in the governance of the Massachusetts Bay commonwealth after the mid-1630s and in later years in inland communities.

Cultural theory is useful in explaining this change, less by locating an agent of causation than by spelling out a relationship between modes of social organization and perceptions of the environment. Cultural theory suggests that corresponding to each viable way of organizing social relations is a distinctive, socially constructed set of perceptions, and that these biases limit "the type of social relations an individual can justify living in." The egalitarian juxtaposition of a corrupt and dangerous outside world with a pure inside stabilizes a set of social relations in which the group believes it can survive only by separating itself from others. Moreover, the egalitarian belief in the goodness and essential equality of uncorrupted human nature justifies a system of social relations in which coercive hierarchies are minimized. The hierarchist, however, perceives human nature as inherently fallible and corrupt, and hence manageable only through well-constructed institutions that closely regulate human behavior. Unlike the egalitarian, who sees institutions as a corrupting influence, the hierarchist fears that without institutions regulating human passions, the social order will come apart.[6]

Although these views of human nature are socially constructed, they are not socially determined. It is possible for our views of the world to change and, at some point, to become incompatible with a current way of life. Such change "occurs when successive events intervene in such a manner as to prevent a way of life from delivering on the expectations it has generated, thereby prompting individuals to seek more promising alternatives." This discrepancy between "the expected and the actual" is termed "surprise."[7] Given a revision in perceptions of the world, cultural theory posits that there will be a corresponding change in one's way of life to more closely accommodate this new reality.

The argument of this chapter is that as the Puritan community consolidated its religious and political institutions in New England, a number of surprises occurred that caused influential Puritans to question the viability of the egalitarian social relations established in the first years of New England settlement. Before, there had been some optimism about the possibility of a just community founded on equality among God's elect, a community that was united by its opposition to a hostile environment. There developed a concern, however, that the obstacles to creating such a community were due not only to the hostility of the world but to the perversity of those within the group. As an increasing segment of the Puritan elite came to see the world in this way, they came to feel that their viability depended not only on maintaining high group boundaries but also in using institutions and authority to regulate and supervise conduct within the group. This change in perception moved Puritan social organization from egalitarianism to hierarchy.

EGALITARIAN BEGINNINGS

To understand the egalitarian origins of Puritanism, we need to go back to England. In reaction to both the traditional hierarchic order of the Anglican church and the disorder brought about by rural depopulation, urbanization, religious decay, and the decline of traditional feudal social organization, a disenchanted element of English society constructed not only an alternate explanation of the world around it but created a corresponding method of organizing its social relations. Michael Walzer refers to this new social organization as one of Calvinist politics, as an essentially egalitarian cadre of saints.

Always in a minority position in England that carried with it a price in persecution, the Puritans "felt themselves alone in a hostile sea."[8] Driven in part by the reality of oppression, in part by an ideology that called for a separation of the elect from the unregenerate, the Puritans erected clearly defined boundaries that separated communicants from noncommunicants and sought to exclude the latter. Rather than retreating from a world seen as corrupt, though, Calvinist ideology offered—even demanded—the transformation of society. Total dedication on the part of the saint was required because the organization sought nothing less than a remaking of the social order. Prospective as well as current members had to exhibit continually a "commitment and zeal" that had to be "tested and proven." Members were subject to constant and intense examination to ensure the ideological purity of the group.[9]

Although external boundaries were pronounced, the internal structure of the English Puritans remained largely undefined. The saints replaced the Anglican hierarchy and the attendant ceremonies, rituals, attire, and distinctions of rank with a "voluntary association of the holy" founded on the equality of all men "within the band of the chosen." The voluntary nature of the group was important, since the transformation of the world was viewed as possible only by a banding together of willing, knowledgeable, and zealous saints. Rather than being differentiated by status, members were "measured by their godliness and by the contributions they can make to the work at hand." Ornate robes were replaced with plain clothing, church decisions would be made by the ministers in "prolonged discussion and mutual criticism" rather than by the bishops, and biblical interpretation would be based on "the Word" rather than on traditional teachings. This new emphasis did not give rise to a loose organization of different minds, though, but one governed by a self-imposed, tight discipline.[10] To the extent that authority was exercised, it was done so collectively rather than individually. Ultimate sanction for the "unrepentant excommunicant," imposed in the name of the group, was exile, a practice common to egalitarian organizations as they seek to purge competing elements from the communal body.[11]

Although the Puritans who arrived in New England were no longer engaged in an immediate struggle with the Anglican leadership, the Puritans still saw themselves as fleeing a menacing world. The corruption of the outer world could be seen in the continued degeneration of England, and the physical environment the Puritans encountered in New England only reinforced their view of the outside world as hostile and dangerous. Certainly the Puritans looked with wonderment at the vast expanse of land in the new world, even marveled at God's creation; but it was a creation that carried a direct threat to their very existence. The wilderness appeared both hostile and unpredictable. Puritan literature is replete with tales of the inhospitality of the wilderness: the bitter winters and the oppressively humid and mosquito-ridden summers. William Bradford writes, for example, of the sudden deaths of nearly half the initial Plymouth community: "But it pleased God to visit us then with death daily, and with so general a disease that the living were scarce able to bury the dead, and the well not in any measure sufficient to tend the sick."[12] During the first winter of Puritan settlement, inadequate housing in the bitter cold created such misery "soe that almost in every family lamentation, mourning and woe was heard, and no fresh food to be had to cherish them."[13]

Although the seacoast native American population had been decimated by a smallpox epidemic and the frontier communities were technically at peace with the natives, the stories of native American attacks were horrifying to the English imagination. The "tawney serpents" attacked "in a monstrous manner" at any time.[14] As the settlers wrote of the abundance of resources and the beauty of the land, they were reminded of the disasters that befell earlier communities. Writing to Governor John Endecott, who claimed to fear no enemies, Matthew Cradock warned of the suffering caused by "too much confidence in Virginia," a reference to the massacre of 347 persons by native Americans in 1622.[15] John Winthrop's journal entries from the early 1630s, as well as William Bradford's recollections, contain numerous references to external dangers and the need to fortify new communities. In the face of this hostile environment, the Puritans maintained an egalitarian form of political and religious organization.

Town Organization

Because not much was written by the Puritans during their first years of settlement, it is tempting to fill in these silences by focusing on later forms of Puritan political organization. Evidence for Richard Bushman's emphasis on the Puritan's concern with order, for example, comes from laws and sermons after 1637.[16] More recently, Theodore Dwight Bozeman's claim that John Winthrop and other Puritan leaders had clearly defined assumptions about "official prerogatives and acts of political officers" rests almost entirely on debates and journal entries that occur after 1636.[17]

The Puritans came to New England having given little thought to the internal structure of the community. There was "no preconceived plan of town organization to guide them in forming a body politic."[18] Certainly the Puritan leaders looked to biblical communities in creating the commonwealth. But the Bible was at best an indeterminant guide for wrestling with the practical exigencies of creating a community. Initially the General Court, the central governing body, consisting of Assistants annually elected by the freemen of the colony and led by a Governor and Deputy-Governor, assumed control over the direction of the Massachusetts Bay Colony; as the Assistants found themselves overwhelmed by commonwealth business, they quickly delegated much of their authority to the nascent towns and their representatives, even though these towns had no legal status.[19] "Each town, each leader, was on his own."[20] In the establishment of Sudbury, for example, the General Court did not define the administrative powers of the town leaders "with any precision" to allow the town to adjust to new situations.[21] One historian even goes so far as to note that "New England society" in these early years "was politically flexible."[22] There is support for this conclusion given Winthrop's ruling principle at this time that "in the infancy of plantations, justice should be administered with more lenity than in a settled state, because people were then more apt to transgress, partly of ignorance of new laws and orders, partly through oppression of business and other straits."[23]

In the early years of settlement, members of the new communities were left to improvise as needs arose. William Bradford, in writing about the election of Assistants in Plymouth in 1624, spoke of the need for a change in persons occupying these positions. If being an Assistant was an "honour or benefit, it was fit others should be made partakers of it"; if, however, "it was a burthen," then "it was but equal others should help to bear it."[24] In the first years of the formation of Sudbury, one sees a similar diffusion of authority. Like the early Boston settlement, the Sudbury government was "still flexible and experimental." Authority was granted to individuals sparingly, and then "for a limited time, at most a year." Power resided with the townspeople, who exercised this authority through monthly town meetings. Rather than there being officially prescribed roles, "When specific jobs had to be done," the nature of these jobs being impossible to predict too far into the future, "the townsmen looked around the meetinghouse to see who was there and who would assume the responsibilities." Over these initial years of town creation the citizens of the town invariably held a variety of posts—field surveyor, tithingman, highway surveyor, fence surveyor—shifting "from one type of job to another quite readily."[25]

The dispersion of authority resulting from this inattention to internal structure could be seen in such important community issues as the legal authority of the towns and the allocation of land. Not until 1636 did the Massachusetts commonwealth finally codify the authority of the town. The first bylaws were recorded in Sudbury only after a year of settlement. Land allocation was made without central direction, even when such direction was intended at the outset. Early land arrangements were often informal, "characterized by inexactness in distribution, inattention to recording, and neglect of the most basic statutory requirements of occupancy and fencing." This "hastily contrived" land system was "one born of convenience and necessity" due to needs for prompt cultivation, uncertain residential patterns, and lack of customs to guide behavior.[26]

This early political organization was not an individualistic one, though, as the community was closely bound together. Religious boundaries served as an important source of demarcation between those included and those excluded from the body politic. That there was a desire to create a tightly knit community is evidenced by early regulations by the General Court that no dwelling could be built more than one-half mile from the meetinghouse. Such actions, even as they failed, "revealed the lingering force of the communal paradigm" as the leaders of the Massachusetts Bay Colony attempted to maintain a cohesive, disciplined community.[27] Efforts were also made to establish barriers to entrance into the political community. In the Dedham Covenant signed by the founders of the community in 1636, the exclusivity of the community is made clear: "That we shall by all means labor to keep off from us all such as are contrary minded, and receive only such unto us as may be probably of one heart with us."[28] The goal was not a pluralistic community but one founded upon a unity of purpose and belief. Candidates for admission into the community were to undergo a public screening process in which the applicant's past was carefully scrutinized. Once admitted to the town, one still had to become a church member to be politically enfranchised.

Church Organization

The development of the ecclesiastical structure of the churches paralleled closely the evolution of town government. The leaders of the Massachusetts Bay Colony "had apparently given little thought to church polity while still in England; their letters to each other and their statements about the reasons for their departure and their intentions are silent on the point."[29] The sense one gets from the writings of these early Puritan immigrants was that the move to America was one of tumult, of a "flight from adversity" where, in John Cotton's words, the choice was to "perish uselessly in prison or leave the country."[30]

The church was seen as composed of a voluntary joining together of people. The foundation of all churches was the covenant in which people committed themselves to each other and to God. The importance of the covenant was that the church had no authority or existence apart from this agreement: "What made their church a church was their commitment to one another and to God, not presbyters or bishops' ordination."[31] The lines of authority in this early form of congregationalism were fluid. The church members elected both their pastor and teacher, a process Charles Gott referred to as an "outward calling which was from the people, when a company of believers are joined together in covenant to walk together in all the ways of God. And every member (being men) are to have a free voice in the choice of their officers."[32] There were also elders and deacons, laypersons who shared the top leadership positions. The ministers were extremely powerful in their authority as voicing God's word, but they were to be constantly monitored by church members for their faithfulness to the Bible. John Cotton, for example, spoke of the responsibility of the congregation "in whom fundamentally all power lyes" to limit the minister's authority.[33]

The Puritan church served as the main source of identity for its members, an identity, as we have seen, that spilled over into political and social practices. The life of the member was devoted not only to Sunday services and weekday lectures but to a "practice of piety" that absorbed the individual into the group. The Puritan life was one of "participation in a whole range of private and public devotional disciplines." Public worship, private meetings in homes designed to integrate "individuals into the devotional matrix of New England spirituality," family devotions, private counseling, the reading and studying of scripture, prayer, and personal writings were all essential to the practice of Puritanism.[34]

The egalitarian nature of Puritanism has been often noted in other studies of Puritanism.[35] But although certain egalitarian features persisted in Puritanism throughout the seventeenth century, egalitarianism becomes less useful in explaining Puritan social organization after the mid-1630s. Although the group remained tightly bound together, perhaps increasingly so, the internal structure of the group underwent significant changes. The fluid authority born of an equality of saints increasingly gave way to oligarchic authority and hierarchical patterns of social relationships.

THE DEVELOPMENT OF A
PURITAN HIERARCHY

By the middle of the 1630s, the Puritan's perception of the New England environment as hostile had subsided substantially. The risk of starvation, of dying from exposure to cold or heat, even of attack by the natives, had greatly diminished. With what had to be some relief, Winthrop noted in March 1637 in his *Journal* that the Pequods had been defeated at Mistick.[36] The references to the dangers of the New England environment that had filled the early pages of Winthrop's *Jour-*

nal declined. The sentiments for building a community of saints, whether as a model to the world or as a settlement in exile, had existed since the departure of the Puritans from England, but the demands of survival had averted any concerted effort toward constructing institutions that went beyond meeting day-to-day concerns to projecting their ideals into the future.[37] The community now turned its attention to consolidating the gains of the first years of settlement to ensure its permanence.

During this change in the "primary task" of the Puritans from "the destruction of traditional order" to the establishment of their own order, the egalitarian roots of the community were shaken as it became increasingly evident that all Puritans were not of one mind about the direction of the community.[38] This concern was not the result of any one event but grew out of a number of seemingly unrelated occurrences. Throughout the 1630s there had been increasing disillusionment among the leaders, for example, with the handling of land settlements. Alarmed by the social problems in England caused by increasing land rents and forfeitures, the leaders of the Massachusetts Bay Colony desired a just community in which all had access to land. By 1634 Winthrop expressed concern that the poor were being forced off their land, notable members of the community were hoarding corn to sell it when it became scarce, and land speculation was increasing. Having emigrated in the belief that it was English institutions and not innate human depravity that caused the pettiness they found all around them, the Puritans viewed with great alarm the persistence of this pettiness in their new community.[39]

The most significant harbinger of the dangers posed by what was seen increasingly as a deviant population was the Hutchinson affair, an event whose resolution was to have an impact beyond the Boston settlement.[40] Anne Hutchinson was to dramatically challenge the Boston leadership in her claim that the Puritan ministers preached a covenant of works rather than grace and that religious authority rested ultimately with private revelation. There is a perceptible shift, particularly in Boston, in the Puritan understanding of the environment after the Hutchinson affair. Where before the Puritan elite had placed some faith in the judgment of communicants, there emerged a growing sense that even those within the group could not be trusted. As Andrew Delbanco notes, in "reducing" Anne Hutchinson "the Puritan community was repudiating not so much an external threat as an uprising part of itself."[41] This anxiety arose because the people were seen as too easily fooled and too easily misled by corrupt principles. Winthrop noted, for example, how the people sympathized with Anne Hutchinson and her supporters and how quickly they condemned the true Puritans (Pastor John Wilson, in this case, whose continuance as pastor of the First Church of Boston had come under attack by the Hutchinsonians).[42]

A substantial number of Puritan leaders, John Winthrop among them, came to see themselves as involved in a sustained effort to prevent these corrupt social patterns and cultural orientations from exercising a significant influence over the definition of emerging social institutions. Winthrop's *Journal* entries, for example, changed from talk of native Americans, fortifications, and the administrative task of setting up new churches, to a preoccupation with corruption within the community.[43] Although depravity had always been central to a Puritan understanding of human nature, hope had been entertained that a community of saints could be established based on a voluntary gathering of God's elect. No longer convinced of this possibility that human nature was in some way retrievable, the Puritans found it increasingly difficult to resist the hierarchical argument for institutional restraints.[44]

The Puritan leadership's increasing concern with corruption did not end with the exile of Hutchinson and her followers. Instead, this anxiety was reinforced, as Stephen Foster has argued, by increasingly militant Puritans arriving in the late 1630s who were disillusioned by the failure of the Church of England to respond to their demand for radical ecclesiastical reforms. The concerns of this new group of Puritan exiles with constructing a purified, exclusive church separate from England reinforced the changing attitudes of the Massachusetts leaders. Adding to their increased anxiety was an influx of what was seen as an "English contagion" of Quaker, Baptist, and Anglican ideas. The Massachusetts Bay authorities, consequently, sought to "construct a theological cordon sanitaire around the inhabitants" that "began at times to approach the obsessive." The leadership, furthermore, attempted to "export its anxieties" to its neighbors by putting pressure on outlying towns to tolerate less dissent.[45] The institutions, at a most vulnerable point, were awash in a sea of corruption.

Town Organization

One can observe in Winthrop's words and actions a changing basis for social and political relations. Governor Winthrop had previously downplayed early efforts to establish a strict internal order. But after 1636, when Thomas Dudley attacked Governor Winthrop for his "lenity" in administering the commonwealth, Dudley's view would prevail; Winthrop would from this point on adopt a more hierarchical stance. Whether he was leading or following this tide, Winthrop was clearly in agreement with the most influential segments of the Puritan community in making this transition. In time, he became one of the most articulate spokesmen for the new oligarchy.

Out of this conflict between Dudley and Winthrop emerged the first significant attempts to centralize the authority of the commonwealth, to create a visible body of leaders who could control the development of civil institutions. Within this centralized body was an egalitarian call for the unity of delegates to the General Court, motivated by a concern that dissension would weaken the authority of this central body. Delegates were to "express their difference in all modesty," to express any disagreement as a question, or even to postpone the issue until time might bring all to agreement (or at least until the issue was no longer relevant). There was to be "more strictness used in civil government and military discipline." More important and more indicative of the move toward hierarchy were the injunctions requiring secrecy. Out of the court, the magistrates "should not discuss the business of parties in their presence, nor deliver their opinions," nor should any dissent in court be shown to others, either "publickly or privately." Secrecy provided an important insulation of the elite from the rest of the group, allowing the court to make and enforce laws without having to answer to public concerns. So important was secrecy for maintaining state control that less than a year later the ministers of the commonwealth would agree that no church officials should publicly question a magistrate for a speech made in the court because "the court may have sufficient reason that may excuse the sin, which yet may not be fit to acquaint the church with, being a secret of state."[46]

The General Court, concerned with the dispersion of power and the substantial discretion the towns had acquired, sought to consolidate its authority through the Town Act of March 3, 1636. The act, argues David Konig, was meant to carefully limit the powers of the towns. Even the powers that were granted to the towns in the Town Act would be overseen by the commonwealth government. "As a way of maintaining control over the towns and of being assured that they would not use their legal powers to gain too much autonomy, the General Court passed the famous Town Act (Order No. 285) only after it had created a supervisory level of magistratical government above the towns earlier that same day."[47]

The move toward a more centralized commonwealth authority was met with resistance, most notably by the town deputies, who had previously exercised substantial discretion. The town deputies saw as a "great danger to our state" the "want of positive laws" that might allow the magistrates to "proceed according to their discretions." The deputies thus proposed that "some men should be appointed to frame a body of ground of laws" that should be treated as "fundamental laws," laws that would presumably limit the arbitrary control of the magistrates. Six years later, in 1641, after a series of committees had worked on drafting just such a code, the Body of Liberties, which spelled out both protections and a range of punishments for different offenses, was finally enacted into law over Winthrop's opposition.[48]

In the development of the Body of Liberties, still more debate arose about the extent of discretion that should be allowed judges in meting out punishments. In 1644 the ongoing dispute between the magistrates and deputies was taken to the elders "to reconcile the differences." Of utmost importance was whether the standing council composed of the magistrates could act in place of the General Court when the court was not in session. After answering in the affirmative, the elders undertook a delicate balancing act with the remaining questions. With some revisions the recommendations of the elders were accepted by the court but for a "few leading men (who had drawn on the rest) [who] were still fixed upon their own opinions. So hard a matter it is, to draw men (even wise and godly) from the love of the fruit of their own inventions."[49]

Less than one year later, in May 1645, this concern of the deputies with the arbitrary power of the magistrates was to directly involve Winthrop. Accused by the town of Hingham of exceeding his authority in dealing with a mutiny against an unpopular court-imposed militia officer, Winthrop chose to defend his actions, in a sense placing himself (or being placed) on trial. The controversy, as Winthrop saw it, was that "two of the magistrates and many of the deputies were of opinion that the magistrates exercised too much power, and that the people's liberty was thereby in danger; and other of the deputies (being about half) and all the rest of the magistrates were of a different judgment, and that authority was overmuch slighted, which, if not timely remedied, would endanger the commonwealth, and bring us to a mere democracy."[50] The different sides may have framed their argument in the language of the Bible, as suggested by Bozeman, but the debate reflected a more generalizable conflict between the egalitarian suspicion of authority and the hierarchical interest in central control.

Having been "acquitted" of the charges, Winthrop made clear in his speech before the court what was at stake if the discretion he had earlier allowed was permitted to continue. In this speech Winthrop provided the understanding of magisterial authority that would be revised only with the overthrow of the Andros regime in 1689. Winthrop announced that the magistrate's authority is from God and that in all but clear cases of error magisterial proclamations must be obeyed or, in his words, "yourselves must bear it." Of fundamental importance for Winthrop was bridging the opposition between liberty and authority. Winthrop declared that moral liberty (as opposed to the license of a beast) depended upon "subjection to authority." Consider Winthrop's example of the proper model of such submission: "The woman's own choice makes such a man her husband; yet being so chosen, he is her lord, and she is to be subject to him, yet in a way of liberty, not of bondage; and a true wife accounts her subjection her honour and freedom, and would not think her condition safe and free, but in her subjection to her husband's authority." We are, as brides of Christ, to "cheerfully submit" to the "yoke" of authority.[51] Gone is the "communitarian" hope enunciated by Winthrop in his famous lay sermon aboard the *Arbella* en route to New England; in its place is a pronouncement of the need for the central authority of the magistrates.[52] Without such authority, the Christian commonwealth risked collapsing from its own sinfulness.

Depicting Winthrop as a transitional figure between an older, traditional time of deference and a more modern, "entrepreneurial" climate, as does Sacvan Bercovitch, is problematic because Winthrop becomes increasingly hierarchical even as he presumably becomes more modern.[53] The "direction" toward free enterprise that Bercovitch sees as "unmistakable" in the utterances of the likes of Winthrop is disputed by the increasing internal prescriptions enacted in the commonwealth. Land was distributed to maintain social distinctions.[54] So, too, a variety of social regulations, "the order on school and college class lists, the seating in many churches, and the use of honorifics ranging from 'goodman' upwards to 'esquire' all registered an individual's place in the social scale, and both the Massachusetts and Connecticut governments lent a hand by passing sumptuary legislation restricting fine apparel to men of quality."[55] We also see the entrenchment of a political elite in which the high turnover in office gave way to an established pattern of the same people being reelected to the same posts.[56]

In the continuing effort to enforce distinctions in the community, the Massachusetts General Court in 1653 sought to regulate lay preaching, which had been a customary practice, by establishing a strict licensing system. In defending the act, the court revealed its anxiety that "persons of bolder spirits and erroneous Principles may take advantage to vent their errours, to the infection of their hearers and the disturbance of the peace of the country." In the face of heavy resistance the court repealed the act only to come back in 1658 to a milder restriction with, in the words of Stephen Foster, "a solemn and awful preface."[57]

So entrenched would this hierarchical view become in Puritanism that Solomon Stoddard—who is often viewed as the most egalitarian of the Puritans because he opened his Northampton church to the community—upheld the importance of hierarchical authority. Stoddard saw the church not as "a confused body of people; but they that are brought into order, and each must observe his proper station: it is compared to a natural body, wherein there are diverse organs appointed to their peculiar services."[58] Consistent with the concern for order, Stoddard wrote of the unfitness of the community to "judge & rule in the Church" and called, instead, for control by the ministers and elders.[59]

To help secure the safety of the group from outside infiltration, group boundaries not only remained high but were enforced with a new harshness. After the Hutchinson affair, restrictions were placed on how long strangers could remain in the town. No household could entertain a stranger for more than a couple of weeks without consulting town authorities, nor could one receive a stranger who had an intent to reside in the town without consent of a member of the General Court or two other magistrates. Anabaptists were identified in colonial law as "infectors of persons" and were whipped.[60] In 1649 and 1650 the Massachusetts leadership was able to convince the Plymouth Colony to suppress "a newly formed Baptist church at Rehoboth, and in the next few years the colony whose deputies had approved universal toleration in 1645 proceeded to put its first comprehensive set of repressive laws on its statute books." In 1658 the Massachusetts General Court passed a law with a penalty of death to punish any nonresident Quakers in Massachusetts. Plymouth, New Haven, and Connecticut would follow with their own anti-Quaker laws.[61] In 1661, after horror was expressed over the execution of four Quakers, the law was repealed and substituted with the Cart and Whip Act. The Puritan elite, having won the battle with the wilderness, was now struggling to maintain the purity of its own community.

Church Organization

Just as the magistrates sought to centralize their authority, creating a more hierarchical form of political organization, so a similar—though less successful—movement occurred in the churches. One treads in dangerous waters in trying to draw general conclusions about the currents and crosscurrents of this church-organization controversy within the Puritan community. Proposals prompted counterproposals; nuanced and carefully crafted compromises were reached that often combined inconsistent aims. Most of all, one must always be aware that underlying the rejection of Presbyterianism in favor of congregational autonomy was a concern not with democracy or equality of the laity with the clerics, but with impurity. Efforts toward interchurch organization were met with lay resistance because such a structure reminded the laity of the corrupt national church they had left in England.

It is possible to identify an increasing concern during the course of the seventeenth century with restraining human impulses. This concern resulted in revisions in both the internal organization of the church and the relationship between churches. Although the hierarchical structures of, say, the Anglican church never appear, there is a perceptible change in the relationship of the ministers to the people, which gained force in the wake of the Hutchinson affair. Where before the ministers shared authority with the laypeople, beginning in the late 1630s a new era in church leadership began, one that appeared more patrimonial. This new style could be seen in two aspects of the minister's relationship with the rest of society: first, in how the minister became associated with a particular congregation and second, in the elevation of the minister's status and power. The concern with controlling the passions of church members also served as an important impetus behind the move toward the expansion of the power of synods.

In the first years of Puritan settlement the minister achieved his position by nature of election, both by God and the congregation. Consistent with what had been the Puritan disdain for artificial distinctions and fear of concentrated power, ordination was often performed by laypeople rather than by other ministers. By the mid-seventeenth century, in most churches the clergy began conducting the ordination ceremony themselves. No longer would authority, even symbolic authority, be shared with the congregation; rather, authority was to be contained within the elite. The power of the clergy was to be conferred by the clergy. By the eighteenth century the ordination day assumed great importance, increasingly seen and insisted upon by the ministry as a solemn occasion, not a day of celebration.[62] The ceremony made clear that ministers occupied a distinct social role. In keeping with this new detachment of the ministers from the congregation, it was argued increasingly that since authority did not derive from the congregations but from something like a universal church, the ministers were free not only to preach (which was always allowed) but also to administer the sacraments in congregations other than their own.[63] How times had changed from the first years of settlement when John Cotton could not baptize his own son at sea because he was not yet elected to a New England church!

The second change in the relationship of the minister to the rest of society was the elevation of the minister's status and power. The early egalitarian church was marked by "a priesthood of all believers," evidenced in the congregation's role in selecting its own ministers and the prominent role of the laypeople in governing the church. The religious elite began to enunciate a view of themselves as preeminent, superior, even elevated above the congregation. Who was fit to be a minister, who was unfit, who would serve in a particular congregation, increasingly became decisions of the ministerial elite and not of the congregation.[64] There also developed "a high-church conception of proper practice" among the Puritans, which recognized "an informal hierarchy of clerical leaders." The oldest minister was considered the religious leader of the area, and informal titles such as bishop were assigned to reflect this different status.[65]

This move to a more centralized authority occurred not only within the congregation but between churches as well. As the congregational church became the established system in New England and became tied to the political order, the state came to have a vested interest in the stability created by uniform standards and procedures. The civil authority, in Winthrop's own words, had become the "nursing fathers to the churches."[66] In 1636 the General Court called for the clergy to agree on "one uniforme order of discipline," a significant statement given the principle of congregational autonomy jealously guarded by the ministry.[67] There was ministerial support for a move to create an interchurch authority. John Cotton in 1644 called for the creation of synods in which leaders from each of the churches would meet and deal with questions of church policy. Under the watchful eye of a central authority, it was hoped, the church leadership could turn somewhere for help, mistakes could be corrected, and purity could be maintained.

In 1646 the magistrates of the Massachusetts General Court, acting in response to an application by some ministers, passed a bill summoning a meeting of the churches, or a synod. As in the Hingham affair involving Winthrop, this bill was met by opposition from the towns, which protested the mandate that the town churches "send their messengers to it" and that any "agreement upon one uniform practice in all the churches" would give disproportionate power to the synod or the General Court. An agreement was reached that the synod would take place by way of invitation rather than by command. The desire of the General Court, as stated in the call for the synod at Cambridge, was to arrive at agreement about "one forme of government & discipline."[68] The synod, wrote Cotton, "is the first subject of that power and authority whereby error is judicially convinced and condemned, the truth searched out, and determined, and the way of truth and peace declared and imposed upon the Churches."[69]

The reason behind the synods, in Cotton's mind, was not so much to correct the ministers as to protect the ministers from a potentially dangerous congregation. Cotton was careful to draw the distinction. A synod could, for example, prohibit "men with long haire, and women to speak in open assemblies, especially to pray with their haire loose about them," but it could not require ministers to "preach in a gown." The synod provided a place for a potentially besieged minister to turn. This was exactly the basis for Cotton's later statement, "In multitude of counsellers is safetie." The synod pointed to a growing separation between the ministers and the church members. If one church lacked "light or peace at home," it could ask "the counsell and helpe" of the other churches. And, perhaps most important, if one church "lyeth under scandall, through corruption in doctrine and practise," then the synodical organization could restore order to the congregation.[70] The result of the Cambridge synod was the Cambridge Platform of 1648, which, although deftly balancing the "unspecified blend of clerical aristocracy and lay democracy," tilted the balance in favor of the clerics.[71] The platform also included a discussion on the functions and powers of synods. Although synods were not absolutely necessary for the well-being of churches, they were seen as essential because of "the iniquity of men, & perversness of times." It was charged to "debate & determine controversies of faith, & cases of conscie[n]ce; to cleare from the word holy directions for the holy worship of God, & good government of the church; to beare witness against mal-administration & Corruption in doctrine or man[n]ers in any particular Church, & to give directions for the reformation thereof."[72] Thus, the synod, as it subordinated individual churches to its direction, would serve as an important institution for restraining and correcting human impulses. The synod provided guidance and support ("safetie," in Cotton's words) through its power to correct mistakes and declare the truth.

The increasing prescriptions intended to regulate behavior within the group were matched by heightened group boundaries. Within the church the noncommunicants were now physically segregated from the communicants. Standards for church membership changed dramatically. Good behavior was no longer sufficient. Rather, as Edmund Morgan suggests, beginning in 1635 proof of one's saving faith became a requisite for membership. As might be expected, new church membership declined. Between January 1637 and December 1638, for example, no new members were admitted. The possibility of moving the churchgoer to salvation, something Winthrop had early on suggested, was now firmly rejected. Cotton, for example, suggested in 1641 that "neither Jews nor any more of the Gentiles should be called until Antichrist were destroyed, viz. to a church estate, though here and there a proselyte."[73] The Cambridge Platform spelled out the function of the officers as "keeping the doors of the Church," allowing entrance only to those who had been "examined & tryed first."[74] Through the requirement of a personal and public confession of faith, the Puritans managed to keep the doors shut to prospective members.

CULTURAL THEORY AND THE
HISTORICAL PROCESS

Cultural theory has not been used primarily as a tool for understanding historical development. Its main objective has been more a Durkheimian one of "seeking transhistorical generalizations about types of social systems" than a Weberian one of understanding how certain social structures develop from earlier ones. This does not mean that cultural theory is ahistorical; rather, it has been argued, employing a distinction made by Samuel Beer, cultural theory has been "more interested in history as past behavior than history as development."[75]

Making explicit what has been implicit in this analysis, I want to suggest that cultural theory makes an important contribution to the Weberian approach of "Verstehen" in understanding the historical process. This method requires the researcher to work "with reference to values, beliefs, and attitudes of a group; the situation confronting it; and the action which has been or will be taken." Through this act of subjective understanding, the analyst in some sense seeks to reconstruct the characters and events of the time with reference to "their values" as they confronted "the forces of the time and place as they saw them." By engaging in this imaginative reconstruction, the analyst attempts to understand and explain the historical actors' "processes of reaction and decision." The model, thus, not only seeks to "describe uniformities of behavior" but also "tells why the uniformities occurred."[76]

A common criticism of this method of "Verstehen" is that the analyst must somehow, through what Samuel Beer calls "mysterious intuition," make an "'intuitive leap' into" the "subjective consciousness" of the historical actors. Beer suggests that no such leap is necessary; rather, "imagination and empathy" allow us to trace the behavioral tendencies of the actors. This imagination is not of a mystical kind, according to Beer, but involves the "capacity for vicarious experience" that allows us in our everyday life to put ourselves in the place of another person.[77]

Such a response is not entirely satisfactory, however, because the sort of empathetic understanding we engage in throughout our everyday lives is rarely systematized. It is at this point that cultural theory proves invaluable in providing a basis (other than our day-to-day practice of empathy) for engaging in subjective understanding. Cultural theory systematizes empathy by providing testable hypotheses about the relationship between perceptions of the world and patterns of social relations. Cultural theory provides a model for understanding the "processes of reaction and decision" by showing how culture orients behavior, and how this is tied to changes in perceptions. In the case of Puritanism, political and religious organizations were transformed from egalitarian to hierarchical as the Puritans revised their understanding of human nature and the external environment.

Egalitarianism, suitable as an ideology for challenging constituted authority, proved insufficient once the Puritans had to establish their own authority. Imbued with a desire to create a community founded on the equality of visible saints, the Puritans found such equality increasingly untenable. The Puritans had always seen corruption in the institutions that surrounded them in England but had always sensed that they could escape this corruption through a voluntary covenant pledging their devotion to God and to each other. The experience in New England, marked by bickering over property and profoundly influenced by the Hutchinsonian assault on the established order, demonstrated the danger of such equality: How could the direction of Puritan institutions be controlled by a people so easily misled and so easily corrupted? Where before institutions were seen as part of the problem in leading a pure life—and thus we see the strong support for congregational autonomy and lay participation in the calling of a minister—the Puritans came to see the institution, with more centralized authority and greater regulation of behavior, as a necessary means to hold human corruption in check. Only by creating hierarchical institutions could the Puritan community be saved from its own sinfulness.

NOTES

Parts of this chapter were first presented at the 1990 American Historical Association in New York City. My thanks to Susan Strandberg for her coauthorship of the earlier version and to Stef Jonkman for her assistance and insightful comments in developing this chapter.

1. Richard L. Bushman, *From Puritan to Yankee: Character and the Social Order in Connecticut, 1690–1765* (New York: W. W. Norton, 1967), 3.

2. See Darrett B. Rutman, *Winthrop's Boston: A Portrait of a Puritan Town, 1630–1649* (Chapel Hill: University of North Carolina Press, 1965); and Kenneth A. Lockridge, *A New England Town: The First Hundred Years, Dedham, Massachusetts, 1636–1736* (New York: W. W. Norton, 1970).

3. Sacvan Bercovitch, *The American Jeremiad* (Madison: University of Wisconsin Press, 1978), 22.

4. See Theodore Dwight Bozeman, *To Live Ancient Lives: The Primitivist Dimension in Puritanism* (Chapel Hill: University of North Carolina Press, 1988).

5. Bushman, *Puritan to Yankee*. It is significant that Bushman's evidence for the concern with order comes from laws and sermons after 1637.

6. Michael Thompson, Richard Ellis, and Aaron Wildavsky, *Cultural Theory* (Boulder: Westview Press, 1990), 25–37.

7. Ibid., 3–4. Also see 69–75.

8. Stephen Foster, "The Godly in Transit: English Popular Protestantism and the Creation of a Puritan Establishment in America," *Seventeenth Century New England* (Boston: Colonial Society of Massachusetts, 1984), 195.

9. Michael Walzer, *The Revolution of Saints: A Study in the Origins of Radical Politics* (Cambridge, Mass.: Harvard University Press, 1965), 318.

10. Ibid., 221, 318, 121, 56–57, 170.

11. Ibid., 55; Thompson, Ellis, and Wildavsky, *Cultural Theory,* 6.

12. William Bradford, *Of Plymouth Plantation,* ed. Samuel Eliot Morison (New York: Alfred A. Knopf, 1952), 95.

13. Samuel Eliot Morison, *Builders of the Bay Colony* (Boston: Houghton Mifflin, 1930), 81.

14. Sumner Chilton Powell, *Puritan Village: The Formation of a New England Town* (Middletown, Conn.: Wesleyan University Press, 1963), 114.

15. Alexander Young, *Chronicles of the First Planters of the Colony of Massachusetts Bay 1623–1636* (New York: De Capo Press, 1970), 136.

16. See Bushman, *Puritan to Yankee.*

17. Bozeman, *Ancient Lives,* 158.

18. Rutman, *Winthrop's Boston,* 41.

19. See John Winthrop, *The History of New England from 1630 to 1649,* ed. James Savage (New York: Arno Press, 1972), vol. 1, 128–129, 132.

20. Powell, *Puritan Village,* 5.

21. Ibid., 80.

22. T. H. Breen, *The Character of the Good Ruler* (New Haven: Yale University Press, 1970), 37.

23. Winthrop, *History,* vol 1, 178.

24. Bradford, *Plymouth Plantation,* 140.

25. Powell, *Puritan Village,* 98–99.

26. David Thomas Konig, "Community Custom and the Common Law: Social Change and the Development of Land Law in Seventeenth-Century Massachusetts," *The American Journal of Legal History* 18(1974), 137–138.

27. Ibid., 30.

28. Lockridge, *New England Town,* 5.

29. Rutman, *Winthrop's Boston,* 47.

30. Bozeman, *Ancient Lives,* 109.

31. Harry S. Stout, *The New England Soul: Preaching and Religious Culture in Colonial New England* (New York: Oxford University Press, 1986), 18.

32. Bradford, *Plymouth Plantation,* 225.

33. Quoted in Stout, *New England Soul,* 19.

34. Charles E. Hambrick-Stowe, *The Practice of Piety: Puritan Devotional Disciplines in Seventeenth-Century New England* (Chapel Hill: University of North Carolina Press, 1982), 23, 138.

35. See Dennis E. Owen, "Spectral Evidence: The Witchcraft Cosmology of Salem Village in 1692," in Mary Douglas, ed., *Essays in the Sociology of Perception* (London: Routledge & Kegan Paul, 1982); and Stephen Foster, "English Puritanism and the Progress of New England Institutions, 1630–1660," in David D. Hall, John M. Murrin, and Thad W. Tate, *Saints and Revolutionaries: Essays on Early American History* (New York: W. W. Norton, 1984).

36. John Winthrop, *History,* vol. 1, 225.

37. For the overriding importance of security, see ibid., 39 (fn.) as well as his journal entry on that page.

38. Walzer, *Revolution of Saints,* 3.

39. Delbanco, *Puritan Ordeal,* 77, 80.

40. For a documentary history of the Hutchinson affair, see David D. Hall, *The Antinomian Controversy, 1636–1638* (Middletown, Conn.: Wesleyan University Press, 1968).

41. Andrew Delbanco, *The Puritan Ordeal* (Cambridge, Mass.: Harvard University Press, 1989), 138.

42. Winthrop, *History,* vol 1, 210.

43. See, for example, ibid., 280; vol. 2, 47, 72.

44. See Thompson, Ellis, and Wildavsky, *Cultural Theory,* 34.

45. Foster, "English Puritanism," 32–33.

46. Winthrop, *History,* vol. 1, 178–179, 214.

47. Konig, "Community Custom and Common Law," 26.

48. Winthrop, *History,* vol. 1, 160.

49. Ibid., vol. 2, 204, 209.

50. Ibid., 226.

51. Ibid., 229–230.

52. Delbanco, *Puritan Ordeal,* 74.

53. See, for example, Bercovitch, *American Jeremiad,* 22.

54. David Hackett Fischer, *Albion's Seed: Four British Folkways in America* (New York: Oxford University Press, 1989), 166–167.

55. Stephen Foster, *Their Solitary Way: The Puritan Social Ethic in the First Century of Settlement in New England* (New Haven: Yale University Press, 1971), 28.

56. Robert Emmet Wall, Jr., *Massachusetts Bay: The Crucial Decade 1640–1650* (New Haven, Conn.: Yale University Press, 1972), 24.

57. Foster, *Their Solitary Way,* 35.

58. Solomon Stoddard, *The Way for a People to Live Long in the Land That God Hath Given Them* (Boston, 1705), 61, quoted in Fischer, *Albion's Seed,* 190.

59. Perry Miller, *The New England Mind: From Colony to Province* (Cambridge, Mass.: Belknap Press, 1953), 234, 258–259.

60. Cited in Winthrop, *History,* vol. 2, 174–177(fn.).

61. Foster, "English Puritanism," 33–34.

62. See J. William T. Youngs, Jr., *God's Messengers: Religious Leadership in Colonial New England, 1700–1750* (Baltimore: Johns Hopkins University Press, 1976), 36–37.

63. See Youngs, *God's Messengers,* 66.

64. See, for example, William Williams, *The Office and Work of Gospel Ministers* (Boston, 1729), 16; Nathaniel Appleton, *Superior Skill and Wisdom Necessary for Winning Souls* (Boston, 1737), 50; Youngs, *God's Messengers,* 67, 35–37.

65. Youngs, *God's Messengers,* 67–68.

66. Williston Walker, *The Creeds and Platforms of Congregationalism* (Philadelphia: Pilgrim Press, 1960), 167, 172; Winthrop, *History,* vol. 2, 330.

67. Quoted in Robert F. Scholz, "Clerical Consociation in Massachusetts Bay: Reassessing the New England Way and Its Origins," *William and Mary Quarterly,* 29(1972), 404.

68. Walker, *Creeds,* 167–168, 170.

69. Quoted in Rutman, *Winthrop's Boston,* 134.

70. John Cotton, *The Keyes of the Kingdom of Heaven, and Power Thereof, According to the Word of God* (London, 1644). Quoted in Rutman, *Winthrop's Boston,* 133.

71. Foster, "English Puritanism," 28.

72. Walker, *Creeds,* 233–234.

73. Rutman, *Winthrop's Boston,* 148; also see 152, 144.

74. Walker, *Creeds,* 222.

75. Richard J. Ellis, "The Case for Cultural Theory: Reply to Friedman," *Critical Review* 7(Winter 1993), 99. See Samuel H. Beer, "Political Science and History," in Melvin A. Richter, ed., *Essays in Theory and History* (Cambridge, Mass.: Harvard University Press, 1970), 41–73.

76. Beer, "Political Science," 55, 51, 48.

77. Ibid., 52, 51.

PART THREE

THEORY

CHAPTER 8

Culture, Rationality, and Violence

Sun-Ki Chai
and Aaron Wildavsky

At first glance, the brutal world of political violence may seem unrelated to the niceties of culture. Nonetheless, culture, conceived as the relationship between shared values and social relations, is a key to explaining the conditions under which individuals and groups will engage in violence and the types of violence that they will employ. Furthermore, although culture and rationality have long been seen as opposing explanations for political phenomena,[1] cultural variables are particularly important for providing coherent rational choice explanations of many types of political behavior, including violent collective action.

In this chapter, we examine two types of rational choice explanations for the use of political violence. One type of explanation assumes that individuals are simply pursuing their material self-interest. We will argue that from such a point of view, numerous aspects of political violence seem paradoxical and irrational. Another type of explanation makes individuals' goals exogenous (i.e., external to the explanatory model), leaving them to be inferred from observed behavior or subject to ad hoc assumptions. But because such explanations cannot account for the nature of goals, they are difficult to use predictively. Cultural theory can help address this gap in rational choice explanation because it explicitly deals with how the goals of individuals are shaped by their culture and how culture is in turn shaped by the constraints of social viability. At the same time, it is quite compatible with the assumption that individuals act rationally to maximize these goals.

We will first address shortcomings in rational choice and nonrational choice explanations of political violence, concentrating in particular on the inability of existing theories to explain why antistate collective violence should occur at all. We will then present a rational choice interpretation of cultural theory, showing how cultural theory's basic assumptions can be incorporated directly into assumptions about individual preferences and beliefs. We will also present an analysis of political violence based on this interpretation, showing how the theory can not only explain the existence of and conditions for violence but also cast light on characteristics of violence that might otherwise appear irrational. In this way, we hope not only to provide improved explanations for political violence but also to open a path to integrating rational choice with cultural explanations of political behavior.

THE "PARODOX" OF POLITICAL VIOLENCE

Any discussion of political violence should begin with an apparent paradox: Under almost all plausible circumstances, it seems irrational for materially oriented, self-interested individuals to engage in collective political violence. The main reason for this apparent irrationality lies not in any presumed inherent hatred of violence but in the so-called free-rider problem.[2] If we assume rationality, there is no reason for individuals to participate in any type of violent activity unless the expected benefit (according to the individual's preferences) from such an activity exceeds the costs. Since most rationalist theories of political action assume that individuals seek only to maximize their personal material welfare, this implies that there must be a material reward involved in political violence that more than compensates for the high risks. However, there seem to be very few cases of collective political violence when this is a reasonable assumption.

As a number of theorists have noted, the participation or nonparticipation in violence of a rank-and-file member of a political group can have only a small effect on the group's probability of success. Furthermore, the member will rarely receive substantial "selective incentives" (personal, nonshared rewards) for participation; his main incentive will be the benefits that result from the advancement of the group as a whole. However, he will generally not be excluded from these benefits even if he has not contributed to their achievement.[3] Hence, the paradox arises: It seems under most circumstances irrational for materialistic, self-interested individuals to participate in collective violent activity.[4]

Several rational choice explanations have been proposed to resolve this and related paradoxes of individual participation in high-risk collective action. An explanation put forward by Samuel Popkin to explain peasant rebellions emphasizes the role of political entrepreneurs who organize efforts either by providing selective incentives to those who participate or by convincing individuals that their contributions are crucial to the achievement of group goals.[5] Another explanation, proposed by Michael Taylor, focuses on how the close monitoring that exists within peasant communities can ensure that contributors can be singled out and selectively rewarded.[6]

Other authors focus on how an individual's effect on a particular collectively desired outcome can be magnified by various aspects of the environment surrounding political groups. Dennis Chong focuses on "all-or-nothing public goods," for example, shared goals that can be achieved only if virtually all the members of the group participate. Such goals increase the incentive for individual members to participate, since each member's participation makes a significant difference in whether the goal is achieved and hence to their own personal benefits.[7] Susanne Lohmann discusses the "signaling" effect of political action on the decisions of government leaders. She posits that government leaders will estimate individuals' positions on a particular issue from their willingness to participate despite the costs that are associated with that participation. Because of this, the signaling effects of participation will increase with its cost, which in turn provides some compensatory benefits.[8]

Although each of these explanations provides plausible reasons that participation in revolutionary activity might be higher in certain cases than predicted by conventional rational choice theories, each has serious shortcomings as a basis for explaining the levels and types of violence employed by different types of revolutionary groups. Those concerned with entrepreneurs and their effect on selective incentives are unclear about the process by which such "violence entrepreneurs" arise and about the basis for their ability to credibly supply selective incentives.[9] Those explanations that focus on close-knit social communities cannot easily be extended to account for high-risk collective action outside those communities, nor can they account for the origin of such communities. Those concerned with all-or-nothing goods are less relevant to antistate violence than they are to nonviolent means of protest such as boycotts, since it is unlikely that the failure of one individual to engage in violence will have much of an impact. Those concerned with signaling effects likewise seem less relevant to violence than to peaceful demonstrations in democratic societies, since the additional incentives provided by signaling effects cannot plausibly compensate for the risks of violent activity.

As a possible antidote to the problems of conventional preference assumptions, some authors put forth explanations that allow for more inclusive preferences, asserting that individuals are seeking various social or expressive benefits from participation rather than simple material gain. The major effort in this direction is the sizable literature on frustration and aggression pioneered by authors such as Ted Gurr and James Davies. Although such theorists accept the notion that individuals are self-interested and materialistic, they also posit the existence of another source of motivation: frustration. According to these theorists, frustration will result from the failure to reach goals, and this frustration will tend to increase aggression independently of whether this aggression promotes material goals. There is no assumption in this literature, however, that individuals are irrational. Instead, the assumption is that while individuals are pursuing material goals, aggression has its own inherent utility in the presence of frustration. It is "innately satisfying."[10] Although this assumption is a possible explanation for how violence can occur despite the presence of free-riding incentives, it does not provide an endogenous theory for explaining the amount of utility that can be gained from aggression given particular levels of frustration. Without such a theory, the exact point at which frustration turns into aggression is not specified.

Other theories of violence are even more inclusive, allowing utility to arise from social status and reputation, altruistic effects, and self-actualization.[11] Clearly, each of these types of preferences can significantly affect the calculation of incentives in revolutionary activity. However, such theories do not provide methodologies to account for the origins of such preferences or to predict the variations in the nature and intensity of those preferences among different individuals. This in turn makes such theories difficult to use as a basis for predicting behavior.

These issues are important not only for rational choice theories but also for theories of political violence in general because virtually all of them implicitly either accept the assumption that actors are maximizing their material welfare or posit the goals of actors as exogenous. Much of current analysis of political violence in the literature on rebellion and revolution is "structural" in the sense that analysts attempt to predict the social and economic conditions under which political violence will occur. Such analysis places much of its emphasis on societies as a whole rather than on the incentives facing the actors within them.[12]

Nonetheless, since violence is after all a type of action, each theory requires at least some model for predicting why political actors behave as they do, even if to claim that structural conditions give them little choice over their actions. Here, theories of political violence generally assume that antistate actors are pursuing their own material self-interest and are doing so in a more or less rational manner. Furthermore, actors are usually not individuals but revolutionary groups or classes that are treated as unitary entities. Such theories simply assume away the free-rider problem without explaining why members would be willing to always act in the collective interest of the group, a shortcoming that has not gone unnoticed by rational choice theorists.[13]

Such theories assume that states, however, can pursue anything from material interest to development to rigid control over society. But the basis of these different goals is not specified; it remains exogenous.[14] More recent explanations emphasize ideological preferences and beliefs as important explanatory variables in revolution,[15] but systematic, deductive explanations of where such preferences and beliefs come from are lacking, hampering the use of such variables as a basis for prediction.

CULTURAL THEORY AND RATIONAL CHOICE

For prediction to be possible, what is needed is a theory that can account for the origin of individual preferences and beliefs, for the group structures that determine the conditions for revolutionary action, and for the form that such action will take. This is exactly what cultural theory can provide.

Cultural theory is more than simply a taxonomy, because each category has a wide range of implications for preferences and beliefs, as well as for action across a wide range of environments. As noted at the beginning of this chapter, cultural theory is completely compatible with the assumption of rationality. Each way of life leads to stable patterns of interactions only if there are certain distinctive shared values, attitudes, and cognitions among those who follow that way of life. Furthermore, the characteristics of each culture can be specified as a set of defining preferences and beliefs that are shared by members of the culture, and as the kinds of rational interactions these preferences and beliefs will engender.

Finally, according to cultural theory's "impossibility theorem," the four grid-group variations reflect the only possible ways of organizing social life that can persist over time.[16] This certainly does not mean that individuals are mentally incapable of other sorts of preferences and beliefs, but it does mean that without such preferences and beliefs, patterns of social interaction will be inherently unstable. Hence those preferences and beliefs that tend to persist over time are those that are capable of supporting viable social institutions.

Low-group cultures are characterized, among other things, by individual preferences that emphasize self-interest and personal welfare; high-group cultures are characterized by some sort of concern for the welfare of the bounded collectivity. High-grid cultures are characterized, among other things, by beliefs and preferences that make adherence to role-based rules of individual conduct utility-maximizing. These include either (1) beliefs that choices besides those prescribed by rules are unviable because of the high costs attached to them or (2) preferences (internalized norms) that value following the rules for their own sake. Low-grid cultures are characterized by beliefs and preferences that make such rules unnecessary for stable patterns of interaction.

The impossibility theorem implies that because only four constellations of individual preferences and beliefs can support stable social institutions, individuals interacting within a particular social institution will in the long run inevitably share one of the four. Hence, cultural theory's assumptions about the constraints on preference and belief rest upon a kind of functional argument, which in turn depends on a natural selection justification.[17] Although some might argue that rationalist and functional analysis are opposed to each other, functional analysis has long been used to justify assumptions about preferences in conventional rational choice theories of behavior. In particular, it has long been argued that firms maximize profits, politicians maximize votes, and states maximize power because these actors who fail to develop such preferences will be "selected out" and cease to exist.[18] Cultural theory applies such arguments to social institutions, positing that for institutions to survive, individuals within them must exhibit certain characteristic preferences and beliefs.

The notion of culturally defined beliefs, in particular, clashes with the assumption often found in rational choice theories that beliefs are derivable either from direct perception or from logical-statistical inferences from that perception—

what is generally referred to as "information." However, this conventional notion is not essential to the assumption of rational choice and lacks verisimilitude over a very wide range of human behavior. Indeed, in many, if not most, political contexts, beliefs based solely on information are insufficient for rendering rational judgments because they do not generate expectations about the relative utilities offered by each available alternative.[19]

In those cases, decisions depend on cultural biases. These biases are preferences and beliefs of individuals that support and are based on a particular way of organizing life. Furthermore, they provide a sufficient basis for rational decision-making under a wide range of circumstances in which information and self-interested materialism are insufficient. Hence, far from saying that culture is the antithesis to rationality, cultural theory says the opposite: Culture is essential for rationality because in many, if not most, situations rational decisionmaking would be impossible without the existence of culturally based preferences and beliefs.

For instance, because fatalists follow a low-group way of life, those within this culture have no special incentives to interact within a bounded social group. Because they are high grid, however, their behavior is prescribed by role-determined rules. However, since there is no strong group to provide these rules, fatalists see their behavior as completely constrained by unvarying forces within their environment. Fatalists will feel so constrained only when they believe they have little or no ability to alter their environment.

Hence, fatalists believe that nature is unpredictable, a lottery where outcomes have little relationship to actions. Given this, there is no reason for them to invest resources and take risks, since they will have to bear the cost of such investments without affecting outcomes one iota. Furthermore, other individuals must be seen as unreliable and opportunistic to the point that any attempts at cooperative action will probably be met with a sucker's payoff because others will fail to cooperate in return. Hence the the only rational behavior is to minimize the expenditure of resources and to act in a noncooperative manner no matter what the circumstances.

Fatalists are generally self-interested in their preferences. Even though it is possible that their preferences contain an element of concern for others, this has little effect on behavior because fatalists believe that there is little they can do to alter their environment—which implies that there is also little that they can do to improve others' welfare. Any resources expended in such an effort will just be lost, with no corresponding gain for the intended recipient.

Given these beliefs and preferences, the behavior of fatalists is rigidly dictated by their existing social and economic roles, and they follow unchanging routines that have provided for survival in those roles in the past. Fatalist peasants plant the same crops year after year in the same way regardless of what other opportunities are available, hoping to provide enough for themselves to subsist upon. Fatalist proletarians do the minimum amount of work necessary to retain their jobs, and they do not voluntarily comply with any attempt to alter their routines because they see such changes as plots to reduce their standard of living.

Because individualists, like fatalists, are low group, they have no special incentives to interact within a particular collectivity. However, because they are also low grid, their behavior does not follow role-based rules. Individualist behavior can lead to stable patterns of interaction only when preferences and beliefs promote decentralized institutions of cooperation, institutions that depend on negotiated exchange.

In order for such institutions to come about, individualists must have an essentially optimistic view of nature and of other individuals. At least where markets are initially being formed, information is usually insufficient for developing well-founded expectations about the return on any investment. Hence, for investments to be made, rational individualists must have a culturally determined predisposition to believe that many types of investments will provide a return that exceeds the costs involved.

A similar logic holds for cooperation. In most types of transactions, it is rational for a person to cooperate only if she expects her counterpart(s) to cooperate as well. However, as rational choice analysts often note, it is impossible to predict from information-based beliefs just how other people will act in most repeated transactions, even given the additional belief that other individuals are rational. Hence, for cooperation to occur, individualists must initially believe that other individuals can and will behave cooperatively under conditions of bargaining and bidding where both individuals' long-term payoffs for mutual cooperation exceed the payoffs for mutual noncooperation. They will themselves be willing to act cooperatively under such situations, barring any overt act of noncooperation on the part of others.

Individualists, like fatalists, generally are self-interested in their preferences. However, they also believe that self-interested actions in a system of open exchange maximize the welfare of all, hence they see no clash between self-interest and concern for others. They believe that any attempt at philanthropy or a redistribution of wealth has negative side effects that result in diminishment of welfare not only for those from whom resources are being taken but also for the intended beneficiaries. Hence, even when an individualist has altruistic preferences, it will be rational for her to act as if she is maximizing only her own welfare.

. Because egalitarians are high group and low grid, they center their social interactions within a bounded group; yet their behavior is not prescribed by any role-based rules imposed by the group. Hence role definition, who should do what, is characteristically vague. Such patterns of social interactions can occur only if group members have shared preferences or beliefs that create special incentives for collective action with each other rather than with those outside of the group.

One way in which such incentives can be provided is through preferences that place an inherent positive value on the welfare of the group as a whole. A number of theorists have noted that such "other-regarding" preferences can have a major effect on the likelihood of cooperative collective action.[20] In particular, an inherent value placed on group welfare raises the relative benefits for cooperation vis-à-vis free riding within the group, hence increasing the likelihood of collective action. Likewise, a negative inherent value placed on the welfare of those deemed outside group boundaries decreases the chances of collective action with those outsiders.

The other primary way in which incentives can be provided is through a set of shared preferences with regard to the nature of society, as well as through shared beliefs about how these preferences can be realized. These shared preferences can be used to define the group boundary, and group activity can be oriented primarily toward realizing them. However, use of shared preferences as the guarantor of unity puts a high price on the maintenance of group consensus. Any dissent can weaken the boundaries of a group by creating the possibility of intragroup conflict and may also lead members to look for allies outside the group. Because the egalitarian culture is low grid, there are no clear rules for resolving disagreements. Hence, even small disagreements about goals can lead to dissolution of group boundaries. This means that such groups must continuously stress the purity of their ideology and make devotion to the group the all-encompassing focus of their members' lives. Furthermore, the need for consensus makes alliances between the group and other groups very difficult because each compromise must be agreed to by all group members before consensus can occur.

Because of egalitarians' need for consensus, one preference shared by all egalitarian groups is a desire for the minimization of inequality (hence their name). Because of the low-grid nature of the group, inequality cannot be justified by formal role differentiation. Hence, any unusual accumulation of resources by a subset of group members creates differences between the goals of these members and those of other members. Such differences tend to weaken group boundaries, hence inequality must be avoided at all costs.

Because of the preference for equality, when egalitarian groups attempt to expand their boundaries to other parts of society, they often try to bring in those who have the most to gain from such goals, that is, those they perceive to be the least fortunate. However, unless the least fortunate are themselves egalitarians, attempts to integrate them will be unsuccessful. Fatalists do not believe that they can gain from joining a group; hierarchists are content with the group that they belong to. Individualists may join as long as they perceive that personal gains can be made from doing so, but they will leave as soon as the group's goals diverge from their own.

Hierarchists, like egalitarians, are high group. Hence they also center their social interactions within the boundaries of clearly defined collectivities. And like egalitarians' interactions, theirs are promoted by preferences that place an inherent positive value on the welfare of the group as a whole, as well as by preferences that place a negative value on the welfare of those outside the group.

However, because they are high grid, hierarchists also maintain their group unity through rigidly prescribed rules that can be attached to formally designated roles of unequal status and power. Such rules specify how members should act in their relationships with other members, depending on their respective designated ranks, as well as the appropriate division of resources and benefits. The rules are confined to within-group interactions and minimize the amount of within-group conflict. Furthermore, since they do not extend outside of group boundaries, they inhibit cooperation with outsiders.

In order for rule adherence to be rational, however, the rules must be internalized, that is, supported by individual preferences and beliefs. Internalization can include preferences that place an inherent value on fulfilling one's designated duty within the group, as well as beliefs that the existing system of roles maximizes both individual and group welfare. Usually, the rules that are internalized are not only those that directly prescribe behaviors for each role but also metarules that endow the occupants of certain leadership roles with the right to set further rules. When hierarchy is defined in this manner, compromise and gradual modification of group structure are possible as long as those who have authority are willing to accept such changes.

CULTURE AND VIOLENCE

Of course, providing a functional, evolutionary argument for the distinctive preferences and beliefs of each culture does not demonstrate that the resulting categories have useful explanatory power. This can only come from applying them to real-world analytical issues. In this section, we apply the categories and their implications to the question of political violence. We discuss the use of violence by each culture, both as state and antistate actors (the sole exception being fatalists, who never take control of the state). As is shown, the "paradox of participation" is hardly the only anomaly that results from materialistic, self-interested assumptions about the preferences of revolutionaries. In fact, there are numerous aspects of strategy followed by revolutionary groups that cannot be made sense of and in fact appear irrational without the aid of cultural theory.

Adherents of each culture are capable of violent action, but the circumstances that foster such action and the nature of the violence employed differs from culture to culture. Furthermore, the particular circumstances and characteristics of violence can be shown to follow logically from the defining preferences and beliefs just identified.

Fatalists

Fatalists do not believe in revolution. The idea that major changes in the governing structure will have any substantial effect on their condition or that of the people around them contradicts their basic beliefs that they have no power to control their environment. The more things change, the more things stay the same. Any involvement in risky activity is out of the question; there are no benefits to compensate for the inevitable costs. Therefore, fatalists try their best to avoid the beckonings of revolutionary entrepreneurs.

This does not mean that fatalists are incapable of violence. However, the type of violence they engage in is personal and the intention is defensive. Fatalists believe that other people are untrustworthy, hence they must under certain conditions be stopped with violence before they can do any damage. In a society lacking strong restraints on the use of violence, this attitude can lead to a tendency to strike before being struck, that is, to anarchic violence.

This fatalistic attitude can explain why violence in fatalistic cultures (the American urban underclass and Southern Italian peasants are two classic examples) is often inwardly directed, directed toward one's own people, rather than toward the state or outside population, which may in fact be blamed for the fatalist's plight. Without the aid of cultural theory, one might be tempted to call such behavior irrational and anomalous. However, it can be seen as rational in light of the fatalist's belief system, in which no one is trustworthy and everyone is out for himself. This belief is rational in equilibrium because it is self-fulfilling: If one believes this of others, then one will rationally behave in an untrustworthy way toward them, which in turn makes it rational for them to behave similarly in return. This in turn means that violence is not aimed on the basis of who is to blame but on the basis of proximity and frequent interaction.

Because they believe that cooperation with others is self-defeating, fatalists are not capable of the large-scale collective action necessary to gain state power. Hence, the question of what sort of violence fatalists demonstrate when they control the state is moot; such control never occurs.

Individualists

The competitive individualist does believe that changes in the governing structure are possible and that such changes can have a major effect on her personal welfare. However, two major factors inhibit her participation in collective political violence. The first is the nature of her preferences. Because she is part of a low-group culture, her preferences are primarily self-regarding; hence she is unlikely to place much emphasis on self-sacrifice for others in her decision on whether to participate in organized high-risk activity. As noted in the earlier discussion, it is thus unlikely that the perceived benefits of participating in political violence will exceed the perceived costs.

Second, individualists in general tend to prefer exiting from an oppressive society to changing it. Unlike complex hierarchies, competitive markets are transportable from one local context to another and can be created anew from disparate elements. Furthermore, individualists do not have any special preferences or beliefs that tie them to a particular group of individuals. Both these factors decrease the costs of exiting a particular society and provide individualists with a viable alternative to staying and attempting at great risk to battle a hostile state. As long as such alternatives exist, individualists will view migration to a foreign land or frontier as an opportunity rather than as a punishment.

This can explain the seemingly paradoxical fact that some of the most entre-preneurial and economically resourceful cultures within a society are often quite passive politically in the face of state oppression, as with the cases of the Jews in Eastern Europe, the overseas Chinese in Southeast Asia, the Indians in East Africa, and the Japanese-Americans in California. Each of these groups gained economic success despite low initial economic standing and a less-than-hospitable political climate. Yet when faced with various forms of political persecution, they generally failed to rise up in active resistance, unlike other minority peoples with seemingly fewer resources.

This behavior would seem irrational in light of theories that emphasize uniform goals among political actors, in which case the probability of resistance would be proportionate to the probability of success, which is in turn proportionate to actor resources. However, it would not be irrational in light of cultural theory, which attributes this passivity not to the individualists' lack of resources but to their self-regarding preferences, which make collective antistate violence irrational. Instead, individualists usually attempt to bargain with the state to minimize its interference in the market and in their personal lives, and, when this is not possible, search for some way of moving elsewhere.

Nonetheless, individualists are capable of violent resistance when there are institutions that allow them to provide selective incentives to cooperators and hence to eliminate free-rider problems. These institutions have often been created for other purposes than the facilitation of collective violence, but they must be capable of being transferred to that purpose. Perhaps the most famous example of such resistance among individualists is the American Revolution: Existing state governments had the institutional wherewithal to raise armies, pay soldiers, and punish those who refused to cooperate. In this case, it was clearly important that the revolutionaries had control over a territory in which they could communicate with one another and strike agreements.

When in power, individualists are in most cases hesitant to use violent coercion against members of the population, since this interferes with the competitive market mechanism. A state composed of individualists is relatively indifferent, however, to the economic harm caused by the market to those who lack the resources to succeed in it. Individualists generally have self-regarding preferences, hence they feel no personal need to rescue someone who has fallen by the wayside. Furthermore, they believe any attempt to rescue such a person will eventually cause him even greater harm by destroying his incentives to compete.

Hierarchists and Egalitarians

The two cultures most likely to foster collective political violence are the hierarchical and the egalitarian. Both are high-group cultures that provide the level of solidarity necessary to engender self-sacrificing revolutionary action. Members feel closely tied to their groups, and this is reflected in strong other-regarding preferences with regard to the welfare of other group members. The usual risks of violent political activity will hence be counteracted by the fact that members can "appropriate" a higher proportion of their contribution to a collective goal than would self-interested individuals because hierarchists and egalitarians care about their entire group's welfare as well as their own. Thus incentives to free ride are reduced. Such preferences, moreover, do not extend toward those outside of the group. In situations of conflict, they can lead to behavior that is both self-sacrificing for the sake of one's own group and quite destructive toward those outside the group. Thus strong solidarity with others, although it may in one sense be the root of benevolence, is also the main facilitator of collective violence.

Hierarchists. Hierarchical revolutionary groups can take two major forms. When the state itself is hierarchical, certain hierarchists within society may still rebel against it because it fails to allocate sufficiently rewarding roles to the members of their group. Because they believe in the optimality of a hierarchical system, such revolutionaries aim not at creating an entirely new system of government but at changing the division of roles among members of society. Because of this, such movements are generally nationalist movements of racial, ethnic, or religious minorities who perceive themselves as oppressed. In this case, violence is directed at the usurpers who have taken illegitimate control over the system, and some care is taken not to damage those parts of the system that can be appropriated once authority has been transferred into rightful hands.

When the state is individualistic, hierarchical revolutionaries seek to change the system completely because they believe that hierarchy is a necessary condition for an optimal allocation of rewards. Such revolutionaries are often seen as atavistic or traditionalist because they often hark back to an earlier, hierarchical form of government. In these cases, violence may be directed both at the occupiers of power and at the economic structures that buttress the competitive market system the revolutionaries are opposed to. It is again important not to see such violence as irrational despite the economic loss that may be involved if and when the revolution is successful. The hierarchist's preferences and beliefs place a high value on a social system with well-defined roles and authority, even at some cost to short-run economic self-interest.

Because hierarchists all share a belief in the optimality of hierarchical institutions, violence within hierarchical groups is caused primarily by clashing beliefs and preferences within the group about the optimal assignment of roles, about the rules attached to those roles, and about which roles provide the authority to set rules. Hence hierarchical organizations are most likely to split on factional lines over disputes about the ascriptive criteria for role differentiation within the organization or, at the very top, about the personalities or families who are to control the organization. Such disputes are particularly likely to arise in cell-structured organizations, which have few cross-linkages between cells at the same level of hierarchy and where each faction can form a viable organization of its own.

Hierarchists in power generally aim violence against those they view as deviants, that is, those who are not willing to accept and perform according to their designated roles. Again, because hierarchists believe that a stable hierarchy provides an optimal allocation of rewards, they view those who oppose the hierarchy as a threat to both group and personal welfare (because of their other-regarding preferences, both types of welfare will be valued). Deviants include not only those who engage in political violence but those who are simply recalcitrant or act in a nonprescribed manner. Because of this, hierarchists are much more likely than individualists to resort to coercion as a means of governing.

Egalitarians. The most radical revolutionaries generally are found among egalitarians. Because existing states are usually predominantly hierarchical or individualist, egalitarians aim for major changes in the governing structure of society. Their violence is directed against all manifestations of authority and power, whether political, economic, or social. Because egalitarians have preferences that value the reduction of inequality for its own sake, it may be rational for them to engage in "leveling" violence even when it does not improve the personal welfare of any individual.

Because egalitarians seek such drastic transformation of the existing state structure, their doctrines are viewed by other cultures as millennial, and such groups are most likely to be viewed by others as crazy or cultlike. These include Western urban guerrilla groups such as the Red Brigades, Direct Action, and the Baader-Meinhoff Gang as well as Third World revolutionaries like the Khmer Rouge or the Sendero Luminoso.

Because the egalitarian system of authority is particularly ill-suited for military action, egalitarian groups face special internal problems of control. Because they have no internalized role-based rules of authority that can resolve disagreements over the means to reach commonly desired goals, such disagreements are the main source of intragroup violence. In various ways, problems of control further increase the levels of violence displayed by egalitarian revolutionary groups. First, egalitarian groups often use initiation as a way of both proving and promoting the commitment of new members to the group and its ideology. Often the most effective way of doing this is by violent activity, which greatly increases the costs of returning to normal society and makes a new member completely dependent on the group. Second, because even small amounts of internal dissent can wreck the group's ability to function, it is rational for group members to expel or eliminate dissidents who cannot be brought quickly back into line. Because of this, egalitarian groups tend to be particularly harsh on perceived turncoats among their own members. Prominent examples include the Japanese Red Army and the Philippine New People's Army.

Furthermore, because consensus is essential to continued existence, egalitarian groups are particularly incapable of compromising with opponents or of forming alliances with other revolutionary groups. Even the smallest dilution in purity can remove the glue that makes such groups viable entities. Because the existence of competing egalitarian groups creates a constant threat of defection and dilution of ideological purity, fellow egalitarian revolutionary groups will be regarded as even greater enemies than the state itself. All this internecine battling and inability to compromise explains in large part why egalitarian groups very rarely achieve power. It also explains why, in the few cases where they have—the Khmer Rouge and the Gang of Four faction of the Chinese Communist Party being the only prominent examples—they have not persisted for long and have often turned against the society that they have set out to transform. But as has been emphasized throughout this chapter, none of this should be seen as irrational—it is part and parcel of the imperatives created by an egalitarian's defining preferences.

CONCLUSION

As the previous analysis shows, cultural theory allows us to ascertain basic preferences and beliefs of individuals from four major cultural types and does so in a way that allows us to predict behavior in a variety of situations. With regard to political violence, it allows us to predict from a few simple assumptions both the conditions under which rational individuals will employ violence and the form that violence will take.

In predicting the conditions for violence, cultural theory resolves the paradox of participation in collective violence in a more satisfactory way than do existing rational choice explanations. For individualists, cultural theorists accept the hypothesis that collective violence can occur only under conditions where institutions and entrepreneurs provide selective incentives for those who participate. However, it does not rely on the questionable assumption that individuals will be able to calculate precisely the risks involved in participation, instead asserting that culturally biased beliefs will determine the perceived efficacy of institutional solutions. Hence fatalists, despite their similarity to individualists in preferences, will not cooperate even if entrepreneurs offer systems of collective incentives because they do not believe that such systems can ever work.

Members of hierarchical and egalitarian cultures will sometimes be willing to engage in violent collective action even when selective incentives do not make up for the potential costs. Because of their strong-group nature and resulting valuation of group welfare for its own sake, the chance to benefit their group or to harm those outside will compensate for the personal risks involved.

Furthermore, cultural theory also provides a clear explanation for empirical phenomena that cannot be explained by other models, including behavior that appears irrational from the point of view of conventional rational choice assumptions about goals and actions. Fatalists will often direct their violence against one another rather than at those outsiders whom they blame most for their plight. This is because their mistrust of everyone creates conflict with those whom they come in contact with most frequently, not necessarily those who have the most control over their condition. Individualists will often be more passive in the face of persecution than those with far fewer resources because they lack the other-regarding preferences that can eliminate free riding without selective incentives. Rebellious hierarchists will generally direct their violence against the occupiers of authority, but not at the institutions that can be appropriated for their own use if they succeed. Egalitarians have a tendency to direct violence at all manifestations of institutionalized power because of their desire to remake the state in their own image. They will also direct violence at members of their own group who depart even slightly from the required consensus that is necessary for their group to be viable.

Hence, far from subverting rationality, cultural theory provides an invaluable resource for rational choice theorizing, enabling rational choice to explain phenomena that have fallen beyond the reach of its conventional assumptions about preferences and beliefs. By specifying and limiting the viable constellations of preference and belief, cultural theory can account for action in cases where conventional assumptions would lead to either indeterminate or inaccurate predictions. In short, just as humans need culture in order to make sense of the world, rational choice needs culture in order to make sense of human behavior.

NOTES

1. The definitive discussion of this is Brian Barry, *Sociologists, Economists and Democracy* (Chicago: University of Chicago Press, 1978).

2. Coined originally in Mancur Olson's *The Logic of Collective Action* (Cambridge, Mass.: Harvard University Press, 1965).

3. See Gordon Tullock, "The Paradox of Revolution," *Public Choice* 11(1971), 89–99; and Morris Silver, "Political Revolution and Repression: An Economic Approach," *Public Choice* 17(1974), 63–71.

4. See Barry, *Sociologists, Economists and Democracy,* 44–46; Barbara Salert, *Revolutions and Revolutionaries* (New York: Elsevier, 1976), 33–38; Allen Buchanan, "Revolutionary Motivation and Rationality," *Philosophy and Public Affairs* 9(Fall 1979), 59–84; T. David Mason, "Individual Participation in Collective Racial Violence: A Rational Choice Synthesis," *American Political Science Review* 82(December 1984), 1041–1043; Jon Elster, *Political Psychology* (Cambridge: Cambridge University Press, 1993), 15–17.

5. Samuel Popkin, *The Rational Peasant* (Berkeley: University of California Press, 1979), chap. 6.

6. See Michael Taylor, "Rationality and Revolutionary Collective Action" in Taylor, ed., *Rationality and Revolution* (Cambridge: Cambridge University Press, 1988), 63–97.

7. See Dennis Chong, *Collective Action and the Civil Rights Movement* (Chicago: University of Chicago Press, 1991), chap. 2.

8. See Susanne Lohmann, "A Signaling Model of Informative and Manipulative Political Action," *American Political Science Review* 87(June 1993), 319–333. In order to be adapted to revolutionary violence, that is, violence that seeks to overthrow the state, the assumptions might be modified so that those being signaled are possible supporters of the revolutionaries rather than a responsive state.

9. On the latter point, see Elster, *Political Psychology,* 18.

10. See Ted Gurr, "Psychological Factors in Civil Violence," *World Politics* 20(January 1968), reprinted in Ikuo Kabashima and Lynn White, *Political Systems and Change* (Princeton: Princeton University Press, 1986), 140–173, quotation at 145.

11. See, for instance, Karl-Dieter Opp, *The Rationality of Political Protest* (Boulder: Westview Press, 1989); and Chong, *Collective Action*, chaps. 3 and 4.

12. For a listing and a more-detailed analysis of these theories, see Jack A. Goldstone, "Theories of Revolution: The Third Generation," *World Politics* 32(April 1980), 425–453, as well as an updated review in John Foran, "Theories of Revolution Revisited: Towards a Fourth Generation," *Sociological Theory* 11(March 1993), 1–20.

13. See, for instance, Taylor's criticism of Theda Skocpol's *States and Social Revolutions* in Taylor, "Rationality and Revolutionary Collective Action," 76–77.

14. See discussion in Goldstone, "Theories of Revolution," 415.

15. See Foran, "Theories of Revolution Revisited," 9–10.

16. See Michael Thompson, Richard Ellis, and Aaron Wildavsky, *Cultural Theory* (Boulder: Westview Press, 1990), 3. The fifth way of life, the hermit, is inherently asocial.

17. See Thompson, Ellis, and Wildavsky, *Cultural Theory*, 103–108, 195–209.

18. See Armen Alchian, "Uncertainty, Evolution and Economic Theory," *Journal of Political Economy* 63(April 1950), 211–221; Anthony Downs, *An Economic Theory of Democracy*, chap. 2, esp. 30–31; and Kenneth Waltz, *Theory of International Politics* (Reading, Mass.: Addison-Wesley, 1979), chap. 5, esp. 88–93.

19. See, for instance, Mary Douglas and Aaron Wildavsky, *Risk and Culture: An Essay on the Selection of Technical and Environmental Dangers* (Berkeley: University of California Press, 1982), chaps. 1–4; Jon Elster, "When Rationality Fails," in *Solomonic Judgements* (Cambridge: Cambridge University Press, 1989), chap. 1, sec. 3; and Douglas North, *Structure and Change in Economic History* (New York: W. W. Norton, 1981), chap. 5, sec. 2.

20. See, for example, David Collard, *Altruism and Economy: A Study in Non-Selfish Economics* (New York: Oxford University Press, 1978), chap. 4; Michael Taylor, *The Possibility of Cooperation* (Cambridge: Cambridge University Press, 1987), chap. 5; and Chong, *Collective Action*, chap. 4.

CHAPTER 9

Cultural Theory and the Problem of Moral Relativism

Charles Lockhart
and Gregg Franzwa

What are we to make of cross-cultural differences in morality? Cultural anthropologists and postmodernists generally expect such differences but are reluctant to label the morality of one culture as better than another.[1] From such relativistic perspectives, moralities are not better or worse, just different. Other scholars, frequently philosophers, follow an objectivist orientation toward morality. That is, they argue that objective moral standards exist and that the practices of some cultures approximate these standards more closely than do the practices of others and are accordingly morally superior. The issue between these camps has attracted much attention in recent years,[2] but this controversy is more complex than popular recent contributions suggest, involving, for instance, at least two distinct levels of inquiry.[3]

On the first, the empirical-normative level, *cultural* relativists such as Ruth Benedict, familiar with empirical differences among the practices labeled "moral" by distinct cultures, become *moral* relativists by denying the legitimacy of cross-cultural moral judgments. These scholars are joined in moral relativism at a second, metaethical level by philosophers who argue that our metaphysical, epistemological, or logical capacities are inadequate for deriving objective moral standards. The latter relativists differ in why they think that objective standards do not exist,[4] but they are united in their belief that first-level empirical and normative claims are inadequate for formulating definitive answers to second-level questions (such as What, if anything, is the meaning of good?[5]) that form the focus of their interests.

Moral objectivists argue that adequate metaphysical, epistemological, and logical grounds do exist for sustaining objective moral standards (i.e., moral assertions are capable of being true). However, they disagree as to what these bases and standards are (and thus on how we assign truth-value to moral assertions).[6]

Thus there are multiple points of contention both within and between the camps of moral relativism and objectivism. Disputes between the two are exacerbated by the camps seeking answers to different questions. Among those whose primary goals include answering empirical questions, moral relativism—an outgrowth of cultural relativism—is common. And although there are moral relativists among contemporary philosophers,[7] moral objectivism, deeply rooted in Western philosophy, has recently enjoyed growing influence. Accordingly, moral relativists in the social sciences and moral objectivists in philosophy frequently talk past one another; the first-level questions that concern social scientists are logically distinct from the second-level questions that occupy metaethicists.

We use cultural theory to build an explicit metaethical argument that will enable us selectively to bridge the gulf commonly separating moral relativists and objectivists. We approach this task in two stages. First, we examine cultural theory's capacity for organizing the empirical and normative variations of cultural relativism. Specifically, we show that cultural theory's version of "constrained relativism" admits sufficient moral pluralism to encompass, predict, and explain a broad range of variation with respect to empirical patterns of acceptance for prominent moral rules. Second, we build an explicit metaethical argument for cultural theory. In so doing we rely on moral pluralism and a functional second-level criterion in order to produce an objectivist account. By moral pluralism we refer to the recognition of multiple and distinct moral goods that cannot be reduced to a common denominator. Our functional criterion resides in the concept of societal viability. We argue that, given a particular context, it is possible to make objective determinations concerning the approximate mix of moral goods—the products of social institutions developed by different "ways of life"—required for societal viability.

CONSTRAINED RELATIVISM AS MORAL PLURALISM

The Seven Deadly Sins

Cultural relativists often contend that moral and social conventions appear in unending variety that cannot be reduced to a limited number of types.[8] In contrast, cultural theory argues for constrained relativism: that is, for variation constrained by a small number of fundamental choices. Cultural theory predicts varying acceptance patterns for moral rules on the basis of a culture's choices. In our first demonstration of this capacity, we consider reactions to four of the "seven deadly sins": avarice, anger, pride, and sloth.[9] Each of these orientations is posited, from either a hierarchical or egalitarian, and thus high-group, perspective, as sinful. Yet in each case at least one cultural bias resists this label and considers the orientation socially constructive.

We start with avarice. Individualists portray humans as industriously procuring nature's bounty in self-regulated ways and making mutually beneficial bargains in the process. Although humans vary in specific characteristics and thus in their relative success in this bargaining process, they are nevertheless "essentially equal" in the sense that none can make certain types of claims to moral advantages—for example, being preferred by a divinity. One implication of this equality premise is a preference for limited external constraints across a variety of social contexts.[10] Such constraints inhibit personal initiative insofar as they restrict individuals' rights to freely pursue their own interests through mutual agreements. And the moral justification of that freedom involves the assumption of the relative equality of the parties to such agreements. For individualists the equality premise further justifies the unequal results of such private bargaining. In the individualistic view, personal success stems less from innate advantages than from hard work and rational self-direction.

In individualistic liberal theory self-interestedness is viewed positively as the key to personal and societal prosperity.[11] Consider Adam Smith's famous passage about appealing not to others' humanity but to their self-interest.[12] If humans were not insatiable accumulators, they would not, according to individualists, be capable of producing wealth. The view of avarice as sin comes from the high-group cultures, particularly egalitarianism. Individualists might agree that avarice, like any other constructive social device, can be misapplied, but it is from their perspective an essential social tool.[13]

For egalitarians humans are not only essentially equal, they have as well no natural social flaws. Thus egalitarians base their preferences for minimal external constraints on a faith in natural social harmony. Yet egalitarians are sensitive to the possibility of corruption by social institutions. The essential evil of institutions lies in their tendency to arrogate some to positions of authority over others. This violates the natural equality of humans and perverts natural human goodness. As a consequence of this aversion to formal authority, egalitarians rarely rule whole societies.[14] In the contemporary period, social democracy represents a regime with egalitarian and hierarchical roots. More commonly, egalitarianism appears on the social periphery[15] in relatively small groups in which authority can be easily shared or is sufficiently informal as to pass virtually unnoticed.

Persons with egalitarian biases do not consider anger necessarily sinful. For them, human institutions are too polluted by pernicious authority or market relations, both causes of inequality, to permit such a label. Jesus' wrath over the money changers in the temple is a case in point. Anger is virtuous; it is the driving force behind purification efforts. Egalitarians perceive their groups to be continually at risk from the false principles that individualists and hierarchists introduce into human social relations. But perpetual vigilance is difficult, and the actions required to counter such social pollution are frequently dangerous. Thus anger is useful. It mobilizes people, and it distracts them from the dangers of their duties. This is not to say that all anger is good; some may be misplaced. But anger is nonetheless a tool essential to the survival of the egalitarian community. As a (feminist) reader of an earlier version of this chapter commented in the margin, "You don't need a model to show that anger isn't universally a sin. Just ask a feminist!"

Hierarchists, who share egalitarians' sense of group membership but who in contrast visualize society as appropriately organized vertically, need tools to maintain their system of social differentiation. They perceive humans as naturally unequal, born with differing talents and characters. Thus hierarchical thinkers such as Plato focus attention on how society can hone natural talents into various forms of expertise available for social purposes while at the same time limiting antisocial activity. Good, skillful humans are the products of sound institutions—families, churches, political parties, and states—that provide external direction for sound development and harmonious living.

Thus humility has distinctly less scope for application in hierarchies than in egalitarian groups. The humble hierarchical leader is a contradiction in terms. Pomp, ritual, and pride are what is called for. Ostentatious public (as opposed to private for individualists) ceremonies and edifices protect and enhance what Machiavelli calls the majesty of the state. Nor is the political leader the only one for whom this is the case. Institutionally developed expertise is revered generally. For instance, the masterpiece through which craftsmen earned their way into medieval guilds was an entirely appropriate source of pride as well. Pride, like avarice and anger, can be misplaced. But to take pride in one's own special contribution is appropriate. And from this perspective the deference required from the lower ranks of society for social order is impossible to achieve in the absence of a sense of pride and self-confidence on the part of their betters.

Can sloth too have supporters? Fatalists may not champion sloth, but only because there is little beyond good luck that their cultural bias supports. Fatalists do not sense membership in larger social institutions, but they do recognize external constraints. They do not play active roles in society. Rather they serve as reservoirs or resources for other, more socially interactive ways of life. Both hierarchists and individualists require a cultural location for those unable to successfully follow their ways of life, and egalitarians need a source of potential recruits for their struggles against authority. Fatalists view human nature as capricious. Social relations have a similarly unpredictable character. Like hierarchists, they see natural flaws in humans but lack faith in social institutions as a remedy.

From a perspective that views social interaction as fruitless in the face of uncertainty or external necessity, there is certainly nothing wrong with sloth. There is little to be said for the hard work the individualist champions, the acquisition of expertise that the hierarchist reveres, or the collective action and sharing favored by the egalitarian. To the fatalist's mind fortune will play havoc with all of these approaches.[16]

What does this exercise with the four "sins" show? Cultural theory claims to be exhaustive with respect to encompassing viable ways of life. Surface variation among societies may be unending, but according to cultural theory, this variation represents incremental differences in the mixtures of the four paradigms and the peculiarities of their interaction with historical contingencies. Exhaustiveness is an ambitious claim that can rarely be demonstrated definitively. Nonetheless, cultural theory—in contrast to some earlier cultural approaches[17]—appreciates the social contributions of multiple, distinct, even contradictory, values. Cultural theory thus exhibits a finite version of moral pluralism that explains how and why distinct, even contradictory, values make important contributions to sustaining societies.

"Universal" Admonitions

A related but distinct test of cultural theory's capacities in this regard is provided by the Golden Rule and the prohibition on murder, rules that are widely accepted across cultural biases. Though these rules are "universal," the form of acceptance varies. Cultural theory predicts distinct practices of these rules across different ways of life. Egalitarians practice the Golden Rule in conjunction with a premise of human equality, frequently applying it among the familiar members of small-scale groups to achieve uniform treatment. We are inclined to think that this assumption, setting, and practice represent the Golden Rule's "home turf."

Hierarchists do not accept the equality premise and generally operate in broader, more varied social settings than do egalitarians. If humans are perceived as unequal, then the treatment that people appropriately receive from one another will vary too. It is possible to rescue a meaning and practice of the Golden Rule in hierarchical circumstances by arguing that each is to be given his or her due. Montesquieu, for instance, refers to this as the principle of honor, each person living up to her or his rank and station. Montesquieu further interprets this principle as holding that, as hierarchists, "we should never do or permit anything which may seem to imply that we look upon ourselves as inferior to the rank we hold."[18] But when what people owe one another varies immensely, the meaning of the Golden Rule has changed sharply from the egalitarian version.

Individualists create yet another practice of the Golden Rule. They share with egalitarians a belief in essential human equality. Individualistic societies have, for example, introduced uniform legal codes that embody a spiritual affinity with the Golden Rule. And within voluntarily created networks individualists cooperate well, creating remarkable accomplishments in the process. But individualistic societies are built on competition as well as cooperation. Consider the verse that Igbo children say to their mother each time she goes off to the village market: "Mother, gain from market people / Market people, lose to mother."[19] In the individualist's view, humans naturally face various forms of competition. Individualists with such perceptions may refrain from doing one another certain sorts of harm, thus limiting the competition to recognized procedures. But individual estrangement in a competitive setting places limits on the sorts of positive cooperation that will be forthcoming.

Let us now consider "You shall not kill." This rule is widely interpreted as proscribing murder (unauthorized killing). But the circumstances in which killing is seen as murder vary among cultural biases. Egalitarians, for whom group purity and equality of members are crucial, may sometimes kill with blessing to achieve these ends. Moses' reaction to the "golden calf" episode and, in our own time, the activities of the Red Guards provide evidence of this blessing.[20] But from the perspective of individualists, killing people for worshiping a different god or arrogating themselves above "the people" and, particularly, doing so without due process is murder. Hierarchists, too, although they might agree with egalitarians in the definition of specific crimes, are apt to have little sympathy for such spontaneous methods.

Hierarchists, who share egalitarians' concern with group preservation, will justify the killing of those who refuse to accept the hierarchy's expertise on proper social orientation. So the act of killing Trotsky, or whoever "has to" be killed in order to affirm the views of the hierarchy's experts, builds deference among various social orders and thus facilitates a stable pattern of social relations. In contrast, individualists may well see social progress as the beneficial consequence of experimenting with nonsanctioned social practices. The killing of political dissidents or social nonconformists is generally murder from their perspective. Egalitarians may have more sympathy with selected results of these hierarchical actions, but minimally their reasons will differ. Sympathy will come from a common concern with group purity. And egalitarians might coincidentally agree that a particular collection of humans had to go. But egalitarians will bridle at hierarchical claims of expertise and thus authoritative action. For a few in high circles to claim superior knowledge by which others may be labeled socially dangerous is a procedure that egalitarians cannot regularly sanction.

Individualists, sharing with egalitarians at least some sympathy for essential similarities among humans, perceive killing as a violation of equal rights to life. In a few instances killing is justifiable and thus not murder. One is self-defense. Additionally, killing by public agents is sanctioned under limited circumstances. The hierarchist may not disagree with killing in these instances, although as we have seen, hierarchy's category of treason is far broader and more open-ended than the individualist's. More important, the hierarchist's rationale for legitimizing such killing will be couched in collective rather than individual terms. Egalitarians will be more hostile to the individualist's defense of killing, arguing that the property rights of individualism create heartless vertical stratification that encourages acts of violence on the part of the disadvantaged. In societies stratified through competition, it is no wonder from the egalitarian perspective that those with the least access to legitimate means of competition use illegitimate means. Blame lies with the perverted social system, not with the individuals who break the system's rules.

As was the case in our examination of the deadly sins, cultural theory's incorporation of moral pluralism facilitates predicting and explaining a range of distinct practices with respect to the Golden Rule and murder. If cultural theory's moral pluralism encompasses the range of values cultures regularly support, it is reasonable to ask if it can be applied in ways that provide objective determinations about the relative merits of various moral views.

CULTURAL THEORY AND METAETHICS

We now explore cultural theory's metaethical implications and offer contributions that reveal a form of moral objectivism. First, we distinguish between the moral stands that cultural theory attributes to adherents of various cultural biases and the ethical position of the theory itself. Cultural theory portrays adherents of various cultural biases as constructing distinctive "stipulated realities" with empirical and normative aspects, in other words, portrays them as objectivists.[21] We think Michael Thompson, Richard Ellis, and Aaron Wildavsky's attribution of relatively inflexible stipulated realities is incorrect for numerous persons in some contemporary pluralist societies, including that of the United States. Persons in these societies are frequently socialized by different ways of life and apply hybrid cultural biases in the varying social contexts of everyday life.[22]

With respect to cultural theory per se, Thompson, Ellis, and Wildavsky argue that each way of life offers distinctive moral strengths and weaknesses. And in conjunction with their view of the internal coherence and interpretative breadth of each cultural bias, this makes them skeptical about the possibility of an external basis for labeling the values or perceptions of one as superior to those of another. In short, these distinctive ways of life have systematic frames of reference for interpreting similar facts and moral issues in different ways. So, if all of the biases contain their own value justifications and fact interpretations such that the assertions of alternative value-fact constructions by each simply beg the questions against the others and if, further, the four biases of cultural theory collectively exhaust the possibilities, only the canons of formal logic would apply universally.

Although we concur that cultural theory's ways of life have contrasting moral strengths and weaknesses, we think these differences leave more common ground than merely formal logic: minimally, at least, a shared goal of social viability. Strictly speaking, the social viability that Thompson, Ellis, and Wildavsky refer to is that which each cultural bias in a society seeks for itself. Viability for single ways of life, however, is fanciful in the long run, since each cultural bias perceives the world in a limited way and needs the other ways of life to provide various supports for its own existence. So we refer to a broader objective: *societal* viability, that is, the viability of the society that multiple ways of life form. By societal viability we mean the resilience a society acquires through developing the distinctive capacities of various ways of life. It is only through participation in a larger, multiperspective society that any particular cultural bias can realistically aspire to viability. All cultural biases thus share an interest in societal viability. We shall make use of this common ground to build selective bridges between moral relativism and objectivism.

We draw first on Geoffrey Warnock's thesis concerning the object of morality. For Warnock, the concept of human nature—an ambiguous, contingent, and variously perceived notion to be sure—includes various needs, wants, and interests.[23] Aspects of the human situation—shortages of resources, information, intelligence, rationality, or sympathy—may jeopardize the fulfillment of these needs and such. Yet some fulfillment is required, both physically and culturally. So the object of morality, according to Warnock, is to nurture conditions—particularly sympathies—that facilitate this fulfillment, thus improving the human situation.

Our concept of societal viability shares a functional orientation with Warnock's conception of morality. Societal viability is a broader concept than morality, involving, for example, empirical judgments about matters such as the feasibility of certain goals in addition to moral preferences about what goals ought to be sought and in which order. A crucial aspect of societal viability, however, involves concern for improvements in the human situation similar to those that Warnock views as the aim of morality. The improvements themselves stem from the activities of the various ways of life. Through their respective social relations preferences, people construct distinct institutions that in turn produce characteristic moral goods. Individualists construct extensive markets that rely on individual rights and enhance productive capacity; hierarchists construct stratified institutions that produce expert knowledge and social order; and egalitarians construct close-knit groups that produce social solidarity. The maintenance of some range—a range that varies with social context—of these goods is required for societal viability. In our view, then, moral goodness resides in the distinctive improvements in the human condition resulting from the disparate social institutions associated with various ways of life.

We share with Warnock as well a response to the questions as to why these are moral goods and why facilitating human survival and some forms of cultural success is morally good. Put simply, we believe that ameliorating the human predicament in these ways produces better consequences. Our approach is thus metaethically similar to that of Peter Railton,[24] who suggests a version of pluralistic consequentialism that draws on multiple, distinct goods—including autonomy, happiness, knowledge, respect, solidarity.[25] Railton holds that these goods cannot be reduced to a single subjective-state measure such as pleasure. Various goods carry different weights, and although Railton does not mention the possibility, these weights—even their valences—may vary among ways of life. For Railton, action aimed at achieving the greatest weighted sum of goods over time generally takes the form of supporting particular institutional arrangements designed to provide these goods.

Railton's formulation works well in conjunction with cultural theory. Persons involved in the various ways of life strive through distinctive institutions to realize largely different goods. Further, realizing some goods may preclude the attainment of others, not only because resources cannot be "spent" twice but also because the institutional arrangements necessary for the realization of some goods are destructive to the prospects for others. For example, Thompson, Ellis, and Wildavsky show that the markets propounded by individualists as means of sustaining individual autonomy and achieving productive efficiency are destructive, as egalitarinans claim, of social solidarity. Likewise, the consensual decision procedures egalitarians promote for achieving social solidarity are rarely capable of providing much in the way of support for productive efficiency. And the social organizations hierarchists use to achieve expertise and orderly patterns of social relations are apt to be too inflexible for improving productive efficiency and too dedicated to vertical distinctions to sustain individual autonomy or allow much feeling of social solidarity. Conversely, markets and groups striving for consensus may offer hierarchists insufficient hope of expertise and orderly social relations.

Cultural theory is neutral among these first-level normative claims of the various ways of life, recognizing the need for the presence of multiple cultural biases.[26] A society composed of institutions devoted exclusively to expertise and social order or to any other narrow range of goods would be insensitive to certain conditions, including some threats to its existence, and would not be viable across the long term. So a fanatical devotion to one portion of the broader range of requisite goods we introduced previously would produce perverse consequences. Our addition to cultural theory at this point is to argue at the metaethical level that fostering the development and maintenance of a variety of social institutions and the consequences they try to produce is morally good. These institutions make distinct contributions (e.g., increases in knowledge, solidarity, etc.) to the improvement of human conditions—contributions that are not reducible to a single measure of goodness but that collectively can increase societal viability.

Our conception of moral goodness requires some means for measuring societal viability.[27] In part this involves assessing the multiple societal accomplishments (e.g., performance with respect to productive efficiency, social order, etc.) that contribute to societal viability. At a rudimentary level societal viability requires at least maintenance of the biological population. But of greater interest for moral theory, we seek measures of cultural flourishing that are bias-specific. Liberal economists have developed numerous measures of productivity (e.g., GNP per capita) that pick up a portion of the contributions of individualism. And we might operationalize hierarchical contributions in part through statistics revealing low levels of serious crimes and other forms of social disorder. Measures of social solidarity beyond the crudest—relative equality of distributions of income and wealth—are not well-developed. Richard Titmus offers an innovative example in this regard involving the practice of voluntary blood donation.[28]

Measuring societal viability also requires examining the relations among its contributing elements. Requisite goods conflict, so increasing realization of one is apt to reduce attainment of others. Optimizing societal viability entails nurturing several goods within limits. But these limits are difficult to specify, and extant efforts to do so even approximately[29] give insufficient consideration to the possibility that optimization may require quite different contributions from various goods in different contexts. Many Americans apply different cultural biases sequentially in varying social contexts. For example, Jennifer Hochschild shows that Americans are more individualistic with respect to the workplace than they are in the social contexts of family, neighborhood, or public policy.[30] We are suggesting a societal-level analogy: Changing circumstances create societal predicaments that require varying amounts of different moral goods. In this vein, Roger Masters suggests that an increased emphasis on hierarchy was essential to building the irrigated agricultural system necessary to support rapid population growth in the ancient Tigris-Euphrates valley.[31]

Charles Maier, focusing on a related, contemporary example, argues that in the 1980s individualistic market economies mastered common economic challenges far better than did their hierarchical rivals in Eastern Europe.[32] Hierarchical institutions are less flexible than their market counterparts,[33] and the economic peculiarities of the 1980s may have pressed Soviet and related economies beyond their endurance. Assuming for the moment that this is so, we argue that societal viability would have been and continues to be objectively served in this case by building individualistic institutions and so establishing more of the moral goods—individual rights, productive flexibility, and efficiency, etc.—that they provide. It is, of course, no easy task for people conditioned to hierarchy to effect such a transformation, and strategies of rapid change are apt to have many pitfalls.[34]

Evaluations of this sort are ultimately grounded on comparative judgments about societal viability. And the more specific the comparisons get, the more complex the supporting arguments become. But at a higher level of generality, the implications of societal viability are intuitively obvious. It seems natural to assert, for example, that a given societal mix of biases may be said to "fit" its environmental niche in better or worse ways when variations of fit represent corresponding differences in moral evaluations. And although the criteria for goodness of fit are necessarily complex, there are general rules implied regarding at least physiological needs. A set of cultural practices, for instance, that lead to decreasing food supplies for an increasing population would surely be difficult to defend as appropriate. And in this situation the further development of institutions that would create more of certain moral goods—productivity (of food) and social order (population control)—would contribute to greater societal viability.

Our earlier discussion of "sins" can also serve to illustrate this argument. Consider, for instance, the view of pride as sinful and envision a society that has thrived under the dominance of individualistic and egalitarian ways of life and thus has a modestly sized and skeptically viewed central government. Now suppose a change in the external environment involving military capabilities (a new technology such as the development of aircraft) or intentions (an expansionist party coming to power in a neighboring country). Under these new circumstances the prevailing, generally negative attitudes toward "the majesty of the state" are apt to serve societal viability less well than in the past. Acquiring more moral goods of a particular sort through the development of a larger, competent, proud, and generally respected central government capable of mastering the new defense needs—as the United States did during the early 1940s—is, prima facie, apt to provide greater societal viability than would exist without such changes.

CONCLUSION

Although hardly without difficulties, this pluralistic consequentialist formulation offers an intuitively appealing means by which to build bridges between moral relativism and objectivism. We do not offer general moral judgments of specific institutions or practices. Rather, we use a second-level criterion, societal viability, to provide objective judgments of specific arrangements *in particular physical and social contexts*. Our transition from a constrained form of relativism to a pluralist version of objectivism is possible because of specific features of the moral views in question. First among these enabling features is a first-level similarity between Thompson, Ellis, and Wildavsky's constrained relativism and Railton's pluralistic objectivism. These two views are distinguished by significant differences, but they share minimally the important similarity of moral pluralism. The second enabling feature is the use of a functional criterion, societal viability, for the objective determination of the mixtures of moral goods associated with better and worse societal responses to specific contexts. This criterion allows us to shift to a second-level objectivist view that, for instance, in a particular context more of the moral goods created by individualistic institutions and less of those produced by hierarchy are required for improving societal viability. In general we think that moral pluralism applied in conjunction with an overarching functional criterion offers a promising avenue for resolving cultural relativism-objectivism issues. Our claim for objectivity in this regard benefits, as do similar claims for science, from the openness of our conclusions to continual empirically based criticism to the effect that support of different mixtures of institutions and thus distinct holdings of moral goods would produce better fits with a given social context.

Additionally, this formulation places boundaries on the goods (Railton) or human needs, wants, and interests (Warnock) that can count as morally good. Although there may be limited exceptions, it is difficult to imagine circumstances under which general practices of malevolence, untruthfulness, or reneging on promises, for example, are likely to contribute to the optimization of societal viability. So our approach affirms normative conclusions consistent with prominent themes of contemporary analytic moral theorists.

We wish to close by focusing attention on some practical questions about our thesis for which we have as yet no sound answers. We have argued that particular cultures produce distinctive, even incompatible, moral goods. How useful particular moral goods turn out to be for certain societies in specific contexts hinges on the fit between the capabilities a culture affords and the demands of the social and physical context. Certain capacities may be crucial in some circumstances but far less helpful in others. So the ultimate moral good in our pluralistic, consequentialist formulation—societal viability—may be served more effectively by different constituent elements, and thus by the cultures that produce them, as societal contexts change. Thus we argue that the fostering of multiple cultures is a desirable feature in societies.[35]

But how such fostering is accomplished remains unclear. The circumstances particular societies face may create obstacles for fostering selective cultures. Is it a coincidence, for instance, that the individualistic, liberal revolution spawned by Hobbes, Locke, Smith, and others took hold in an island rather than a continental society? It is hard to envision a claim similar to Hobbes's—that when the sovereign's command endangers one's life, the obligation to obey vanishes—gaining influence among the elites of a society encircled by adversaries, such as Germany or, more recently, Russia. And is it accidental that the societies that accepted individualistic ideas more quickly and thoroughly—the United States, Canada, Australia, and New Zealand—shared aspects of Britain's physical isolation?[36] Also the need for different cultures and their distinctive moral goods can arise quickly and—from the perspective of a society's elites—unexpectedly. If our earlier analysis is correct, for instance, the development of hierarchy that brought the Soviet Union the remarkable triumph of victory in World War II led, by virtue of its success and the consequent progressive repression of other cultures, to societal dissolution in the face of the economic challenges of the 1980s. Extraordinary success of one culture's institutions in one, particularly a high-profile, context may hamper societal elites' recognition of the need to foster other institutions for coping adequately with different circumstances in the near future.

Further, although we disagree that the end of either ideology or history is at hand,[37] we are curious whether the desirability of fostering multiple cultures provides any particular benefits for societies with strong individualistic cultures. All three of the socially interactive cultures hold partial or mythical visions of how the world works and attempt to convert the adherents of other cultures to their own viewpoints, but individualism is inherently more tolerant of differences. In spite of the intuitive appeal of this notion, we are hesitant to guide cultural studies back toward the difficulties of the 1950s. One of the virtues of cultural theory, as we have seen, is its evenhandedness with respect to different cultures and their distinctive moral contributions. And toleration of cultural diversity is not unknown among other cultures: Witness the hierarchical Islamic toleration of the frequently more egalitarian Christian and Jewish communities. Clearly, our current knowledge about the varying empirical implications of cultural theory's pluralistic consequentialism is inadequate, but these uncertainties offer fascinating intellectual opportunities.

NOTES

We are indebted to Michael Thompson, Richard Ellis, and Aaron Wildavsky for the ideas that gave rise to this chapter and for their comments on it. In addition, we have received support from many others. Richard Galvin's assistance has been particularly valuable, and we are grateful as well for help provided by Larry Biskowski, Claudia Camp, Richard Coughlin, Dennis Coyle, Michael Dodson, Alexis Durham, Jean Giles-Sims, Bob Grady, Mike Katovich, Hugh Heclo, Gene McCluney, Andy Miracle, Larry Preston, and Joseph White. Earlier versions of this chapter were presented at the annual meetings of the American Political Science Association, San Francisco, August 31, 1990, and the Western Political Science Association, San Francisco, March 19, 1992.

1. See, for example, Ruth Benedict, *Patterns of Culture* (Boston: Houghton Mifflin, 1959); and Michel Foucault, *The Archaeology of Knowledge* (New York: Harper and Row, 1972), respectively.

2. See Ruth Benedict, *Patterns of Culture;* Clifford Geertz, *Local Knowledge: Further Essays in Interpretative Anthropology* (New York: Basic Books, 1983); Hadley Arkes, *First Things: An Inquiry into the First Principles of Morals and Justice* (Princeton: Princeton University Press, 1986); Allan Bloom, *The Closing of the American Mind* (New York: Simon and Schuster, 1987); and Bernard Gert, *Morality: A New Justification of the Moral Rules* (New York: Oxford University Press, 1988).

3. See J. L. Mackie, *Inventing Right and Wrong* (New York: Penguin, 1977).

4. See C. L. Stevenson, "The Emotive Meaning of Ethical Terms," *Mind* 46(January 1937), 14–31; R. M. Hare, *Freedom and Reason* (Oxford: Clarendon Press, 1963); and Gilbert Harman, "Moral Relativism Defended," *Philosophical Review* 84(January 1975), 3–22.

5. The wording here is taken from Louis P. Pojman, ed., *Ethical Theory: Classical and Contemporary Readings* (Belmont, Calif: Wadsworth, 1989), 352.

6. See Immanuel Kant, *Groundwork of the Metaphysics of Morals* (New York: Hutchinson's University Library, 1961; orig. pub. 1873); John Stuart Mill, *Utilitarianism* (Indianapolis: Hackett, 1979; orig. pub. 1863); G. E. Moore, *Principia Ethica* (Cambridge: Cambridge University Press, 1903); David Brink, "Moral Realism and the Sceptical Arguments from Disagreement and Queerness," *Australasian Journal of Philosophy* 62(June 1984), 111–125; and Alan Gewirth, *Reason and Morality* (Chicago: University of Chicago Press, 1978).

7. See, for instance, Alasdair MacIntyre, *Whose Justice? Which Rationality?* (Notre Dame, Ind.: University of Notre Dame Press, 1988).

8. See, for instance, Benedict, *Patterns of Culture,* 237–238.

9. We focus on four rather than all seven to save space. The arguments in the cases of gluttony, envy, and lust would be similar to that for avarice.

10. Locke sought to constrain relatively interventionary monarchs and thus, against this background, sought limited government; but the notion of a self-regulating economy had not yet developed, so limited government meant something different to Locke than it does to contemporary libertarians. See Ian Shapiro, *The Evolution of Rights in Liberal Theory* (New York: Cambridge University Press, 1986).

11. See Albert O. Hirschman, *The Passions and the Interests: Political Arguments for Capitalism Before Its Triumph* (Princeton: Princeton University Press, 1977).

12. Adam Smith, *Wealth of Nations* (New York: Penguin, 1982; orig. pub. 1776), book 1, chap. 2, para. 2.

13. It is reasonable to object that lines of demarcation between constructive and sinful activity are not so clearly drawn among the four cultural biases, that, for instance, avarice is the term everyone—the individualist included—uses to describe situations in which a focus on acquisition is carried too far. We do not disagree. A conception involving adherents of various cultural biases crying foul at various junctures as a particular type of activity becomes progressively more extreme; although more demanding to introduce, such a conception probably provides a more faithful representation of reality. In adopting this complication, however, we should keep In miind that egalitarians and hierarchists have less appreciation for the socially beneficial contributions individualists perceive in avarice even if particular instances are too modest to draw their condemnation.

14. For some exceptions, see Karl D. Jackson, ed., *Cambodia: Rendevous with Death* (Princeton: Princeton University Press, 1989); and Lucian W. Pye, *The Mandarin and the Cadre: China's Political Cultures* (Ann Arbor: Center for Chinese Studies, University of Michigan, 1988).

15. See Mary Douglas and Aaron Wildavsky, *Risk and Culture: An Essay on the Selection of Technical and Environmental Dangers* (Berkeley: University of California Press, 1982).

16. See Edward C. Banfield, *The Moral Basis of a Backward Society* (Glencoe, Ill.: Free Press, 1958).

17. Gabriel A. Almond and Sidney Verba, *The Civic Culture: Political Attitudes and Democracy in Five Nations* (Princeton: Princeton University Press, 1963); and Lucian W. Pye and Sidney Verba, eds., *Political Culture and Political Development* (Princeton: Princeton University Press, 1965) exhibited a clear preference for stable, Westminster-style democracy.

18. Baron de Montesquieu, *The Spirit of the Laws,* translated by Thomas Nugent (New York: Hafner, 1949), vol. 1, 32.

19. Victor C. Uchendu, *The Igbo of Southeast Nigeria* (New York: Holt, Rinehart, and Winston, 1965), 5–16.

20. On the latter, see Pye, *The Mandarin and the Cadre.*

21. For some exceptions to this objectivist portrayal, see Michael Thompson, Richard Ellis, and Aaron Wildavsky, *Cultural Theory* (Boulder: Westview Press), 265–267.

22. See Jennifer L. Hochschild, *What's Fair? American Beliefs About Distributive Justice* (Cambridge, Mass.: Harvard University Press, 1981); Michael Walzer, *Spheres of Justice* (New York: Basic Books, 1983); and Charles Lockhart and Richard Coughlin, "Building Better Social Theory Through Alternative Conceptions of Rationality," *Western Political Quarterly* 45(September 1992), 802–804.

23. See Geoffrey Warnock, *The Object of Morality* (London: Methuen, 1971).

24. Peter Railton, "Alienation, Consequentialism, and the Demands of Morality," *Philosophy and Public Affairs* 13(Spring 1984), 134–171.

25. Two caveats are in order here. First, on the complexities of "moral pluralism" see Richard Galvin, "Moral Pluralism, Disintegration, and Liberalism," in Cornelius Delaney, ed., *The Liberalism-Communitarianism Debate* (Totowa, N.J.: Rowman and Littlefield, 1993). Second, we are not claiming that all human needs are morally good, only that some are.

26. See Thompson, Ellis, and Wildavsky, *Cultural Theory.*

27. One implication of our moral pluralism is that we do not regard societal viability as unified and cumulative a measure of morality as utility is for utilitarians. For us, moral goodness resides in the distinct specific improvements produced by the disparate institutions of the various ways of life. Societal viability, although including these various moral components, is best understood as a measure of the capacity of a society to cope with particular circumstances it confronts.

28. See Richard M. Titmus, *The Gift Relationship* (New York: Random House, 1971).

29. See Abraham Maslow, *Motivation and Personality* (New York: Harper and Row, 1970); and Douglas and Wildavsky, *Risk and Culture.*

30. See Hochschild, *What's Fair?*

31. Roger D. Masters, *The Nature of Politics* (New Haven: Yale University Press, 1989), 221–223.

32. Charles S. Maier, "Why Did Communism Collapse in 1989?" unpublished paper, Cambridge, Mass., 1991.

33. See Charles E. Lindblom, *Politics and Markets* (New York: Basic Books, 1977), chap. 5.

34. Harry Eckstein, "A Culturalist Theory of Political Change," *American Political Science Review* 82(September 1988), 789–804.

35. The societal "learning" process we project bears some similarities to learning as portrayed by Gerald M. Edelman, *Bright Air, Brilliant Fire: On the Matter of the Mind* (New York: Basic Books, 1993).

36. Unfortunately for this generalization, another prominent island society, Japan, has not—spontaneously at any rate—developed a similar powerful individualistic culture.

37. See Daniel Bell, *The End of Ideology* (New York: Free Press, 1960); and Francis Fukuyama, *The End of History and the Last Man* (New York: Free Press, 1992), respectively.

CHAPTER 10

Conceptualizing and Operationalizing Cultural Theory

Richard P. Boyle
and Richard M. Coughlin

Cultural theory holds that the patterns of social interaction within which people live their lives come to shape, in predictable ways, their worldviews and in turn their attitudes and behavior. A huge accumulation of observation and research within the social sciences and psychology supports the general contention that people are shaped by their social experiences, so the problems lie in finding ways to specify, constrain, and operationalize these relationships. Mary Douglas provides a simplified starting point by proposing that two dimensions of social relationship adequately describe the patterns of social interaction that generate four clearly identifiable worldviews (at least at the level of whole cultural systems). The cultural theory equation therefore says that

Social Relations	—>	Worldview	—>	Attitudes,
(measured on grid-		(Type 1, 2, 3, or 4)		Behaviors
group dimensions)				

We will focus discussion here on the question of measuring the four basic cultural biases at the individual level using the standard instruments of survey research. In order to do this, we need a way to represent social relations as an approximate summary of each individual's lifetime experience of social interaction. There are various ways to go about doing this, but none of them are easy and all have limitations and costs. Aaron Wildavsky has proposed that individuals' preferences about the kinds of social patterns they would like to spend their time in affects the development of other preferences. "If the interests that we consider ours are indeed the products of social relations," he writes, "then the origins of our preferences may be found in the deepest desires of all: how we wish to live with other people and how we wish others to live with us."[1] By using preferences for social relationships as a mediating construct between previous experience and present worldview, we arrive at this expanded equation:

Experience in   —>   Preferred   —>   Worldview   —>   Attitudes,
Social Rela-   Social Rela-
tions   tions   (Type 1–4)   Behaviors

When the relationships are represented in this way, there are three causal links connecting the four conceptual components of cultural theory. In order to test the theory, we need to operationalize each component independently of the others and then analyze the relationships between each set of measures, preferably over time. This is not a simple task. We begin by reviewing the two main categories of existing research and then highlighting the problems that remain.

THE RELATIONSHIP BETWEEN
SOCIAL PATTERNS AND WORLDVIEWS

A methodology for analyzing groups and organizations along the grid-group dimensions was developed by Jonathan Gross and Steve Rayner. Their procedure requires a detailed inventory of questionnaire responses about group membership and hierarchy, leading to the development of "polythetic scales" consisting of a weighted combination of a number of separate indices. In addition, Gross and Rayner stress that these indices need to be combined with extensive ethnographic fieldwork to cross-check their validity. Admittedly, this method is "expensive of time and resources and is therefore principally applicable to small-scale units."[2] Perhaps for this reason, their methodology has not, as far as we know, been used in actual research.

James Hampton developed a survey instrument in which grid and group are measured by a series of forty-two questions about the current work situation and family life of respondents. These measures of social pattern are then correlated with "cosmology" responses to from nine to twelve questions (some questions are used more than once) for each of the four basic grid-group types. In an empirical test using this methodology, Hampton found that "only 8 of the 26 cosmology questions showed no significant association with the grid-group measures," a failure rate he characterized as "encouragingly low."[3] Therefore, Hampton's work provides moderate support for a direct association between social relations and worldview. However, since his analysis is correlational, no imputation of causality can be made—we don't know whether respondents chose their jobs because of their worldviews, had their worldviews modified over time by workplace social patterns, or both.

THE LINK BETWEEN
WORLDVIEWS AND ATTITUDES

Possibly because of the complexity and difficulty of operationalizing grid and group without the resources available to, say, Melvin Kohn and Carmi Schooler for their longitudinal study of the effects of the grid dimension of work settings on attitudes and personality variables,[4] most empirical research in cultural theory has bypassed the direct measurement of social patterns. Instead, attitudinal measures of the four basic cultural biases have typically been constructed and then used to predict a variety of other attitudes, opinions, perceptions, or beliefs.[5] Since research of this kind focuses exclusively on the final link of the causal diagram, linking worldviews to attitudes, the implicit assumption is that worldview scales reflect the predicted grid-group combinations in social patterns. This kind of assumption is by no means unreasonable, but it presents certain problems, particularly for the validity of the attitudinal measures used.

CURRENT METHODOLOGICAL PROBLEMS

The most pressing problem is to find good methods for operationalizing grid and group for both actual and preferred social patterns. Hampton made a good start here, but his failure to analyze the internal structure of the grid and group items or provide clear instructions for translating responses into dimensional scores, combined with the apparently weak level of the correlations, points toward the need for developing better self-report instruments. Kohn and Schooler have provided methods for doing this for grid with their measures of occupational self-direction in the workplace.[6]

Until now no work has been directed at operationalizing Wildavsky's idea about preferences among social patterns. We address that issue in the section on the University of New Mexico (UNM) survey.

Aside from Hampton's work, there is amazingly little direct evidence at the individual level that the grid and group dimensions of social patterns (however measured) actually predict worldviews. Since this is the heart of cultural theory and is by no means intuitively obvious to many people, research strategies that bridge the social pattern–worldview link are particularly needed.

Merely having grid-group measures for social relations (either actual or preferred) does not resolve all problems, however; there remains the issue of what kind of conceptual space they define. One debate concerns whether the intersection of grid and group is most appropriately viewed as a typology (i.e., four basic categories in a 2 × 2 table) or as the coordinates of a Cartesian surface. The consequences of adopting one approach over the other are not trivial, particularly in any attempt to develop operational measures for empirical analysis.

The heuristically more powerful approach is to view the intersection of grid and group as a typology. The implicit assumption here is that there are discontinuities between the four basic categories, and this underscores the distinctive worldviews associated with each type. This approach provides the least ambiguous portrayal of how various combinations of group identification and external constraint produce different perceptions and valuation for a broad range of phenomena in the social and natural environment. This approach also has the value of parsimony in that it yields 4 basic types of cultural bias—not 40 or 400. Not surprisingly, then, the main contributors to cultural theory have tended to emphasize pure (or "extreme") examples of grid and group intersection as discrete categories.[7] A person is thus described as an individualist or a hierarchist, an egalitarian or a fatalist, not some combination of these tendencies. This sort of discrete categorization yields the fourfold typology shown in Figure 10.1a.

The logical alternative to discrete categories of grid and group is to conceive of them as continuous axes of a two-dimensional space in which individuals (or groups) vary across the map according to changes in intensity along the gradients of grid and group. This seamless two-dimensional space can be visualized by removing the horizontal and vertical axes in Figure 10.1b. Conceptually this approach offers several advantages: It allows greater flexibility in characterizing varying degrees of grid and group, enabling us to explore the possibilities of hybrid types associated with various regions of the grid-group space;[8] it reduces the chance of small errors in measurement leading to miscategorization of any particular case; and it tends to correspond better to prevailing notions of how various cognitive attributes are actually distributed in the population, that is, as increments along a continuum rather than as discrete lumps.

Michael Thompson suggests a way of combining the fourfold typology with a two-dimensional map.[9] The question, he argues, hinges on the thickness of the lines separating the categories. At one extreme, where the lines are conceived of as infinitesimally thin, there are indeed four and only four categorical types possible. If a line is crossed in any direction, a "phase shift" occurs in the physical universe, in which a small change in base conditions yields a sudden, radical transformation to another state. In contrast, where lines are thick, "pure" types (corresponding to the quintessential categories) occupy only small regions near the corners of the quadrants (illustrated by the small boxes in the corners of Figure 10.1c), and transitional gray areas consume most of the area of the map.

These possibilities demonstrate that in addition to finding ways to measure grid, group, and each worldview type, we need to make decisions about the best way to represent their interrelationship—discrete or continuous, linear or nonlinear, additive or interactive, with or without zero points, independent or correlated, and so on. At this early stage of development, the approach that is most useful may vary with the specifics of the research project in question. In empirical research using mass survey data, for example, cultural bias is most readily operationalized as continuous scales of individualism, egalitarianism, hierarchy,

a. Grid and group as dichotomous variables; their effects on each worldview scale occur only with the cell for which that worldview is appropriate.

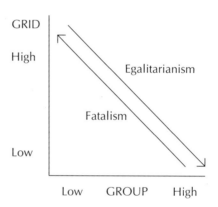

High   Low

GRID

High | Fatalism | Hierarchy |

Low | Individualism | Egalitarianism |

GROUP

b. Grid and group as continuous dimensions of an open coordinate system, with worldview scales related to grid-group across the full surface (hierarchy and individualism scales not shown here).

GRID

High

Egalitarianism

Fatalism

Low

Low   GROUP   High

c. Grid and group as continuous dimensions but related to worldview scales only at the extremes.

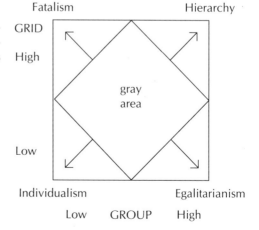

Fatalism   Hierarchy

GRID

High

gray
area

Low

Individualism   Egalitarianism

Low   GROUP   High

FIGURE 10.1 Alternative representations of grid, group, and their effects on worldview scales.

and fatalism. In other research—for example, case studies focusing on exceptional groups such as radical environmental activists or rural peasant communities[10]—the simple fourfold typology may be superior.

THE GENERAL SOCIAL SURVEY

An initial attempt by Charles Lockhart and Richard Coughlin to develop indicators of the four types of cultural bias using data from large representative national
samples in the General Social Survey (GSS) compared worldview scales with
specific attitudes.[11] Lockhart and Coughlin selected attitude items from the GSS
that best approximated the character of individualism, egalitarianism, hierarchy,
and fatalism. They constructed additive indices of these items, ran standard tests
for scale reliability, and used the indices as independent variables in multiple regression models predicting responses to a set of other survey items. In the language of research methodology, this approach is described as *content validity*—
the items appeared to capture the content of the thing they set out to measure.[12]
Although attitude indices constructed in such a way can be reliable and internally
coherent, their validity is limited to the attitude domains they study.

  Support for content validity derives almost solely from general acceptance
among researchers that the measures are indeed valid. Lockhart and Coughlin
also subjected the attitudinal measures in the GSS data to a stronger test of validity—*construct validity*.[13] Coughlin and Lockhart identified categories of respondents in the GSS sample that they hypothesized (on the basis of content validity)
represented distinct combinations of grid and group[14]—for example, Catholics
who characterized their religious convictions as strong and who reported attending church services once a week or more were selected as a putative high-grid–
high-group category.[15] The purpose was to test whether the attitudinal items selected by Lockhart and Coughlin to index specific worldviews were associated
with the social categories assumed to represent grid-group combinations. The
GSS enabled them to identify categories that allowed at least a crude test of the
construct validity of their worldview items.

Individualists

Coughlin and Lockhart selected self-employed respondents in the highest income
category as prototypical individualists. Although it was not possible to directly
measure the grid-group position of these respondents, it was a plausible assumption that high-income, self-employed people would be, on average, likely to correspond to a social context low on both group identity and external constraints.

Hierarchists

In addition to Catholics who characterized their religious convictions as strong
and also reported attending church services once a week or more, members of vet-

erans' organizations were assumed to represent people belonging to high-grid–high-group organizations.

Egalitarians

Blacks who reported taking part in consumer boycotts motivated by racial considerations or other civil rights activities and women who reported being active in feminist organizations were selected as prototypical egalitarians. Because of lack of data on these measures for certain years, however, several combinations of variables were used to classify respondents as egalitarians. On some items, where neither direct nor indirect measures of participation in collective action were available, "all blacks" was used as a surrogate group for "black activists" (these instances are noted in Table 10.1 and should be interpreted with more than usual caution).

Fatalists

Three categories of respondents were included as possible fatalists: low-income farmers, people who described themselves as lower class, and people who admitted to having been arrested. Of these, low-income farmers were hypothesized to best approximate low-group identity and high external constraint.[16] However, the number of respondents in this category in the GSS samples was often too small for meaningful analysis. The inclusion of two other categories—respondents who placed themselves in the lower class (a self-description that is significant because the overwhelming majority of Americans in every socioeconomic stratum describe themselves as middle class) and those who admitted to having been arrested—yielded enough respondents for analysis.[17]

Each of the social context categories was coded as a dummy variable, 1 if a respondent was included in the category, 0 if not. The correlations between each of these categories and the attitudinal items used in constructing the cultural bias indices were then examined. The purpose here was to determine if the attitudinal items met two conditions: (1) the items should form internally consistent clusters that clearly approximate predicted aspects of each worldview (content validity); (2) the items, and the clusters, should clearly differentiate the predicted social categories (construct validity).

Table 10.1 shows the variables that fared best in this test. Items concerning government trying to do too many things that should be left to individuals and private business (HELPNOT), the benefits of business profits (EQUAL2), and America offering the opportunity to live well (EQUAL6) all correlated positively with the individualist category (high-income, self-employed persons). These items are useful in differentiating individualists from the larger sample at a critical statistical significance level of p < .05.

Two of these items (HELPNOT and EQUAL2) also correlated positively with membership in at least one of the hierarchist categories. In addition, all three

TABLE 10.1 Correlations of Attitudinal Items with Social Context Categories

Survey Item	High-Income Self-Employed (I)	Black Activists (E)	Women Activists (E)	Devout Catholics (H)	Veterans' Org'tions (H)	Lower Class (F)	Low-Income Farmers (F)	Ever Been Arrested (F)
(EQUAL2) Economy can run only if businessmen make profits, benefiting all in the end	++ [a]	−^ [bc]	na [d]	0 [e]	++	0	0	−
(HELPNOT) Gov't is trying to do too many things that should be left to individuals/private business	++	−	−	+ [f]	+	− − [g]	0	0
(EQUAL6) Overall, one can live well in America	++	−^	na	0	0	− −	0	0
(USCLASS7) Differences in social standing are acceptable because they reflect what people made out of opportunities	+	0^	na	0	0	0	0	0
(USCLASS4) What one gets in life does not depend on own efforts, but on the economic situation, job opportunities, union agreements, and gov't	− −	++^	na	0	0	++	+	0
(EQUAL3) Gov't should employ everyone and keep prices stable, even if rights of businessmen restricted	− −	++^	na	0	−	++	0	0

Item								
(EQUAL4) Gov't should meet everyone's needs, even in sickness, poverty, unemployment, and old age	− −	+ +∧	na	0	− −	+ +	0	0
(HELPPOOR) Gov't should do everything possible to improve standard of living of the poor	− −	+	na	−	−	+ +	0	0
(HELPBLK) The government should help improve standard of living of blacks	−	+ +	na	0	−	+	0	0
(HELPSICK) Gov't should help pay for medical expenses	− −	+ +	na	0	0	+ +	0	0
(USCLASS5) Personal income should not be determined by one's work. Everybody should get what they need to provide for family	− −	+ +∧	na	0	0	+ +	0	0
(USCLASS2) What one can achieve in life depends upon one's family background	− −	+ ∧	na	0	0	+ +	0	+
(USCLASS3) What a person achieves depends on abilities and education	0	− −∧	na	0	0	−	0	0
(EQUAL7) Generally, business profits are distributed fairly in the U.S.	0	−∧	na	0	+ +	−	0	−

(continued)

TABLE 10.1 (continued)

Survey Item	High-Income Self-Employed (I)	Black Activists (E)	Women Activists (E)	Devout Catholics (H)	Veterans' Org'tions (H)	Lower Class (F)	Low-Income Farmers (F)	Ever Been Arrested (F)
(EQUAL5) High welfare benefits make people not want to work	0	—^	na	0	0	0	+	0
(GETAHEAD) People get ahead by hard work, rather than lucky breaks or help	+	–	0	0	0	–	–	–
(ANOMIA5) Lot of average person is getting worse	– –	+	+	–	–	++	0	+
(ANOMIA6) Unfair to bring child into the world the way future looks	– –	0	+	– –	0	++	+	+
(ANOMIA7) Most officials uninterested in problems of average person	– –	+	+	–	+	++	+	+
(HELPFUL) People are just looking out for themselves	–	++	+/–[h]	– –	–	++	0	+
(FAIR) Most people would try to take advantage of you if given the chance	–	++	+/–	–	0	++	0	+
(TRUST) You can't be too careful in dealing with people	– –	++	0	– –	0	+	0	0

(USCLASS8) Overall social differences are justified	0	− −[c]	na	0	+ +	− −	0	0	0
(PORNMORL) Agree sexual materials lead to breakdown of morals	−	0	0	+	0	0	0	+	−
(HOMOSEX) Think sexual relations between two adults of the same sex is wrong	−	0	0	+	+	+	0	+	−
(LETDIE1) When a person has an incurable disease, law should allow patient's life be ended	+ +	− −	na	− −	+	+	−	−	+
(SUICIDE1) Person has the right to end own life if ... has an incurable disease	+	− −	na	− −	0	0	−	−	+
(SUICIDE2) ... has gone bankrupt	+	−	na	− −	−	−	0	0	+
(SUICIDE3) ... has dishonored family	+	−	na	− −	−	−	0	0	+
(SUICIDE4) ... is tired of living and ready to die	+	−	na	0	0	0	0	0	+

[a] + + = r > .05, p < .05.
[b] − = r < .02, p < .05; p < .10 for small subsamples.
[c] ^ = all blacks.
[d] na = data not available.
[e] 0 = r not significant.
[f] + = r > .02, p < .05; p < .10 for small subsamples.
[g] − − = r < −.05, p < .05.
[h] +/− = opposite signs for different subsamples.

items correlated negatively with at least one of the egalitarian and fatalist categories and so are possible indicators (with appropriate adjustment of signs) of egalitarianism and/or fatalism. Only one item, concerning individuals making the most
out of opportunities they had (USCLASS7), picked up the individualist category
alone.

A similar pattern is apparent in the various items on social and economic
equality. Items dealing with government intervention to provide employment
(EQUAL3), meet everyone's needs (EQUAL4), improve the condition of the poor
(HELPPOOR) and blacks (HELPBLK), and help pay for medical expenses
(HELPSICK); the suggestion that personal income be determined by need rather
than by one's work (USCLASS5); and the impact of family background on what
one achieves in life (USCLASS2) all correlated positively with the egalitarians
(black activists) and one of the fatalist categories (lower class). Conversely, these
items showed consistently strong negative correlations with individualists and, to
a lesser extent, hierarchists.

Items related to fatalism showed nearly the same pattern. A tendency to regard
lucky breaks or help from others as important to getting ahead (GETAHEAD), to
see officials as not interested in the average person (ANOMIA7) and the lot of the
average person as getting worse (ANOMIA5), and to mistrust the motives of
others (HELPFUL, FAIR, TRUST) all correlated with two or more of the fatalist
categories.[18] These same items also tended to be positively correlated with egalitarians and negatively correlated with both individualists and hierarchists.

A different pattern was observed in items related to hierarchy, particularly with
respect to traditional morality. Although disapproval of euthanasia (LETDIE1),
suicide (SUICIDE1 to SUICIDE4), pornography (PORNMORL), and homosexuality (HOMOSEX) runs high among hierarchists (a tendency more pronounced
among the devout Catholics than among the veterans' organization members),
these views are also found to some extent among egalitarians and in at least some
of the fatalist categories. In contrast, individualists show the opposite correlations
on these items, meaning that they are less likely than the rest of population to dis-
approve.

Some items intended to serve as indicators of cultural bias turned out to have
no correlation with the social context variables. For example, responses to "A
person's social standing depends on whether he or she belongs to the upper or
lower class" showed no variation across the groups examined. An item saying the
"younger generation should be taught to think for themselves, even if not approved of by elders" did not vary across social categories. More surprising,
"Only if differences in income and social standing are large enough is there incentive for individual effort" showed virtually identical distributions among individualists, egalitarians, and hierarchists. Finally, a few items showed associations
that contradicted some predictions of cultural theory: For example, a question
asking respondents to locate their view of human nature on a scale running from
"essentially good" to "evil and perverse" found egalitarians (and fatalists) view-

ing humans as evil, with hierarchists (and individualists) tending to see people as essentially good.

Broadly speaking, the pattern of correlations between attitudinal items and social context supports cultural theory's core notion that different combinations of grid and group produce different biases. However, some clusters of items showed rather stable distributions across social categories. Three broad patterns emerged:

1. Responses to questions about economic activity and government intervention correlated positively with individualist (and, to a lesser extent, hierarchist) categories and negatively with egalitarian and fatalist categories.
2. Items questioning faith in societal institutions and revealing pessimism about the future correlated positively with egalitarian and fatalist categories and negatively with individualist and hierarchist categories.
3. Questions related to morality (euthanasia, suicide, pornography, and homosexuality) tended to divide individualist from hierarchic categories, with some inconsistent association between egalitarians and fatalists.

To explore this further, we reanalyzed the Coughlin and Lockhart data by grouping the items in Table 10.1 into several clusters.

Free Market:	EQUAL2, EQUAL3 (reversed), and HELPNOT.
Achievement:	USCLASS2 (reversed), USCLASS4 (reversed), USCLASS7, GETAHEAD.
Welfare State:	EQUAL4, HELPPOOR, HELPSICK, USCLASS5.
Social Pessimism:	ANOMIA5, ANOMIA6, ANOMIA7.
Distrust:	HELPFUL, FAIR, TRUST.
Traditional Morality:	PORNMORL, HOMOSEX.
Right to Die:	LETDIE1, SUICIDE1.

We assigned scores to these clusters in the following, admittedly crude, way: Significance levels coded "++" in Table 10.1 were given 5 points; "+," 4 points; "o," 3 points; "–," 2 points; and "––," 1 point. These scores were summed and the means used to rank order the social categories on each cluster. The rankings are similar across five of the seven scales, with the high-income self-employed, members of veterans' organizations, and devout Catholics always at one end; blacks or black activists and the self-identified lower class are (with one minor exception) at the other end. On both of the remaining scales, the self-employed and people who have ever been arrested are the most permissive; Catholics and to a slightly lesser extent low-income farmers are least permissive. These results suggest that two attitudinal dimensions can provide consistent differentiation between the social categories. But it is less clear how these two dimensions relate to grid and group.

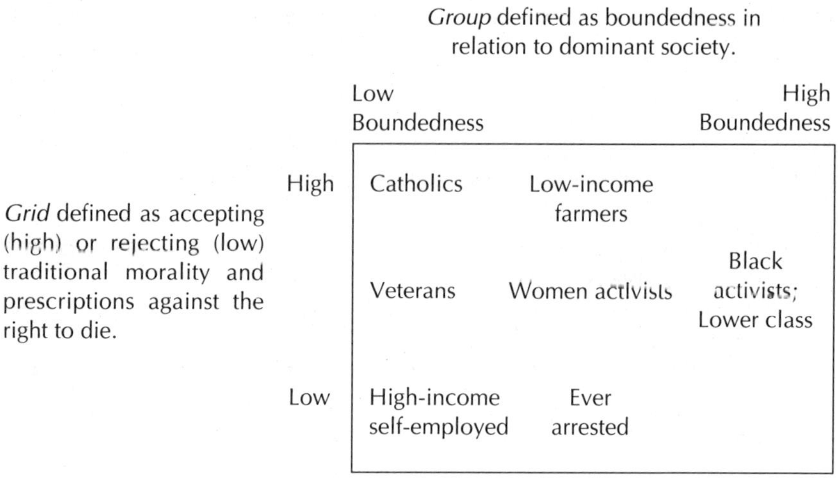

Group defined as boundedness in
relation to dominant society.

	Low Boundedness		High Boundedness
High	Catholics	Low-income farmers	
Grid defined as accepting (high) or rejecting (low) traditional morality and prescriptions against the right to die.	Veterans	Women activists	Black activists; Lower class
Low	High-income self-employed	Ever arrested	

FIGURE 10.2 Eight social categories plotted on the grid-group map.
Note: Categories are implied by combining the rankings for free market, achievement, welfare state, distrust, and social pessimism as group and the rankings for traditional morality and the right to die as grid.

The second dimension, which combines traditional moral precepts with attitudes about a human's right to die, reflects grid in the sense of closely constraining cultural norms. The first dimension has nothing to do with group in the usual sense of close interpersonal ties but can be interpreted in terms of boundedness between in-group and out-group, an emphasis that is central to the Douglas-Wildavsky tradition.[19] High rankings for "distrust" and "social pessimism" can indicate alienation from the dominant society (out-group); high rankings for "free market" and "achievement" reflect support for and commitment to the existing U.S. socioeconomic system; "welfare state" indicates rejection of the existing system and asserts an alternative system that is more favorable to the in-groups that make up some of the social categories. Therefore, we argue that these two dimensions can be interpreted as grid in the sense of a narrow or permissive attitude toward cultural norms, and as high or low group in the sense of accepting or rejecting the dominant U.S. social system. The opposition of the latter to the dominant society defines them as a bounded group in opposition to the dominant society (high group).

This is an exercise to suggest where future research should lead, not a definitive test of cultural theory. The analysis has produced distinctive patterns, even if they are not quite what we expected. Figure 10.2 plots the eight social categories. The high-income self-employed, as prototypical individualists, resemble devout Catholics and veterans in their strong identification with the dominant society but differ from them in their permissive approach to cultural norms—here their closest neighbors are people who have been arrested (in the words of Robert Merton, these are "innovators"[20]). Low-income farmers are closest to devout Catholics because their preference for restrictive norms is combined with ambivalence about, but not rejection of, the dominant system. Finally, blacks and black activists map onto the same position of people who identify themselves as lower class, another group that clearly does not see itself as benefiting from the dominant system. We could imagine adding "radical egalitarians"[21] in the bottom-right corner, and in the upper-right, perhaps an alienated religious cult such as the Branch Davidians.

The fit between grid-group location and imputed worldview occurs as predicted for some social categories, especially the high-income self-employed, but locations for other groups are surprising, such as black activists and the lower class together on the boundary between hierarchy and egalitarianism, and devout Catholics and veterans in the fatalism quadrant. We suggest there are two reasons for these surprises. First, the GSS data provide a limited sampling of the universe of attitudinal items that are relevant to worldviews and the range of social categories that can be assumed to populate the grid-group map. Second, although boundedness is clearly an important aspect of the group dimension—if it were not, why would it have emerged here so strongly?—it also clearly is not the whole story. Our second research project, involving undergraduate students, was designed to examine a wide range of alternative ways to operationalize group and grid, so we will have a chance to see what difference it makes when group is not defined as boundedness.

THE UNIVERSITY OF NEW MEXICO STUDENT SURVEY

We surveyed undergraduates in order to test the hypothesis that preferences for social relations can be used as proxies for actual experience in social contexts. Our measures for the grid (control vs. autonomy) and group (density and character of social relationships) dimensions of social relations were developed from questions about a variety of social relationships in different contexts (see Table 10.2). The items used to elicit preferences concerning parenting styles were adapted from Diana Baumrind[22] and Sanford Dornbusch et al.,[23] and those for work-situation preferences were adapted from Hampton,[24] Geert Hofstede,[25] and the literature on occupational values. All of the grid items correlated fairly highly with one another, so we combined them in a single scale.

The group items showed no such consistency. Items 4–6 of Table 10.2, which suggest a preference for friendly, cooperative sociability, correlated fairly strongly with each other and weakly but significantly with items 1 and 8, but not with anything else. Furthermore, this cluster (group items 4–6) did not correlate with any of the worldview scales. Apparently, responses to items 4 and 5 do not provide useful information for inferring positions on the group dimension. One

TABLE 10.2   Questionnaire Items Used to Measure Grid and Group in the UNM Student Survey

Parenting style: "Here are some different ways parents can behave in raising their children. Please rate each statement in terms of how you think parents *should* behave." (Five-point scale)

Grid

1. Parents should try to shape the beliefs and values of their children in accordance with what they themselves believe.

2. Parents should set clear rules and standards, using commands and physical punishment when necessary to enforce them.

3. Parents of teenagers should emphasize obedience and respect for what people in positions of authority say.

Group

1. Parents of teenagers should not impose decisions but should talk things over and try to work out an agreement about what should be done.

2. Parents should emphasize that as members of a family their children have responsibilities and obligations to others that take priority over their own personal interests.

3. Parents should show as much warmth and affection for their children as they can.

Work situation: "How would you rate each of the job characteristics listed below in terms of their importance to you?"

4. Work in a situation where so long as I follow the rules things will be OK.

5. Work in a situation where I get clear directives from above and can expect the people below me to carry out my orders.

6. When people work for an organization, they should follow the rules completely, even when they think breaking a rule would be in the organization's best interests.

7. When a subordinate and his or her superior disagree, it is best for everyone concerned for the subordinate to simply do what the superior says.

4. Work as part of a team with people who cooperate well with one another.

5. Have warm, friendly relationships with my supervisor and co-workers.

6. Work at a job where the people I work with get together socially off the job.

7. Know that my loyalty to the organization will be rewarded in the long run.

8. Work for an organization that allows all employees to participate in decisionmaking, particularly in their own unit.

(continued)

TABLE 10.2   (continued)

Grid	Group
Management style:	*Most enjoyable situation:*

8. Managers in work organizations use a variety of different management styles. Which kind of manager would you prefer to work under? A manager who:

a. Makes decisions promptly, communicates them clearly and firmly, and expects subordinates to carry out the decisions loyally, whether or not they agree with those decisions.

b. Consults with subordinates and takes their advice into account before reaching a decision but then expects all to wòrk loyally to carry out the decision whether their advice was heeded or not.

c. Calls a meeting when there is an important decision to be made and has the group discuss the issue until a consensus emerges that everyone can accept.

d. Sets broad policy guidelines and then leaves each subordinate to make his or her own decision about how to do the best job.

9. Which of the following social situations do you think would be the most enjoyable? Imagine yourself in each of the four situations and then choose the *one* that sounds the most enjoyable.

a. Being loved and accepted unconditionally, whether I have earned it or not.

b. Being popular and successful, admired by the people around me.

c. Being free to do whatever I feel like at the moment without worrying about what people around me think or might do.

d. Fitting in harmoniously and reciprocally as part of a group in which people understand and trust each other.

reason may be that when people think about work, other considerations (intrinsic or extrinsic rewards, opportunities for advancement, etc.) are more important than social relationships and therefore distort the results.

Group items 2 and 7 in Table 10.2 were designed to get at the long-term commitment and boundedness that cultural theory usually considers to be an important aspect of group. However, although these two items were moderately correlated with the grid scale (i.e., high-grid respondents preferred them), they showed little or no association either with each other or with the worldview scales. Group item 3 also proved unsatisfactory because (not surprisingly) more than 90 percent of the students considered warmth and affection to be "extremely important" in parenting. Therefore, we conclude that at least as used in the present study, items 1–8 do not show promise as instruments for measuring group.

Finally, item 9 was intended to reflect not preferences within specific contexts but preference for a particular type or quality of social experience. Responses to this item did not correlate strongly with any of the other group preference items but, as we will see, showed interesting relationships with the worldview scales. Our efforts to develop a group scale therefore concentrated on item 9.

We derived the grid scale used here from the mean of responses to grid items 1–8.[26] Although we used only one group item, developing a linear scale from the four possible responses to item 9 was more difficult. When we designed the questionnaire item, we had in mind that responses b ("being popular and successful, admired by the people around me") and c ("being free to do whatever I feel like at the moment without worrying about what people around me think or might do") reflect individualistic orientations. Response b was chosen to represent a somewhat competitive, status-conscious orientation; the orientation implied by c seemed more purely independent of other people. Responses a and d represent close, intimate relationships, but in different ways. We derived response a ("being loved and accepted unconditionally ...") from discussions of the yearning of the Japanese for a state of *amae*,[27] assuming that Japan is a high-group, relatively hierarchical culture. Response d was chosen to reflect a more symmetric relationship in which all members of the group both give and receive: "fitting in harmoniously and reciprocally as part of a group in which people understand and trust each other." We hypothesized that this response would appeal to egalitarians.

Responses chosen for item 9 elicited information not only about group but about grid as well, as we anticipated. When we classified responses b and c as low group, and responses a and d as high group, the mean grid score for each response was

Low Group		*High Group*	
b. Popular and successful	.17	a. Unconditional love	.09
c. Free to do whatever ...	−.07	d. Harmonious group	−.11

By adding the grid mean corresponding to the student's group response to the grid score for that student, we obtained a single, dichotomous classification of group and a continuous measure of grid.[28] Dichotomizing the adjusted grid scale at its mean yields a 2 × 2 grid-group table.[29]

Relationships Between Preferred
Social Relations and Worldviews

Our concern here was to test the prediction that the students' grid-group classifications will be related to scales measuring the four distinctive worldviews. The worldview scales were created with the GSS items used in the first study; with items reported by Karl Dake to scale fatalist, egalitarian, individualist, and hierarchist worldviews; and with some items developed specifically for this study. After factor analyzing the questionnaire items, we used eight scales to measure the four worldviews. Each scale was computed as the mean of responses to its component items ranging from 5 (strongly agree) to 1 (strongly disagree). A high score therefore indicates strong agreement with the items scaled.

Hierarchy. An authority scale was defined as the mean response to these three items:

I believe people should do what the government tells them to do,
   whether they think it is right or wrong.
Sexually explicit materials lead to a breakdown of morals.
The police should have the right to listen in on private telephone
   conversations when investigating crime.

The strongest agreement with these items comes, as predicted, from the high-grid–high-group combination (see Table 10.3).

In addition, students in the high-grid–high-group cell were considerably more likely to agree both that "the Bible is the actual word of God and is to be taken literally, word for word" and that "homosexual relations between two consenting adults are morally wrong" (significance for both p < .001). According to cultural theory, a commitment to traditional structures of morality is basic to the hierarchist worldview. And, in keeping with the similarity noted earlier between psychological research on dependency and cultural research on hierarchist worldviews, these students were significantly (p < .001) more likely to agree with the statement, "I feel uncomfortable when I make a decision that is different from what other people seem to be doing."

Egalitarianism. The low-grid–high-group combination was not associated with favoring policies that assign responsibility to the government for achieving egalitarian goals.[30] However, an egalitarian concern about specific disadvantaged groups is evidenced by the high levels of agreement with these statements (all significant at p < .01):

The rights of homosexual persons should be protected by law.
Racial injustice is a very serious problem in society today.
I support intensified federal efforts to eliminate poverty.

Cultural theory further predicts that egalitarians will be strongly pro-environment.[31] This prediction is supported by the responses of students in the low-grid–high-group cell to several items, especially this one:

Which of the following statements comes closest to stating the way you feel about our relation to the environment?

a. Humans should exercise dominion over nature; the environment is to be used but cared for responsibly.
b. The physical resources of the environment should be used for the economic advantage of those who successfully take advantage of the opportunities.
c. Humans are equal participants with the environment in a cooperative life process; nature has sacred qualities and should be protected.
d. Nature's forces are powerful, mysterious, and threatening, so human efforts to control the environment are limited and temporary.

Egalitarians chose response c; hierarchists were the most likely to choose response a (see Table 10.3).

Finally, the cultural theory prediction that low-grid–high-group conditions will be associated with a distrust of science and technology is supported only weakly in our analyses, and the prediction that egalitarians will be distrustful of "bigness" in general is refuted—it is the students in the low-grid–low-group cell who most often agree with these statements:

The human goals of sharing and brotherhood are being hindered by the
    growth of big institutions and the technologies they use.
Giant corporations have too much influence on the lives of ordinary
    people.

In sum, as predicted by cultural theory, a low-grid–high-group combination is associated with pro-environment attitudes and a concern about minorities and disadvantaged groups. The difference between high and low grid on these attitudes is strong; the group dimension has a much weaker effect. Students in the low-grid–low-group cell respond almost as favorably to these items as do students in the low-grid–high-group cell. Students in the low-grid–low-group cell did not answer

TABLE 10.3   Summary of Attitudes Relevant to Worldviews

Scale or Item	Cell 1[a]	Cell 2[b]	Cell 3[c]	Cell 4[d]	Sig <
Authority scale	1.66	1.95	1.35	1.44	.001
Welfare state scale	2.22	2.29	2.41	2.27	ns
Redistribute wealth scale	1.91	2.18	2.17	2.21	ns
Environment: percent saying					
"Humans have equal role"	.52	.50	.74	.70	.001
"Humans have dominion"	.39	.42	.17	.17	.001
Fatalism scale	2.14	2.01	1.62	1.95	.02
Distrust scale	1.34	1.24	.95	1.06	.002
"Need large corporations"	2.33	2.00	1.65	1.79	.001
"Need struggle of life"	2.05	1.78	1.32	1.47	.001
Self-interest scale	2.07	1.78	1.42	1.46	.001
Market economics scale	2.58	2.51	2.12	2.26	.001
"Avoid competition ..."(%)	.65	.61	.59	.70	ns
"Prefer self-employment" (%)	.19	.18	.31	.42	.01

[a]High grid, low group.
[b]High grid, high group.
[c]Low grid, high group.
[d]Low grid, low group.

our questions in the way expected of individualists. But before we take up the individualist cell, it will be useful to take a closer look at the fatalist cell.

Fatalism. Three scales apply here:

Fatalism:

It is not always wise to plan too far ahead because many things turn out to be a matter of good or bad fortune anyhow.
The future is too uncertain for a person to make serious plans.

Distrust:

A person is better off if he or she doesn't trust anyone.
Cooperating with others rarely works.
There is no use in doing things for people. You only get hurt in the long run.

Political alienation:

I don't worry about politics because I know I have no influence anyway.
It seems to me that, whoever you vote for, things go on pretty much the same.

Cultural theory says that a high-grid–low-group combination will produce the highest scores on each of these scales, and these predictions are supported. The link with political alienation is not statistically significant (p > .10), so we concentrate on the other two. We should note here also that students in the egalitarian cell are less fatalistic and distrustful of other people; the scales for fatalism and egalitarianism seem to measure the same diagonal vector, inversely correlated (see Table 10.3).

Students in the low-group–high-grid cell are the least likely to feel that racial injustice is a serious problem in the world today, the most likely to oppose gay rights, the least supportive of government efforts to eliminate poverty, and the most likely to agree that "concern about the environment restricts industry too much." They also showed the strongest agreement with

A prosperous economy requires concentrating production in large
    corporations; and with
It is just as well that the struggle of life tends to weed out those
    who cannot stand the pace.

Taken together, therefore, the high-grid–low-group combination of preferences seems linked not only with fatalism but also with higher levels of alienation (both from other people and from the political system), with less activist social and environmental views, and with more support for big business and social Darwinism. The high-grid–low-group category appears to combine aspects of two worldviews—fatalism and individualism; cultural theory predicts that the individualist worldview should occur only in the low-grid–low-group cell.

Individualism. Two scales emerged from the factor analyses that appear to tap elements of the worldview of individualism:

Self-interest:

Programs designed to help poor people only end up destroying individual
    initiative.
If people are poor, it's because they don't try hard enough.
It is not the government's responsibility to improve the standard of living.
    Everyone should take care of himself or herself.

Market economics:

In order to survive and prosper, a free society must allow private enterprise
    the opportunity to pursue its own ends with a minimum of regulation.
In a fair system, people who achieve more should earn more.
If businesses make good profits, that benefits everyone in the end.

Surprisingly, the low-grid–low-group combination is linked not with high scores on these scales but with low scores. The students who best approximate the individualist worldview are found in the high-grid–low-group cell, which appears to include both fatalism and individualism (see Table 10.3).

To explore this further, we looked for the predicted competitiveness of individualists by using the statement, "Competition should be avoided as much as possible because it leads people to be in conflict with each other." Students in the low-grid–low-group cell were slightly more likely than others to *disagree* with this statement, and acceptance of competition is spread fairly evenly across all grid-group combinations (see Table 10.3). Rather than competitiveness, the distinguishing feature of the low-grid–low-group students seems to be *independence*. When asked whether, ten years from now, they would prefer to be working for government or private-sector organizations, to have started companies of their own, or to be working as self-employed individuals, far higher proportions of these students chose self-employment (see Table 10.3). Consistent with this preference for self-employment, the low-grid–low-group students were also most likely to rate these two characteristics of a job as extremely important:

> work in a situation where the person who does the best job is
>   rewarded; and
> have a job in which I carry out the work by myself

There is one additional distinguishing characteristic of the students in this group: They scored substantially higher than all other groups in saying that parents should encourage self-direction on the part of their children:

> Parents should encourage children, and especially teenagers, to
>   question what they are taught and make up their minds for themselves.
> Parents should allow teenagers as much autonomy and self-regulation
>   as possible.

When we look at students in the two low-group quadrants, therefore, we find differences between those with high-grid and those with low-grid preferences—but not exactly the differences that cultural theory predicts. Rather than seeing a contrast between fatalists and individualists, we seem to have distinguished *competitive* individualists (the high-grid category) from *independent* individualists (the low-grid category). From a global perspective these findings make sense. On a grid-group map of the world population, a sample of American college students would be expected to concentrate well below the midpoint of the grid axis and probably to be centered somewhat on the left, or low, side of the group axis. What the analysis reported so far has done, in essence, is superimpose a 2 × 2 table over this distribution by using the means to divide the sample in two. Thus, our tables primarily distinguish very-low-grid from medium-low-grid students—so our finding that the former are more independent and the latter more competitive is consistent with the basic qualities of individualism they share.

These findings introduce new questions for future research to consider: (1) Can the distinction between independent and competitive individualists as a function of grid scores be extended generally to similar populations? (2) Is there a relationship between our independent individualists and what cultural theory has discussed as the "hermit"?[32] (3) What should be made of the apparent similarity between independent individualists and egalitarians on social issues, on orientations toward the environment, and on a generally favorable view of human nature?

Furthermore, if we assume, as we did previously, that most of the students in our sample would rank as low-grid in world terms, then why did the students in our high-grid–high-group category fit so well the description of hierarchists? Howard Schuman, Lawrence Bobo, and Maria Krysan have recently argued that measures of authoritarianism are more meaningfully related to other attitudinal orientations at higher educational levels than at lower educational levels,[33] which supports the validity of our findings and suggests the importance of further research on hierarchy among educated Americans.

In sum, our survey of undergraduate students supports the contention that locating people on a grid-group surface through their preferences about social relationships makes possible good predictions about attitudes, values, and perceptions that have no prima facie relationship to attitudes about social relationships. The fundamental proposition that social patterns have a significant, and predictable, influence in shaping worldviews is therefore supported.

CONCLUSION

The purpose of both studies reported here was to develop survey methods for measuring grid and group and then to test the cultural theory postulate that worldviews (as measured by specific attitude scales) can be predicted from grid-group combinations. Our general conclusion is that this postulate seems to be true for survey research on individuals as well as for ethnographic comparisons of cultures, although the linkages between grid-group and worldview were not always what cultural theory predicts. However, if we interpret these results by situating the samples or categories we examined in the larger framework of a (hypothetical) representation of the world population, what initially appear to be contradictions become reasonable extrapolations of the basic logic informing cultural theory. Although we arrive at a consistent statement, however, the consistency depends on the methods used to produce and interpret the findings. We conclude by reviewing our findings from a methodological perspective.

1. Grid seems to be a robust dimension. All of our measures of grid correlated with each other, and their associations with worldview and attitudinal items were in line with cultural theory predictions. This was true even when, in the first study, a very narrow aspect of grid—restrictive or permissive attitudes about certain traditional norms—was used to represent the dimension as a whole.

2. Group poses serious measurement problems. In the first study (where no measures equivalent to the independence-interdependence distinction were available), the dimension that emerged quite strongly had to do with positive or negative attitudes toward the dominant socioeconomic system of the United States. If we equate opposition to the dominant system with boundedness of the in-group and then assume that boundedness indicates a high-group position, we obtain results that are clear but often at variance with cultural theory predictions. What does this mean? Our conclusion is that boundedness (particularly in the sense of in-group versus out-group) is quite different from other measures of group and in future research should probably be treated as an independent dimension until other measures have been analyzed. In the second study, we found that good predictions about worldview items could be made on the basis of a distinction between independence from or interdependence with other people as expressed through preferences for the kind of social situation the respondent thinks would be most enjoyable. To the best of our knowledge, no questionnaire item like this has been used before either in cultural theory research or in the general literature on personality and attitude scaling.[34] There are, therefore, two tasks ahead: to see whether the results we obtained with this item will be replicated in other studies and to improve on the item by trying different phrasings and modes of presenting this idea to survey respondents.

3. Once grid and group are measured, there are further problems in using them to represent a two-dimensional system. We prefer conceptualizing grid-group cross-classifications as continuous Cartesian coordinate systems. But in our second study, grid and group were collapsed at their midpoints into a 2 $\times$ 2 table, which makes the quadrants appear to be representing the prototypical categories of cultural theory. Since a sample of American college students scarcely represents the world's population, we made assumptions about the region of a "universal" grid-group map in which our sample might reasonably be located, and on the basis of those assumptions we were able to integrate our results with cultural theory postulates in a consistent way. However, assumptions of this kind should always be questioned and investigated, and the challenge for future research will be to apply similar methodologies to other cultures or to groups representing other segments of the U.S. population.

4. The issue of how to measure worldviews (or even what a worldview consists of) is by no means resolved. It was suggested earlier that if we think in terms of scales to measure worldviews, the appropriate conceptualization would plot each scale as a diagonal vector pointing toward the corner it represents. In this case, scales for diagonally opposite corners should be inversely correlated. We found some evidence for this in the second study, but in the first study we found such indices of fatalism as distrust correlating positively with such indices of egalitarianism as welfare state. The most likely reason for this is that the first study emphasized social categories that were either supportive of or antagonistic toward the dominant system of the United States—the in-group–out-group dimension was

highlighted, and responses to the attitudinal items reflect this. The student sample appeared to be much less polarized on this dimension.

A final, related, note: In both of the studies we report here we must plead guilty to blurring the distinction between worldviews and specific attitudes, and this may be responsible for some of the problems just discussed. We suggest that it may be preferable to conceptualize worldviews in terms that clearly reflect the basic structure they are assumed to acquire from grid-group patterns: Fatalism and distrust are appropriate measures for the high-grid–low-group corner; scales of traditional morality or attitudes toward authority are reasonable for the high-grid–high-group corner; and distinctive orientations toward the environment are appropriate for all corners. But more specific attitudes toward political and economic policy issues may be too context-dependent to be useful for comparisons over time or across cultures. For example, the meaning of responses to the free market and welfare state items used here may well have been different at the time of the undergraduate student survey, given the collapse of the Soviet system (often seen as discrediting centrally planned systems), than it was during the mid-1980s when the GSS surveys were conducted.

In sum, the findings reported here both emphasize the usefulness of grid and group measures of social patterns along with worldview items and provide guidance in how to incorporate these measures in survey research. We suspect that as more empirical research inspired by cultural theory proceeds, similar modifications will likely need to be made along with the introduction of greater complexity in the relationships actually observed. We are confident that such adjustments and appropriate modifications will only improve the explanatory and predictive power of cultural theory.

NOTES

1. Aaron Wildavsky, "Choosing Preferences by Constructing Institutions: A Cultural Theory of Preference Formation," *American Political Science Review* 81(March 1987), 4.

2. Jonathan Gross and Steve Rayner, *Measuring Culture: A Paradigm for the Analysis of Social Organization* (New York: Columbia University Press, 1985), 115.

3. James Hampton, "Giving the Grid/Group Dimensions an Operational Definition," in Mary Douglas, ed., *Essays in the Sociology of Perception* (London: Routledge & Kegan Paul, 1982), 75.

4. Melvin Kohn and Carmi Schooler, *Work and Personality: An Inquiry into the Impact of Social Stratification* (Norwood, N.J.: Ablex, 1983).

5. See, for example, Karl Dake, "Orienting Dispositions in the Perception of Risk: An Analysis of Contemporary Worldviews and Cultural Biases," *Journal of Cross-Cultural Psychology* 22(1991), 61–82; and Hank C. Jenkins-Smith and Walter K. Smith, "Ideology, Culture, and Risk Perception," in this volume.

6. Kohn and Schooler, *Work and Personality.*

7. See, for example, Michael Thompson, Richard Ellis, and Aaron Wildavsky, *Cultural Theory* (Boulder: Westview Press, 1990).

8. See Charles Lockhart and Richard Coughlin, "Building Better Comparative Social Theory Through Alternative Conceptions of Rationality," *Western Political Quarterly* 45(September 1992), 793–809.

9. Michael Thompson, "A Three-Dimensional Model," in Douglas, ed., *Essays in the Sociology of Perception,* 31–63.

10. Edward C. Banfield, *The Moral Basis of a Backward Society* (Glencoe, Ill: Free Press, 1958).

11. See Lockhart and Coughlin, "Building Better Comparative Social Theory."

12. Content validity was also the basis for the studies discussed earlier of relationships between worldviews and specific attitudes.

13. This follows Edward Carmine and Richard Zeller's proposal that "first, the theoretical relationship between the concepts themselves must be specified. Second, the empirical relationship between the measures of the concepts must be examined. Finally, the empirical evidence must be interpreted in terms of how it clarifies the construct validity of the particular measure" (*Reliability and Validity Assessment* [Newbury Park, Calif.: Sage Publications, 1979], 23).

14. Richard Coughlin and Charles Lockhart, "Cultural Theory and Political Ideology: An Empirical Test," presented at the annual meeting of the Western Political Science Association, San Francisco, March 19–21, 1992.

15. Characterizing all such Catholics in the GSS sample as hierarchists is an admittedly crude approach, especially given the often problematic relationship between the Vatican and many American Catholics on such issues as birth control and the ordination of women. Yet our central purpose here is exploratory: to shed light on whether the attitudinal measures identified as indicators of hierarchical views correspond at all to social categories likely to have a higher than average incidence of hierarchist tendencies. So it is not of great consequence that some American Catholics may cleave to more permissive, egalitarian values as long as these tendencies do not neutralize the expression of hierarchical values that constitute the traditional, formal relationships embodied in the church.

16. Farmers, especially those who enjoy little financial success, are doubly constrained: first, by the vagaries of the natural environment, which may wipe out a crop by drought, or flood, frost, or pestilence; second, by remote and often fickle commodity futures markets that dictate the prices that crops will fetch. It is not surprising, then, that farmers more than others will tend to see success or failure as less a function of individual effort and more the outcome of forces beyond individual control—in short, fatalism.

17. To guard against contamination of the fatalist category with egalitarians, the categories "lower class" and "ever arrested" were examined separately both including and excluding blacks. The pattern of results remained unaffected.

18. The small number of low-income farmers made it difficult to achieve statistically significant correlations.

19. For example, Mary Douglas explicitly excludes hunter-gatherers, usually considered the most egalitarian of societies, from the egalitarian category because they are not sufficiently bounded (*How Institutions Think* [Syracuse, N.Y.: Syracuse University Press, 1986]).

20. Robert Merton, "Social Structure and Anomie," in *Social Theory and Social Structure* (Glencoe, Ill.: Free Press, 1957), 131–160.

21. See Aaron Wildavsky, *The Rise of Radical Egalitarianism* (Washington, D.C.: American University Press, 1991).

22. Diana Baumrind, "Parenting Styles and Adolescent Development," in J. Brooks-Gunn, R. Lerner, and A. C. Petersen, eds., *The Encyclopedia of Adolescence* (New York: Garland, 1991), 746–758.

23. Sanford M. Dornbusch, Philip L. Ritter, P. H. Leiderman, D. F. Roberts, and M. J. Fraleigh, "The Relation of Parenting Style to Adolescent School Performance," *Child Development* 58(187), 1244–1257.

24. See Hampton, "Giving the Grid/Group Dimensions an Operational Definition."

25. Geert Hofstede, *Culture's Consequences: International Differences in Work-Related Values* (Beverly Hills; Sage Publications, 1980); and *Cultures and Organizations: Software of the Mind* (London: McGraw-Hill, 1991).

26. More specifically, we (1) adjusted responses to items 1–7, which were coded on a scale from 1 to 5, for response bias by subtracting each student's response to each item from his or her mean response for the full set of fourteen all-work preference items; (2) dichotomized item 8 such that response $a = 1$ and all other responses = 0; and (3) summed the resulting scores and divided by 8.

27. See especially Helen Markus and Shinobu Kitayama, "Culture and the Self: Implications for Cognition, Emotion, and Motivation," *Psychological Review* 98(1991), 224–253.

28. These two scales were found to be only weakly correlated.

29. The n's were distributed as follows: 63 fatalism (high control, independence from others), 84 hierarchy (high control, interdependence with others), 53 individualism (low control, independence from others), and 94 egalitarianism (low control, interdependence with others).

30. Two scales of attitudes toward the welfare state and wealth redistribution were indicated by factor analysis. However, neither of these scales produced statistical significance (see Table 10.3). One interesting feature of Table 10.3 is the low (antiegalitarian) score on "Redistribute Wealth" for students in cell 1, which indicates that at least the scale measures a worldview dimension extending diagonally across the table.

31. See, for example, Mary Douglas and Aaron Wildavsky, *Risk and Culture: An Essay on the Selection of Technical and Environmental Dangers* (Berkeley: University of California Press, 1982).

32. See, for example, Thompson, Ellis, and Wildavsky, *Cultural Theory,* 28–32.

33. Howard Schuman, Lawrence Bobo, and Maria Krysan, "Authoritarianism in the General Population: The Education Interaction Hypothesis," *Social Psychology Quarterly* 55(1992), 379–387.

34. See, for example, John P. Robinson, Phillip R. Shaver, and Lawrence S. Wrightsman, eds., *Measures of Personality and Social Psychological Attitudes* (San Diego: Academic Press, 1991).

CHAPTER 11

The Theory That Would Be King

Dennis J. Coyle

Cultural theory, or grid-group analysis, is a marvelous, mysterious beast. A compelling tool of social analysis, it is nonetheless viewed with wary fascination by the social science community, which tends to be intrigued by its aspirations toward comprehensiveness yet put off by some of its more exotic applications and terminology. My purpose here is to explore some of the implications of the theoretical framework and its place in the social sciences. I hope to provide some food for thought for political and social scientists and for the considerably smaller universe of cultural theorists, as indeed we hope this entire book has. I make no pretense of speaking for any other contributors to this volume, or of summarizing its themes. This chapter is intended not as a conclusion, but as a beginning.

Some grid-group scholars may feel that a critical review at this stage is not constructive. But I am confident grid-group analysis is promising enough that it can only gain from being put under the microscope. I will largely focus on the book *Cultural Theory* by Michael Thompson, Richard Ellis, and Aaron Wildavsky, which has played an important role in introducing this particular cultural approach to the political and social science community,[1] and on the foundations of grid-group analysis laid by anthropologist Mary Douglas.[2] Most reviews of cultural theory are by scholars with little or no background in grid-group analysis,[3] and a critique by a fellow traveler might be constructive.[4]

Cultural theory is ambitious. Although not claiming to be entirely original, it has sought to "capture the wisdom of a hundred years of sociology, anthropology and psychology."[5] Although recognizing that culture may not entirely explain all human action, cultural theorists do assert that the grid-group model is applicable to any society, ancient or modern, large or small, primitive or postindustrial, and that the three, four, or five ways of life generated by the model exhaust the basic possibilities for social organization. "Regardless of time or space," the authors of *Cultural Theory* say, "individuals always face (and, as long as human life exists, always will) five ways of relating to other human beings."[6] Anywhere. Always. Period. Humble it is not. But that's part of the attraction.

Grid-group analysis is commonly referred to as cultural theory, or even Cultural Theory. This can seem presumptuous, as cultural theory exhausts neither definitions of culture nor theories about it, any more than Weber defines sociology or Marx defines historical analysis. My preference is to cling to the clunky term "grid-group analysis," although I have compromised with the predominant usage of "cultural theory" by using the terms interchangeably.[7] Others recognize that cultural theory is a troubling title but reject "grid-group" or other more informative phrases as "less felicitous" or lacking "instant recognition."[8] But whatever it is called, the grid-group approach is unlikely to be instantly recognized in homes across America, so we might as well be informative. And it is only through usage that terminology will become felicitous.

CULTURAL BOXES AND THE WANDERING ZERO

Skeptics might say "cultural" theory ignores culture altogether in that it places individuals from throughout time and around the world in the same categories without adequately appreciating the differences in their beliefs and practices, the uniqueness of the cultures in which different groups are embedded. The criticism is exaggerated because the grid-group approach, if used cautiously, need not deny important differences within any way of life. Cultural theorists need only assert that the dimensions they employ are fundamental and that the categories enable fruitful comparisons between different settings. The caution against oversimplification is well taken, however, and this may be especially a problem when the four cultures are seen as rigid boxes into which persons must be placed. This problem can be guarded against by regarding grid and group as continuous, rather than dichotomous, variables and by regarding the four corners they produce as ideals or theoretical extremes rather than the loci of individuals. We can then better account for gradations in commitment to particular cultural perspectives by placing individuals at points between the four corners. Rather than expecting dramatic changes when someone passes through no-man's-land from one culture to another, we can recognize that the passage may involve only a series of modest, incremental shifts in the weighting of preferences. When I speak of a libertarian, for example, I am referring to someone whose arguments, policy positions, or preferences favor a low-grid, low-group way of life even though she may accept many hierarchical institutions and appreciate voluntary community. Relative to other parties in a dispute or to existing policies, this person would advocate less constraint and less group control and would rely on libertarian arguments to make her points. A person need not be an individualist in every aspect of her preferences and social relations to be meaningfully described as a libertarian. As Douglas advocates, "Each included member [of a cultural classification] only needs to show a majority of the features in the class. An advantage of this method is that it does away with sharp dichotomies."[9]

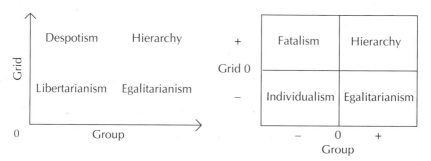

FIGURE 11.1 The grid-group model with 0 in the lower left, in the middle, and with alternative terminology.

Another way to phrase the issue of "boxes" versus continua is to ask where zero is in the grid-group model. Placing zero in the middle, at the intersection of the midpoints of each variable, does not rule out continua, but it creates a clear dividing point between the four cultures, making it easier to discount cultural variation within each "box" (see Figure 11.1). If, however, zero marks the lower-left corner of the diagram, the point where both the grid and group dimensions begin, then it becomes easier to see grid and group as two continua along which an individual, argument, or group (depending on the subject of analysis) can theoretically be located at any point.[10] Douglas has not been consistent on the location of zero.[11] But she does generally view the variables as continua, such as when she says, "There is not reason to expect sudden breaks in continuity from one context (and its supporting cosmology) to another."[12]

A centered zero suggests that it must be possible for individuals to occupy or at least pass through a state in which they lack any trace of social group or constraint. When zero is in the lower left, although the characteristics of the location are the same, there is no implication that such a point could be occupied. Social relations may be minimal, but never entirely absent. Douglas seems to agree that zero is unattainable when she writes, "The zero would represent a blank, total confusion with no meaning whatever."[13]

If zero is placed in the middle, grid and group must then generate negative as well as positive values. The concept of negative group is particularly odd, as one cannot have less of a group than none at all.[14] It may be that low-group social relations are more aptly characterized by another term, such as "network," but that is essentially a loose group rather than a negative of it. If, however, a network is qualitatively different from a group, and not just different in degree, then network and group do not lie on the same axis, and the typology breaks down.

Negative grid is also a troubling concept. Those who employ it place individuals in this location if they are constraining or controlling others, pushing them to the periphery of the network; the "big men" of New Guinea are a common example.[15] This seems to me an incomplete conception of the low-grid, low-group way of life and a distortion of the nature of social relations, as I will explain further on, and it also leaves a rather empty box. Short of God and perhaps Ross Perot, it is hard to conceive of anyone who is not constrained or "gridded" in any way, who is immune from pressure from others yet somehow able to pressure them. Negative grid is especially difficult to imagine when applied to egalitarians; they, like individualists, would be "negative grid," but surely the essence of their social relations is not that they are "gridding" hierarchists, who, like fatalists, would be "positive" grid. If negative and positive grid apply only to individualists at the center of networks and the fatalists they manipulate and do not apply to hierarchists and egalitarians, then the typology succumbs once again. We then have four labels for cultures, but no longer any persuasive deductive claim that they are exhaustive and rooted in two common variables.

OF HERMITS AND INDIVIDUALISTS

When zero is placed in the middle, the question arises of who might reside there. Who is neither negatively nor positively grouped, neither "gridding" nor "gridded"? The answer given by some cultural theorists has been the hermit, the person who has withdrawn from social relations because she wishes to be neither coerced nor coercive.[16] (See Figure 11.2.) Descriptions of the hermit can be quite romantic, evoking the natural man of Rousseau unsullied by civil society.[17] Although I haven't known many hermits, I would suppose that is in part because there are not many of them and because they are, well, antisocial. If culture is a social phenomenon, as cultural theory argues it is, it seems curious to make a small group removed from social relations one of the basic ways of life. As social scientists, I'm not sure why we should care much about a category so removed from society, and I doubt that such an existence in the eye of the storm of social life, removed from social relations, is even possible. Michael Thompson, who developed the hermit category, acknowledges that at best the hermit "keeps his [social] network to a minimum ... and avoids placing heavy demands on such networks as he has."[18] Even hermits in the deepest recesses of the wilderness were products of social relations that shaped their perceptions and preferences.

The hermit category is often omitted in empirical applications, and this may be a discreet way of acknowledging that the category is dubious. But it's important to challenge this fifth way of life directly not only because of the attention it was given in *Cultural Theory* but also because of the implications it has for the low-grid, low-group way of life, libertarianism. I prefer to use this label rather than individualism, which I identify with the low end of the group scale, including both the low-grid and high-grid cultures. Libertarianism, I argue, is the combination of autonomy (or low grid) and individualism (or low group). This is a relatively fine distinction, and I don't think the term "individualism" necessarily does violence to the low-grid, low-group culture as long as it incorporates autonomy. Libertarianism also emphasizes the key social value that is pursued within the culture— liberty—and associates that corner of the grid-group map with a significant intel-

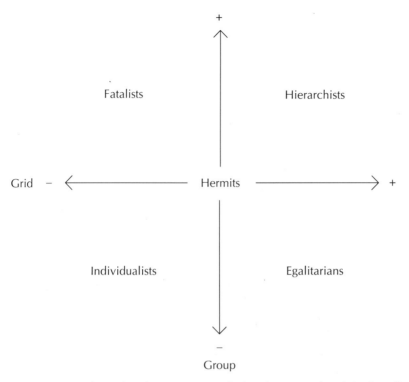

FIGURE 11.2 The cultural categories, including hermits, placed in five discrete locations. *Source:* Adapted from Michael Thompson, Richard Ellis, and Aaron Wildavsky, *Cultural Theory* (Boulder: Westview Press, 1990), 8.

lectual perspective in modern policy debates, just as egalitarianism is more lucid than sectarianism, the older term for the low-grid, high-group way of life. Egalitarians pursue equality, and libertarians pursue liberty, and this straightforward approach can remove much of the mystery when introducing grid-group analysis to other scholars.[19]

Hermits, I suggest, essentially are libertarians with a preference for being left alone, and interpretation of this culture is distorted when hermits are excluded.[20] Libertarianism stresses the freedom to make decisions in one's own interest, and that freedom entails the choice not to participate, be it by not voting in politics, by not working for a corporation or buying consumer goods, or by withdrawing from social contact altogether. As long as no one is preventing the hermit from riding back into the settlement, she remains free. Originally, the hermit was very close to Douglas's description of low-grid, low-group social relations, which were characterized by sparse population, infrequent interaction, and material sacrifice.[21] The problem arises when this corner of the model is identified exclusively with market competition or acquisitive materialism and the hermit is sent packing to her own category of the model.[22] Douglas took her off the map entirely, writing that "this diagram does not deal with the possibility of voluntary withdrawal from society," although she noted the similarity to low-grid, low-group culture.[23]

Much of my personal introduction to the "hermit" perspective came while hanging out, so to speak, on the cliffs of the Shawangunk Mountains some twenty years ago. Rock climbers are highly individualistic, and the "Gunks" gang was notoriously so.[24] The young climbers who frequented the cliffs were competitive, hedonistic, and somewhat reckless. All in all, great fun. Ropes linked climbers in temporary networks, which lasted as long as was mutually beneficial. Even between partners competition could be intense. Solo, unroped climbing was revered by many, but gravity dictated that having a partner was prudent. The alpine climbs in distant mountain ranges that were admired and much talked about were solos and fast, small group ascents, not large expeditions that demanded heavy doses of cooperation and sacrifice to the greater good of the group. The climbers wished to escape, however briefly, from the conformity of mainstream society, like the hermits of cultural theory.[25] In short, climbers were largely libertarians who, living in the wake of the 1960s, felt uncomfortable with that identification, which they tended to equate with greedy capitalist oppression, much as some cultural theorists would later do.

When hermits are awarded their own cultural category, the implication is that they could not be in the lower-left corner of the model because they are not coercing anyone. This version of cultural theory suggests that low-group social relations must be dog-eat-dog; persons are either individualist dogs who are eating or fatalist dogs who are being eaten, so to speak. In *Cultural Theory,* the classic individualist is characterized as a manufacturer who is "unashamedly manipulative."[26] Asserting that control of others is fundamental to low-grid, low-group relations[27] is, I think, a mistake that arises in part from placing zero in the middle and then attempting to conceive of what "negative grid" might be. This paints cultural analysis into a corner, as when Douglas concludes that the "jazz man, though down grid" doesn't quite fit the low-grid, low-group culture because he is "not trying to exert control over others."[28] Not all social relations are coercive;[29] people interact all the time simply because they like it or find it useful, and they are free to walk away. The low-grid social relations of libertarianism do not require a downtrodden class of fatalists to step on;[30] rather, fatalism frustrates libertarianism because it erodes trust, initiative, and self-reliance.[31]

Classifying only successful elites as individualists, and assuming that those who work under them are fatalists, is problematic.[32] In libertarianism, "size of following" is not the only "way of reckoning success."[33] Libertarian success does not require large accomplishments, just the freedom to choose.[34] A self-employed handyman who does as he wishes would be as libertarian as a prosperous entrepreneur.[35] Douglas and Wildavsky come closer to the mark in *Risk and Culture* when they write that the market individualist "cannot claim autonomy for himself without setting it up as universally valuable, a right of his fellow citizens, too. He will claim for everyone the rights freely to contract and freely to withdraw from contractual obligations."[36] Libertarianism is a culture of freedom that may include entrepreneurs, the working class, hermits, or anyone else for that matter, even taxi drivers.[37]

Freewheeling libertarianism may well leave in its wake a rubbish heap of fatalists, "disenfranchised derelicts who cannot be reincorporated into the system which excludes for poor performance."[38] Such fallout is not an essential aspect of libertarianism, however, and considering it such distorts the cultural model and the libertarian ideal that is an animating force in policy debates. A robust group of individualists might interact freely without any sense of oppression or utter failure.

Having said that, I think it is interesting to note that the self-reliance espoused by libertarians can lead them to discount social problems, which in turn can discredit libertarianism in the public forum. This vulnerability has not gone unnoticed, and libertarians have joined the public fray, arguing that social ills such as poverty and environmental degradation can best be addressed through individualist mechanisms such as fully defining property rights and lowering governmental barriers to economic activity. "Even if individual self-interest were their only motivation," Douglas writes, "the debate must necessarily be conducted in terms of the collective interest, since the forum in which collective support is mustered is public."[39] In effect, social interest is in the self-interest of libertarians if they are to sustain their culture, just as they argue that self-interest serves the social interest.

OF FATALISTS AND DESPOTS

When individuals are free from group responsibility (that is, low group), life is not always "Little House on the Prairie." When the norms of free choice are violated by an oppressive leader, this is not libertarianism but despotism. On the cultural map, it is the upper-left corner, where low-grid, each-for-himself individualism still reigns but where autonomy has been subverted by constraints. The despot is responsible to no one but herself and oppresses others, who might still be termed fatalists, merely to serve her own ends.

Shifting the oppressive leader from the low-grid to high-grid corner clarifies libertarianism, and it also makes the high-grid, low-group location a coherent culture, with leaders as well as followers. It allows this culture to be more comparable to the other three, more than just their rubbish bin. It may be that fatalism is largely "the squeezed-out residue" of other cultures,[40] but this is not the entire story. Despotism makes, if not a virtue of rubbish, at least a coherent set of social relations, by describing high-grid, low-group leadership.

What might such a leader be like? The answer, if cultural theory is indeed a predictive, deductive theory, should be rooted in grid and group. The leader would constrain, or grid, everyone else, not for the good of the whole group but only for herself; she would seek to impose grid without group. An unstable high-grid, high-group society might have several aspiring despots, all vying to stick it to each other. Labeling this locale "despotism" makes clear it is an "ism," that is, a theory of organizing, albeit one that does not have much to recommend it, except to the despot.[41] Fatalists may be unable to participate in hierarchies or sects or markets, but from the fatalist perspective, it's all despotism. That is, they're getting the shaft; they're being constrained by others who do not take their interests into account, and it doesn't much matter to them what the internal social relations of the shaft are. Although "fatalist" is a reasonable term for the grunts in the upper-left corner,[42] "despotism" may more fully describe their predicament.

Locating oppressive leaders in despotism also clarifies the nature of hierarchy. Hierarchy does not need a "lowerarchy" of fatalists to oppress.[43] The hierarchical ideal entails each individual understanding and accepting his role, and devotion to the greater good by leaders as well as followers. Each person is "gridded," not just those near the bottom. "The distinguishing feature of hierarchy is that every decision is referred to the well-being of the whole," Douglas writes. "Since no one can be eliminated, all have to be assigned places in the system, and the claims of the places have to be recognized. ... The distinctive point is that people can drop down, but not out."[44]

If the leaders maintain power only by coercing the alienated fatalists below them or use the status quo to their selfish ends, then the hierarchy has failed, not succeeded. As *Cultural Theory* puts it, "Hierarchists strive hard to internalize their externalities" rather than impose costs on others.[45] But sustaining the communication and restraint important in hierarchy is difficult; cooperation can become coercion through ignorance, fear, accident, and avarice. "It is a truism of organization theory," Douglas notes, "that sending commands down is easier than receiving news from below, as a truly collegial hierarchy would require. The subversion of the hierarchy into a tyranny is easy."[46]

Hierarchies, like libertarian markets, are never perfect: "On the fringe of markets are individuals who have little scope for trading; on the fringe of hierarchies are other individuals who are very weakly enfranchised."[47] But these imperfections are not necessary to the viability of the cultures, and incorporating relations with fatalists into hierarchy or libertarianism only distorts the ideal types that are important sources of preferences and arguments in politics and public policy. Similarly, fatalists may be excluded by egalitarian sects, but that is not a fundamental aspect of egalitarian social relations and preferences. Again, even when fatalists are oppressed by exclusion from hierarchies, sects, and individualist networks, the latter three cultures, unlike despotism, do not describe their relations with the fatalists.

Even when despotism is added to fatalism, this way of life is still not an equal participant in the struggle over ideas and institutions. In many policy contexts, only hierarchy, egalitarianism, and libertarianism are important cultures. There are two reasons for this. First, it's generally inadvisable to advocate despotism.

Who knows what lurks in the minds of candidates and interest-group leaders, but proclaiming one's despotic ambitions rarely wins votes. In democracies, even hierarchy is viewed with suspicion and often couched in terms of economic, military, or environmental necessity.[48] Second, those on the bottom of this culture, the fatalists, largely lack either the ability or the motivation to join the public forum. If you believe life is arbitrary and capricious, entirely beyond your control, there's little point in having preferences, let alone advocating them; if you're actually constrained from participation, you're out of luck. As Douglas writes, "By definition the fourth type is politically mute."[49]

UNREQUISITE VARIETY, OR
JUST WHAT IS BEING CLASSIFIED?

The argument I have been making implicitly rejects the requisite-variety principle. *Cultural Theory* insists there are five viable ways of life, yet "each way of life needs each of its rivals, either to make up for its deficiencies, or to exploit, or to defend itself against,"[50] and so "none of these modes of organizing social life is viable on its own."[51] These are hardly fundamental, viable cultures in themselves if they are dependent on the presence of their competitors.[52] It may be that a modern society will almost always be a mix of cultural types, perhaps all four, and that cultural variety enables adaptation to changing circumstances and provides a "safety valve" for individuals to adjust their preferences.[53] But that does not mean that any society must be a mix of the four cultures, or that they do not represent distinct and theoretically viable ideals. Requisite variety can become a crutch used to explain away the cultural diversity or inconsistencies typically found in any population or even in individuals. It would be better to reconceive the object of analysis rather than seek refuge in the requisite-variety rule.

Each corner of the typology can be usefully thought of as an ideal type, a form of organization that provides the basis for preferences and arguments among which individuals choose as they seek to cope with the world, influence policy, and so on. Individuals need not promote a single cultural line, although they should recognize the conflicts between different perspectives. Preferences about social relations are not the same as the relations themselves, and thus measuring social preferences is an imperfect substitute for measuring relations. But analyzing preferences is the strength of grid-group analysis, at least when applied in the social sciences. People largely do battle in politics, public policy, and social life over their preferences, using arguments about how they wish to live. When cultural scholars put a greater emphasis on actual social relations, it is easy to get lost in the thicket of trying to find significant differences in individuals' social relations and correlating these with political or policy preferences.

Measuring social relations accurately is not easy.[54] If we trust people's accounts of their relations, preferences may cloud their self-assessments. To avoid this screening effect, we could follow people around all day, surreptitiously so as not to trigger a Hawthorne effect. Getting a large enough sample for comparison could require an army of graduate students. Grid-group analysts struggle to find a simpler substitute. Charles Lockhart and Richard Coughlin, for example, try type-casting socioeconomic groups, but that requires heavy presumptions about social habits.[55] Gross and Rayner run into the same problem, such as when they categorize door-to-door salesmen, supermarket cashiers, disabled or elderly persons as high-grid, low-group (that is, fatalists) when they might well be individualists or contented hierarchists.[56] Even if we can accurately inventory social relations, using small variations to find candidates for the four cultures may obscure more important differences in preferences. Especially in liberal, capitalist societies,[57] most people live of necessity as individualists, with a degree of hierarchical regulation thrown in, but that doesn't mean they like it. The conceptual distinctions among preferences and arguments that make grid-group analysis useful in understanding social and political conflict can disappear if we insist on placing an individual in one corner or another based on actual social relations.

In many cases, cultural theorists have implicitly shifted the object of study. Typically it is statements about social relations—how we wish to live and how we think others should live—rather than the relations themselves that take center stage. Thus Gross and Rayner use grid-group analysis to classify "strategies of disputants in familiar types of debates,"[58] Douglas emphasizes that "data are either actions or statements in defense of actions,"[59] and Schwarz and Thompson analyze "not only the outcome of the public policy process, but also the kinds of selection criteria and justifications that policy actors adopt."[60]

In an excellent article comparing cultural theory favorably with other explanations for risk perception, Aaron Wildavsky and Karl Dake conclude that "individuals perceive a variety of risks in a manner that supports their way of life." That might suggest empirical support for the policy importance of actual social relations, as "ways of life" incorporate both social relations and "cultural biases," defined as "worldviews ... entailing ... values and beliefs defending different patterns of social relations." But what they actually measure is *preferences* about social relations, an aspect of cultural bias. Thus, they earlier conclude, more precisely, that "worldviews best account for patterns of risk perceptions."[61] This is an important finding in itself, and a good example of how cultural theory can reveal important relations between social preferences and political and policy preferences, values and beliefs.

Especially perhaps in a liberal democracy, policies and institutions are constantly vulnerable to revision, and it is through the public forum that individuals both develop and seek to implement their policy and institutional preferences. Douglas states well the centrality of political argument, broadly conceived, to cultural analysis: "From the first [individuals] involve one another in a primitive form of constitution making. Each individual who enters a social relation is drawn at the same time into a debate about what the relation is and how it ought to be conducted. This is the normative debate on which cultural analysis fastens attention."[62]

Cultural theory posits that most individuals, not just elites, participate in the give-and-take of policy and institutional development. Indeed, what first attracted me to the grid-group approach was its ability to make sense of the animated debates I had witnessed while covering local politics and policies as a reporter. People clearly understood that, for example, a major housing development would have consequences for how they lived their lives, and they freely expressed their strongly held views that it would affect larger values such as freedom, community, prosperity, and equality. Yet the literature on ideology tells us that everyday people largely lack the capacity to think ideologically. Culture provides the missing link by packaging preferences and experiences in a way that economizes choice. As Douglas observes, "Anyone who has attended a town meeting or a board meeting knows that the normative debate is a fumbling, half-coherent process. ... Decisions ... rest on tacit assumptions, not on argued syllogisms."[63] Culture supplants articulation.

DIVERSITY WITHIN CULTURAL TYPES

The grid-group model provides a manageable number of basic cultures, allowing us to make meaningful comparisons despite great differences among societies in size, location, degree of development, or era. As Douglas puts it, "This is the central argument of cultural theory: culture itself is constrained. It cannot make any number of combinations and permutations."[64] Cultures may be few, but it is more difficult to argue that individuals, whether we are measuring them by their preferences or their relations, are as constrained. Issues, arguments, and especially individuals do not always fit neatly into the corners of the grid-group model. To paraphrase Jefferson, it may be fair to say, "We are all libertarians, we are all egalitarians, we are all hierarchists," in that we may appreciate the virtues of these conflicting social and political arrangements. If the grid-group model is correct, we will recognize a tension between them, and most people, I would agree, tend to have a gut preference for one of the three major cultures.[65]

Once we acknowledge that persons may be torn between cultures, it becomes important to consider the significance of the "multicultural life." Douglas writes, "Personally, I believe the limits are real, that it is not possible to stay in two parts of the diagram at once,"[66] although this does not eliminate the possibility that an individual might be located on the fringe of a culture, partly under the sway of a competing culture. That is, a person might be a cultural fence sitter, aware of the tensions between values and beliefs, but not be a contented advocate of different cultural extremes with no sense of conflict. But *Cultural Theory* suggests that it is quite possible for an individual to reside in one culture during part of his day (say, being a hierarchist at work) and another culture during another part (perhaps a despot at home!), reducing dissonance through compartmentalization.[67] Whether we are speaking of preferences or social relations, the "multiculturalist" must reconcile the conflicting pressures of different cultures. How this is done, and how this dynamic of cultural tension affects preference formation, merit further exploration.[68]

The strength of grid-group analysis—restricting cultural variety—can also be a shortcoming, as cultural theorists tend to give less attention to the great variety within any one culture. The grid-group approach yields important insights about the commonality of hierarchical organization in diverse times and environments, for example, but it tends to gloss over significant differences between hierarchical organizations that are not easily explained by moving along the axes of grid and group. How can a small traditional group in a desert be distinguished from a large, formal organization in modern capitalism or government? Is there a significant difference between a hierarchy structured by bureaucratic rules and one held together by implicit moral obligations? A recent paper by Richard Mumford that delineated similarities between Amish and Japanese cultures illustrates the problems of collapsing variety.[69] Although he did not use the grid-group model, the approach was comparable, helping us to see fundamental social similarities in diverse settings. But his approach also sweeps tremendous social differences under the rug and underestimates the variation in each society. As another example, Douglas has lumped "bureaucratic systems," "monastic life," the "military," and a "stable tribal system" together as hierarchies without providing a framework for distinguishing them.[70] In my own work, I have argued that order is the key value of hierarchy,[71] but there are many different ways to create order.

Variation within egalitarianism and libertarianism also merits attention and may be more easily accommodated within the grid-group framework. The egalitarian ideal posited by cultural theory is one of voluntary, participatory community, yet egalitarians in public policy debates often advocate government coercion to further equality. This may represent something of a pact with the devil, a resort to "high grid" means, much as Lenin saw the dictatorship of the proletariat as the first step toward the withering of the state. It is important to recognize these very different approaches. If we lump coercive egalitarians with others, we may superficially promote the model, but we beg the question of whether grid is an essential dimension if it fails to distinguish between them, and of whether egalitarianism is a plausible category. Either the grid-group criteria should be modified, or, as I prefer, an effort should be made to delineate the significance of different locations within the low-grid, high-group corner of the model. Jacksonian Democrats might lie along the group line toward libertarianism; redistributive regimes would be higher grid. Similarly, describing both deep ecology and redistributive housing policies as egalitarian can be surprising, and it is important to clarify just where they lie within the low-grid, high-group realm.[72] If we view grid and group as continuous rather than dichotomous, with many viable combinations of values, then these finer distinctions do not undermine the model.

Within the libertarian realm there may be considerable difference between hermits communing with nature, climbers dangling from cliffs, taxi drivers battling on the streets of New York, and computer nerds designing innovative products in their garages. Just as in the case of hierarchy, this variation may require incorporating additional factors, and a large degree of variation may be explained by shifting grid and group values. For example, resort to courts to enforce contracts introduces a minimal hierarchical element,[73] a slight rise on both the grid and group scales; organizing a freewheeling research and development unit within a corporation may be an attempt to bring the virtues of individual competition into a strong group setting.

In attempting to provide a comprehensive typology of social relations and preferences, grid-group analysis paints with a very broad brush. It may be that individuals face the same basic choices whether in ancient or modern society, in a pastoral village or an industrial city, and a universal model enables valuable comparison. But there are major differences as well, and glossing them over can leave the impression that cultural theory bludgeons nuance. To fully explain social and political phenomena, we must give greater attention to variation within cultures and consider the possibility that other dimensions are important. This might take the form of a more elaborated grid-group model, or it may mean making the model part of a larger social theory.[74]

CONSTRAINTS ON
CULTURAL RATIONALITY

Cultural theory shows that when it comes to social relations, there is more than one way to organize. It reveals that creating institutions and policies is a value-laden process. Choices are rational—that is, they make sense—if they further one's cultural preferences. "Rational people support their way of life," assert the authors of *Cultural Theory*,[75] and there are "competing social definitions of what will count as rational."[76] In seeking to shape society to their ends, individuals may have many different motivations, and they are not easily reduced to a single rational actor, as Chai and Wildavsky point out.[77]

But a good thing can be taken too far, leaving the impression that decisionmaking and preference formation are purely matters of values and beliefs. True, social implications may affect preferences, and actions may appear irrational to us that are appropriate in their cultural settings. Yet rationality may be constrained not only by culture but by other factors such as material self-interest and environmental context. Economists and rational choice theorists may be inattentive to the social and experiential components of preferences;[78] in contrast, grid-group scholars tend to slight self-interest.[79] Whether biological in origin or an inevitable product of early socialization, material self-interest may be a powerful motivating force that transcends culture. Social scientists commonly describe actions that further self-interest as rational, and even *Cultural Theory* notes that "what is culturally rational may conflict with (and even lose out to) individual self-interest."[80] Yet cultural theory doesn't adequately specify what a self-interest that goes beyond social or cultural interest might be, since it emphasizes that "needs and resources ... are socially constructed."[81]

Similarly, environmental factors that might constrain cultural choice are often deemed to be only social, as when Douglas writes that "the environment is defined to consist of all the other interacting individuals and their choices."[82] Douglas has also declared that "there is nothing natural about the perception of nature; nature is heavily loaded with political bias."[83] In *Risk and Culture,* Douglas and Wildavsky write that "the choice to worry most about [different] risks is never made directly but is settled by a preference among kinds of favored social institutions."[84]

Culture plays an important, and often underappreciated, role in determining attitudes toward institutions or the natural environment, but that is not to say that each assessment of environmental risks is equally accurate, or that the process is entirely social. When "cultural theory insists there are five rational and sustainable solutions to every problem," it reduces policy to values and contradicts itself. Thompson, Ellis, and Wildavsky also note that "ways of life ... cannot exclude reality altogether. ... As ways of life do not pay off for adherents, doubts build up, followed by defections."[85] But if there are four or five answers to every social problem, why should doubts arise? Much is made of "surprise," of dissonance between expectations and experience, as leading to cultural change, but the argument is largely hypothetical and based on assertions.[86] Factors other than culture must be at work, but these have not been adequately explored.

The risks associated with nuclear power, for example, may be exaggerated by egalitarians who distrust centralized authority, but they are real enough to suggest that an unregulated libertarian regime could be hazardous. Or, say, one might advocate small communities of independent farmers, but such communities are easier to establish in temperate regions of the eastern United States where rainfall is plentiful than in the Central Valley of California, where huge water projects are used to irrigate arid areas. Automobiles, personal computers, modems, and faxes might facilitate individualist networks; large, costly systems such as railroads and mainframe computers may entail hierarchy. A high degree of uncertainty or disagreement might be more conducive to individualism; their opposites might encourage hierarchy. Douglas has noted that "another dimension which is not on the diagram, that lying between density and sparsity," may be especially important.[87] Most cultural theorists would not entirely dismiss the importance of technological or environmental factors, but a tendency to make sweeping statements about the primacy of culture can give that impression.

Matching cultural forms with their environmental conditions may be especially useful as grid-group analysis is adapted to the social sciences, particularly public administration and policy, where the search for better institutions and ideas is constant. Cultural theory posits alternative clusters of preferences but is reticent to specify why one might be preferred over another. Douglas acknowledges that "as a theory it has very little to say about people's choices between social forms."[88] Suggesting simply that solutions depend on cultural bias sells grid-group analysis short. Yes, it is important to consider values in policymaking and to consider the social consequences of policies. But many factors—such as the state of technology, the abundance of natural resources and the knowledge of how to use them, agreement on values to be pursued, and knowledge of methods—may make certain cultures more viable than others. Careful empirical investigation and theoretical development of the relationships between these factors and cultural choices would help realize the potential of the grid-group approach as a tool of policy analysis.

CONCLUSION

Grid-group analysis is not yet king, and that news will be a relief for the legions of social scientists who are seeking to make careers through original contributions. But it is invigorating in its audacity, and promising in its achievements. I have tried to suggest important areas for further research and theoretical refinement in the hope that the influence of grid-group analysis will grow among scholars and students. Despite its imperfections, the grid-group method may be the most promising theoretical approach in the social sciences today. The more students and scholars from throughout the disciplines apply it, the more rigorously it will be developed. There is no patent on grid-group analysis, although no one is likely to match the foundational contribution of Mary Douglas, and secondarily the work of Aaron Wildavsky, in adopting it to social science unless by, say, integrating the best of grid-group into public choice, critical theory, and what have you and producing the Grand Theory That Explains All. Even if cultural theory does not reach its loftiest aspirations, it is at least, as Douglas says, "a good little typology" that goes a long way in helping us understand the world around us.[89]

NOTES

I would like to thank Mary Douglas, Michael Thompson, Karl Dake, and Richard Ellis for their comments on this chapter. This chapter is better for it, although to say that the errors that remain are my own is an understatement. I hope cultural theorists will read this chapter in the constructive spirit it is intended.

1. Michael Thompson, Richard Ellis, and Aaron Wildavsky, *Cultural Theory* (Boulder: Westview Press, 1990). An earlier address to the American Political Science Association by Wildavsky, published as "Choosing Preferences by Constructing Institutions: A Cultural Theory of Preference Formation," *American Political Science Review* 81(1987), 3–21, was also significant in this regard.

2. See Mary Douglas, *Natural Symbols: Explorations in Cosmology,* 1st ed. (London: Barrie & Rockliff, 1970), especially the chapter "A Rule of Method"; Douglas, *Natural*

Symbols: Explorations in Cosmology, 2nd ed. (London: Barrie & Jenkins, 1973), especially the chapter "Grid and Group"; Douglas, "Cultural Bias," in *In the Active Voice* (London: Routledge & Kegan Paul, 1982) (originally Royal Anthropological Institute Occasional Paper 35, 1978); Douglas, "Introduction to Grid/Group Analysis," in Douglas, ed., *Essays in the Sociology of Perception* (London: Routledge & Kegan Paul, 1982). These remain timeless, essential works for understanding the core of cultural theory, although Mary Douglas and those who have followed in her path, including Steve Rayner and Michael Thompson, continue to produce a large body of important work. Douglas's recent excellent collection of essays, *Risk and Blame: Essays in Cultural Theory* (New York: Routledge, 1992), expands on many of her earlier themes. For reviews and critiques of Douglas's work, see Shaun Hargreaves Heap and Angus Ross, eds., *The Enterprise Culture: Themes in the Work of Mary Douglas* (Edinburgh University Press, 1992); James V. Spickard, "A Guide to Mary Douglas's Three Versions of Grid/Group Theory," *Sociological Analysis* 50(1989), 151–170; and Robert Wuthnow, James Davison Hunter, Albert Bergesen, and Edith Kurzwell, eds., *Cultural Analysis: The Work of Peter L. Berger, Mary Douglas, Michel Foucault, and Jurgen Habermas* (Boston: Routledge & Kegan Paul, 1984). For those interested in the myriad ways in which grid-group analysis has been developed and applied, *Cultural Theory* contains an extensive bibliography of related work.

3. See, for example, reviews of *Cultural Theory* in *American Political Science Review* 85(September 1991), *Contemporary Sociology* 20(September 1991), *Journal of Politics* 54(November 1991), *Perspectives on Political Science* 20(Fall 1991), and *Social Forces* 70(December 1991).

4. My own applications can be found in "'This Land Is Your Land, This Land Is My Land': Cultural Conflict in Environmental and Land-Use Regulation," in this volume; "Takings Jurisprudence and the Political Cultures of American Politics," United States Court of Federal Claims Symposium, *Catholic University Law Review* 42(Summer 1993), 817–862; *Property Rights and the Constitution: Shaping Society Through Land Use Regulation* (Albany: State University of New York Press, 1993); "A Critical Theory of Community," Working Paper 87-5, Institute of Governmental Studies, University of California–Berkeley; and two articles coauthored with Aaron Wildavsky, "Requisites of Radical Reform: Income Maintenance Versus Tax Preferences," *Journal of Policy Analysis and Management* 7(Fall 1987), 1–16, and "Social Experimentation in the Face of Formidable Fables: Why FAP Failed Though It Might Have Succeeded," in *Lessons from the Income Maintenance Experiments* (Boston: Federal Reserve Bank, 1988), 167–184.

5. Douglas, "Introduction to Grid/Group Analysis," 1.

6. Thompson, Ellis, and Wildavsky, *Cultural Theory,* 22. See also Douglas, "Introduction to Grid/Group Analysis," 1: "The infinite array of social interactions can be sorted and classified into a few grand classes."

7. Cultural Theory, the uppercase version favored by Richard Ellis, at least distinguishes this approach from generic theorizing about culture, thereby recognizing that there can be other approaches to the topic. But capitalization can suggest that the grid-group model is the only cultural approach that merits inclusion in the Realm of Great Ideas.

8. Ellis and Wildavsky acknowledge that "grid-group" is "the more precise if less felicitous phrase" ("A Cultural Analysis of the Role of Abolitionists in the Coming of the Civil War," *Comparative Studies in Society and History* 32[January 1990], 92, n. 13). The authors of *Cultural Theory* write that "a theory of sociocultural viability" might be more

accurate but reject it because it is "stylistically awkward and does not convey the instant recognition we seek" (Thompson, Ellis, and Wildavsky, *Cultural Theory,* 1, n. 5).

9. Douglas, "Cultural Bias," 201.

10. This "sliding" along the axes does not weaken the theory as long as persons in the middle recognize and articulate the conflicts and tensions between the cultures.

11. In the first edition of *Natural Symbols,* for example, Douglas employs two different graphs, one placing zero in the middle, the next in the lower left, and simply notes that "We can redraw the diagram this way," even though the implications of the two schemes are different (1970, 60). In the second edition, only the graph with zero in the middle is retained 1973, 83–84). Perhaps not coincidentally, this edition may be her weakest statement of the grid-group model. A few years later, in "Cultural Bias," the graph with zero in the middle has disappeared, and Douglas emphasizes that the low values of grid and group lie in the lower-left corner (35). This may partially account for why "Cultural Bias" is probably her strongest early exposition of grid and group. Also compare the differences in the grid-group diagrams in Douglas, *Risk and Blame,* 106, 178, 201, 287. Spickard also notes that Douglas presents different variants of her grid-group model. Spickard, "Guide," 152.

Gross and Rayner place zero to the lower left and assign grid and group values from zero to one, avoiding the hazards of negative value (Jonathan L. Gross and Steve Rayner, *Measuring Culture: A Paradigm for the Analysis of Social Organization* [New York: Columbia University Press, 1985] ix, 7); Wildavsky has implicitly done the same. Grid, for example, is measured by whether the individual is "subject to many or few prescriptions" (Wildavsky, "Choosing Preferences by Constructing Institutions," 6). *Cultural Theory* returns zero to the middle and speaks of "negative grid" but also refers to grid and group as matters of degree, which at least suggests the possibility of continua (5–8).

12. Douglas, "Cultural Bias," 205. In *Risk and Blame,* she writes that "there is no absolute hierarchy—organizations are merely more or less hierarchical" (177). See also *Natural Symbols* (1970), 59, and *Natural Symbols* (1973), 84.

13. Douglas, *Natural Symbols* (1973), 83.

14. Attempts to conceive of "negative grouping" led, I think, to basic confusion of grid and group in the second edition of *Natural Symbols,* where negative group is conceived as pressure on others (see pp. 83–84, 89).

15. Thompson, Ellis, and Wildavsky, *Cultural Theory,* 96. See also Michael Thompson, *Rubbish Theory: The Creation and Destruction of Value* (Oxford: Oxford University Press, 1979).

16. Michael Thompson, "The Problem of the Centre: An Autonomous Cosmology," in Mary Douglas, ed., *Essays in the Sociology of Perception* (London: Routledge & Kegan Paul, 1982). See also Thompson, Ellis, and Wildavsky, *Cultural Theory,* 7, 13, 223.

17. "Hermits ... seek to become one with nature. ... They do this, not in a misery of self-imposed privation, but in joyous participation in nature's fruitfulness." Thompson, Ellis, and Wildavsky, *Cultural Theory,* 11.

18. Michael Thompson, "A Three-Dimensional Model," in Mary Douglas, ed., *Essays in the Sociology of Perception* (London: Routledge & Kegan Paul, 1982), 37.

19. Common language is preferable when it can be used accurately, and I defend "grid-group" only because it refers more clearly to the particular model developed by Douglas than does "cultural theory," not because I prefer obfuscation. Speaking of which, new audiences often pause at the term "hierarchy." In comparing this culture with libertarianism

and egalitarianism, I stress that the key value pursued by hierarchies is order. The term "hierarchy," although accurate, is nonetheless awkward, but "orderists" or "ordians" would surely be worse. "Order" is also not as precise a term, as in a very broad sense each culture offers a different form of order, although in a narrow sense I think it reasonably conveys the more tightly controlled and predictable system of hierarchy. "Communitarianism" is close but may also apply to egalitarianism. Perhaps the problem is that hierarchy typically is not advocated as openly today as other cultures, and thus the term seems more exotic.

20. "Networks" is the term Thompson uses to describe individualist social relations, and he notes that hermits maintain very weak networks. That would suggest that hermits belong in the individualist culture. Thompson, however, argues that the hermit's desire to withdraw from networks, rather than energetically participate in them, and his disinclination to manipulate others merit a separate category. Thompson, "A Three-Dimensional Model" and "The Problem of the Centre." See also Thompson, Ellis, and Wildavsky, *Cultural Theory*.

21. Douglas, *Natural Symbols* (1970), 60.

22. See the discussion of Thoreau in Richard Ellis, *American Political Cultures* (Oxford: Oxford University Press, 1993), 140–150.

23. Douglas, "Cultural Bias," 204, 232. Again, I argue that the hermit either is irrelevant to social analysis or belongs in the libertarian culture.

24. Gunks culture had been shaped a decade earlier by the Vulgarians, a rude lot that had offended their more genteel predecessors through their gross behavior and superb climbing.

25. It is interesting that in their chapter in this book, Boyle and Coughlin find some individualists to be similar to hermits.

26. Thompson, Ellis, and Wildavsky, *Cultural Theory*, 7.

27. See Douglas, "Cultural Bias," 202. Control of or by others may more appropriately be an indication of the high-grid cultures of hierarchy and despotism.

28. Douglas, "Cultural Bias," 244.

29. *Cultural Theory* sees all four ways of life as fundamentally about coercion: "In the grid-group framework individuals are manipulated and try to manipulate others. ... Coercive social involvement is what the ... ways of life [other than the hermit] are about" (6, 29).

30. *Cultural Theory* asserts that "wherever there are 'big men' ... there must be 'rubbish men'" (96).

31. Witness the difficulties of developing a culture of capitalism in the former Soviet Union. Douglas notes that trust is essential to individual markets. *Risk and Blame*, 140.

32. See Thompson, Ellis, and Wildavsky, *Cultural Theory*, 7. Doing so creates complications, such as how fatalists can be simultaneously incapable of social relations and capable of socioeconomic success. According to *Cultural Theory*, "Movement out of fatalism is likely to be involuntary because, once established there, people lose independent initiative," yet "From Fatalist to individualist is the familiar 'rags-to-riches' story." More gradually, it is "pulling yourself up by your bootstraps" (pp. 94, 76). If we avoid characterizing those in lowly economic positions as fatalists, then the rags-to-riches move is more plausible.

33. Douglas, "Cultural Bias," 208. See also Thompson, Ellis, and Wildavsky, *Cultural Theory*, 7.

34. Gross and Rayner note that a low-grid, low-group culture may be small-scale or on the frontier, in contrast to the New Guinea "big men," who dominate their society (*Measuring Culture,* 7).

35. Indeed, corporate leaders may well be more hierarchical if they have come to value status and order.

36. Mary Douglas and Aaron Wildavsky, *Risk and Culture: An Essay on the Selection of Technological and Environmental Dangers* (Berkeley: University of California Press, 1982), 80. I think this is more accurate than to suggest that individuals in all four cultures are necessarily "maximizing their social transactions" (Thompson, Ellis, and Wildavsky, *Cultural Theory,* 13).

37. Taxi drivers have been offered as a classic example of hermits (see Thompson, Ellis, and Wildavsky, *Cultural Theory,* 10). But taxi drivers who withdrew from social relations would have considerable trouble doing business.

38. Douglas, *Risk and Blame,* 227.

39. Ibid., 134.

40. Michiel Schwarz and Michael Thompson, *Divided We Stand: Redefining Politics, Technology and Social Choice* (Philadelphia: University of Pennsylvania Press, 1990), 43, 74. See also Thompson, Ellis, and Wildavsky, *Cultural Theory:* "Fatalists ... are the cultural equivalent of compost" (93).

41. Although a group of sadomasochists might find it agreeable.

42. "Isolates," as employed recently by Mary Douglas (see *Risk and Blame,* 105–106), may be more appropriate because it emphasizes that the individual is isolated from those who control his life, "gridded" by constraints yet excluded from group.

43. Douglas agrees that fatalists "are not the low-grade citizens of the bottom echelons of hierarchy" (*Risk and Blame,* 227).

44. Ibid., 226.

45. Thompson, Ellis, and Wildavsky, *Cultural Theory,* 64.

46. Douglas, *Risk and Blame,* 144.

47. Ibid., 145.

48. Despotism comes into policy debates as a pejorative label for competing perspectives. Libertarians, for example, might argue that high-group cultures are essentially despotic because they shackle the individual. Hierarchists might see despotic dangers in an egalitarian regime, dismissing it as a dangerous fancy that would allow those in power to coerce others while freeing them of any meaningful obligations or checks to make them consider the welfare of all. Egalitarians may see the happy loyalty of hierarchy as a myth that legitimates despotism by obscuring it.

49. Douglas, *Risk and Blame,* 145.

50. Thompson, Ellis, and Wildavsky, *Cultural Theory,* 4.

51. Wildavsky, "Choosing Preferences by Constructing Institutions," 7.

52. This assertion also suggests that cultural partisans suffer a form of false consciousness. The hierarchist, egalitarian, or libertarian might think her way of life is independently viable or even superior, but this would be self-delusion.

53. In his chapter in this volume, "Cars and Culture in Munich and Birmingham: The Case for Cultural Pluralism," Frank Hendriks nicely illustrates the advantages of cultural pluralism in the policy process.

54. Placement decisions are simpler if the individuals are fictitious, as was the case in Gross and Rayner, *Measuring Culture.* This strategy can help clarify how grid and group

might be operationalized but also can encourage suspicions that grid-group analysis is inapplicable to the real world.

55. Charles Lockhart and Richard Coughlin, "Building Better Comparative Social Theory Through Alternative Conceptions of Rationality," *Western Political Quarterly* 32(September 1992), 398–409. See also the chapter by Boyle and Coughlin in this book.

56. Gross and Rayner, *Measuring Culture,* 9.

57. Since sensation is unavoidably solitary, individualized social relations may be fundamental in any setting, presenting a challenge to other cultures, but the rapid change and decentralized political and economic systems of Western society exaggerate this effect.

58. Gross and Rayner, *Measuring Culture,* 18.

59. Douglas, "Introduction to Grid/Group Analysis," xxi.

60. Schwarz and Thompson, *Divided We Stand,* 76.

61. Aaron Wildavsky and Karl Dake, "Theories of Risk Perceptions: Who Fears What and Why?" *Daedalus* 119(Fall 1990), 57, 43–44, 47, 56.

62. Douglas, *Risk and Blame,* 133. See also 127–128.

63. Ibid., 136.

64. Ibid.

65. "Most individuals do find themselves inhabiting one way of life more than the others," according to Thompson, Ellis, and Wildavsky, *Cultural Theory,* 267. I would modify this statement to say that most individuals prefer one way of life, shifting the emphasis from actual social relations, which might be implied by "inhabiting," to preferences about social relations.

66. Douglas, "Introduction to Grid/Group Analysis," 4.

67. Thompson, Ellis, and Wildavsky, *Cultural Theory,* 265.

68. A related set of questions concerns the person who lives or advocates a pluralist life within a single culture. A hierarchist who spends his entire existence in a single tightly ordered group will have a different experience from one who moves between different hierarchical organizations over time, be it a day or a lifetime. Yet unless we view grid and group as continuous and allow that individuals may be located anywhere on the diagram, it seems difficult to accommodate these variations within the grid-group model. Similarly, what about an individualist who interacts regularly with the same network of associates, as compared with one who constantly faces new social situations? Transaction-cost economics might suggest that the first situation will lead to greater organization, or hierarchy. See Oliver E. Williamson, "The Economics of Organizations: The Transaction Cost Approach," *American Journal of Sociology* 87(1981), 548–577.

69. Richard Mumford, "The Japanese and the Amish: Opposite Roots, Similar Values," presented at the International Conference on Amish Society, Elizabethtown, Penn., July 22–25, 1993.

70. Douglas, *Natural Symbols* (1973), 87.

71. Coyle, "'This Land Is Your Land, This Land Is My Land,'" this volume, and *Property Rights and the Constitution.*

72. Ibid.

73. See Douglas, "Cultural Bias," 208.

74. Michael Thompson, building on his hermit category, has suggested that a third dimension of manipulation might improve the model. I don't think this is fruitful, as should be apparent from my earlier discussion of hermits and individualists, but it is illustrative of how the model might be enlarged. See Thompson, "A Three-Dimensional Model."

75. Thompson, Ellis, and Wildavsky, *Cultural Theory,* 98. See also Wildavsky, "Choosing Preferences by Constructing Institutions," 16.

76. Thompson, Ellis, and Wildavsky, *Cultural Theory,* 22.

77. Sun-Ki Chai and Aaron Wildavsky, "Culture, Rationality, and Violence," in this volume. See also Mary Douglas, *Risk and Blame,* 189–198. She notes that even Oliver Williamson, the founder of transaction-cost economics, "believes firms vary, but not individuals" (*Risk and Blame,* 192).

78. As *Cultural Theory* aptly puts it, "Social institutions generate preferences (to use Marx's phrase) 'behind the back' of individuals" (58). Douglas writes that "social choice" theory ignores "the effect of institutional forms upon moral perception" ("Introduction to Grid/Group Analysis," 6).

79. See Aaron Wildavsky, "Why Self-Interest Means Less Outside of a Social Context: Cultural Contributions to a Theory of Rational Choices," *Journal of Theoretical Politics* (forthcoming).

80. Thompson, Ellis, and Wildavsky, *Cultural Theory,* 270.

81. Ibid., 39.

82. Douglas, "Cultural Bias," 198.

83. Douglas, "Introduction to Grid/Group Analysis," 7.

84. Douglas and Wildavsky, *Risk and Culture,* 187.

85. Thompson, Ellis, and Wildavsky, *Cultural Theory,* 270, 69.

86. See ibid., 3–4, 69–75. See also Michael Thompson and Paul Tayler, "The Surprise Game: An Exploration of Constrained Relativism," Warwick Papers in Management no. 1, Institute for Management Research and Development (Coventry: University of Warwick, 1986). We are told, for example, that individualists believe in the myth of nature as benign, assuming nature is "wonderfully forgiving" of unregulated exploitation, and that this is accurate if "there is an excess of opportunity over existing investment" (*Cultural Theory,* 73, 26). In other words, resources are plentiful. Yet even if we believe the nature-as-perverse/tolerant or nature-as-ephemeral myths, in which we assume nature may harshly punish human error, a laissez-faire system may be justified if we lack the knowledge of how to proceed safely, as markets can be discovery mechanisms. If it turns out the nature-as-perverse/tolerant myth is correct, *Cultural Theory* tells us, markets must give way to bureaucracies because the "excess has vanished and there is no longer anything for the hidden hand to get hold of" (74). But economists argue that it is precisely these conditions of scarcity when markets function best. The cause-effect assertions of cultural surprise theory are thus not the only plausible ones. Adequate incorporation of environmental factors will entail greater attention to empirical investigation and more nuanced theoretical development.

87. Douglas, *Natural Symbols* (1973), 92. Earlier in her work, as I noted earlier, Douglas considered sparsity to be a defining element of low-grid, low-group relations. See Douglas, *Natural Symbols* (1970), 60.

88. Douglas, "Introduction to Grid/Group Analysis," 7.

89. Douglas, *Risk and Blame,* 137.

About the Book

This new set of original case studies is designed to offer an empirical counterpart to *Cultural Theory* (Westview, 1990), the landmark statement of political culture theory authored by Michael Thompson, Richard Ellis, and Aaron Wildavsky, and to extend and challenge the analysis developed there. Here, the theoretical concepts laid out in that book are operationalized and applied in textbook fashion to key areas in methodology, public policy, and history. Highlights include essays on risk perception, environmental regulation, and mental health policies and a never-before-published piece on "Culture, Rationality, and Violence," by Sun-Ki Chai and Aaron Wildavsky.

Dennis J. Coyle is assistant professor of politics at the Catholic University of America. **Richard J. Ellis** is assistant professor of political science at Willamette University.

About the Contributors

Richard P. Boyle is a lecturer in sociology at the University of New Mexico. He received a Ph.D. and M.A. in sociology from the University of Washington and was a postdoctoral student in mathematical sociology at Harvard University. He has taught at several schools, including the University of California–Los Angeles. He has published articles in *American Sociological Review, Sociometry, American Journal of Sociology,* and other journals.

Sun-Ki Chai is a Ph.D. candidate in political science at Stanford University. He received a B.S. in mathematical science and an M.S. in computer science from Stanford. He is completing a dissertation on rational action and political development and has published an article on political violence in *Comparative Politics.*

Richard M. Coughlin is a professor of sociology at the University of New Mexico. He earned his M.A. and Ph.D. in sociology at the University of California–Berkeley, and his B.A. at Harvard University. His articles have appeared in several edited collections and in *Western Political Quarterly,* the *Journal of Behavioral Economics, Social Science Quarterly,* and other journals. He is the author of *Ideology, Public Opinion and Welfare Policy* (Institute of International Studies, Berkeley, 1980) and a novel, *The Conversion Factor* (Manor, 1980), and editor of *Morality, Rationality, and Efficiency: New Perspectives on Socio-Economics* (Sharpe, 1991) and *Reforming Welfare: Lessons, Limits and Choices* (New Mexico, 1989).

Dennis J. Coyle is an assistant professor of politics at the Catholic University of America in Washington, D.C., and a visiting associate professor of policy sciences at the University of Maryland Graduate School–Baltimore. He received his Ph.D. and M.A. in political science from the University of California–Berkeley, and his B.A. from the University of Connecticut. He has been a visiting fellow at the Social Philosophy and Policy Center in Bowling Green, Ohio, and a visiting lecturer of the University of California–Davis. He is author of *Property Rights and the Constitution: Shaping Society Through Land Use Regulation* (State University of New York Press, 1993). He has published articles on political culture, public policy, and constitutional law in the *Catholic University Law Review, Journal of Policy Analysis and Management, Public Interest,* and other journals.

Richard J. Ellis is an assistant professor of political science at Willamette University in Salem, Oregon. He received his M.A. and Ph.D. in political science from the University of California–Berkeley and a B.A. in politics from the University of California–Santa Cruz.

He is coauthor of *Dilemmas of Presidential Leadership: From Washington Through Lincoln* (Transaction Press, 1989) and *Cultural Theory* (Westview Press, 1990) and author of *American Political Cultures* (Oxford University Press, 1993) and *Presidential Lightning Rods: The Politics of Blame-Avoidance* (University of Kansas Press, 1994). He has published articles on political culture and American political history in a number of journals, including *Western Political Quarterly, Studies in American Political Development, Journal of Theoretical Politics,* and *Comparative Studies in Society and History.*

Gregg Franzwa is an associate professor in philosophy at Texas Christian University. He received an M.B.A. from the University of California at Berkeley and a Ph.D. in philosophy from the University of Rochester. His areas of interest include the history of modern philosophy and theories of human nature. He has published on these and other topics in philosophical journals, magazines, and newspapers.

Dean C. Hammer is an assistant professor of government at Franklin and Marshall College. He received his Ph.D. and M.A. from the University of California–Berkeley, and his B.A. from Augustana College. He has published articles in *Polity, Journal of Popular Culture, Presidential Studies Quarterly,* and *PS: Political Science and Politics.*

Frank Hendriks is completing his Ph.D. in public administration at Leiden University. His dissertation is on traffic policymaking in Birmingham, England, and in Munich and Rotterdam. He has also studied public administration at Erasmus University, Rotterdam, and Indiana University. His research interests include cultural and institutional studies, policy analysis, and comparative government.

Hank C. Jenkins-Smith is a professor of political science at the University of New Mexico and is director of the UNM Institute for Public Policy and UNM'S Survey Research Center. He received his B.A. at Linfield College in Oregon, and his M.A. and Ph.D. from the University of Rochester. He spent several years as a policy analyst for the Office of Policy Analysis at the U.S. Department of Energy and subsequently taught at Southern Methodist University in Dallas, Texas. He has published books, reports, and articles on policy analysis, risk perception, energy policy, methodology, and long-term policy change. His most recent book is entitled *Democratic Politics and Policy Analysis* (Brooks/Cole, 1990). Other published works have appeared in the *American Journal of Political Science, PS: Political Science and Politics, Policy Sciences, Journal of Operations Research, Public Administration Review, Journal of Policy Analysis and Management,* and *Natural Resources Journal,* and he has written numerous book chapters.

Charles Lockhart is professor of political science at Texas Christian University. He received his Ph.D. from the State University of New York at Buffalo, and from 1971 to 1974 he taught at the Defense Information School while on mandatory military service. His most recent book is *Gaining Ground: Tailoring Social Programs to American Values* (University of California Press, 1989). His research has appeared in many journals, including *Journal of Politics, Western Political Quarterly, Review of Politics,* and *Polity.* His current research focuses on the nexus between policy and culture.

Gary Lee Malecha is an associate professor of political science at the University of Portland. He graduated with a B.A. in political science at the College of St. Thomas, St. Paul, Minnesota, and earned his M.A. and Ph.D. in political science at the University of Notre Dame. He has been a visiting assistant professor at California Polytechnic State University at San Luis Obispo and Trinity College in Hartford, Connecticut, and associate professor at Weber State University in Ogden, Utah. Research interests include public policy, the presidency, and political culture.

Walter K. Smith received his B.A. in journalism and his M.A. in political science from the University of New Mexico. He is an analyst for the Arbitron Company in Laurel, Maryland, where he is involved in the development of electronic-based survey measurement methods.

Brendon Swedlow is a recent graduate of the University of California, Hastings College of the Law, and is currently completing a doctorate in political science at the University of California–Berkeley. With Aaron Wildavsky, he is author of chapters on American political culture (in *The Rise of Radical Egalitarianism,* American University Press, 1991) and American environmentalism (in *But Is It True? On the Relationship Between Knowledge and Action in the Great Environmental and Safety Issues of Our Time,* Harvard University Press, 1994).

Aaron Wildavsky was Class of 1940 Professor of Political Science and Public Policy at the University of California–Berkeley. Among his numerous books are *Risk and Culture* (University of California Press, 1982), *Cultural Theory* (Westview Press, 1990), *The Rise of Radical Egalitarianism* (American University Press, 1991), and *But Is It True?* (Harvard University Press, 1994). Collections of his papers on rational choice, cultural theory, the environment, federalism, and budgeting are being published posthumously.

Index